Aulus Gellius, William Beloe

The Attic Nights of Aulus Gellius

Vol. 2

Aulus Gellius, William Beloe

The Attic Nights of Aulus Gellius
Vol. 2

ISBN/EAN: 9783337773700

Printed in Europe, USA, Canada, Australia, Japan

Cover: Foto ©ninafisch / pixelio.de

More available books at **www.hansebooks.com**

THE

ATTIC NIGHTS

OF

AULUS GELLIUS:

TRANSLATED INTO ENGLISH,

BY THE REV. W. BELOE, F. S. A.

TRANSLATOR OF HERODOTUS, &c.

IN THREE VOLUMES.

VOL. II.

LONDON:

PRINTED FOR J. JOHNSON, ST. PAUL'S CHURCH-YARD.

M DCC XCV.

THE
ATTIC NIGHTS
OF
AULUS GELLIUS.

BOOK VI.

CHAP. I.

The reply of Chryfippus to thofe who denied a Providence.

'T HEY *who think that the world was not produced on account of the Deity and of man, and deny that human affairs are governed by Providence,*

think

' The beginning of this chapter was wanting in all the editions with which I am acquainted; but I have reftored it from Lactantius's Epitome of his Divine Inftitutions, Chap. 29. It is a whimfical circumftance enough, that the greater part of this very Epitome fhould have lain hid till the prefent century. St. Jerome, in his Catalogue of Ecclefiaftical Writers, fpeaking of Lactantius, fays, " Habemus ejus Inftitutionum Divinarum adverfus gentes libros feptem et Epi-

think that they urge a powerful argument when they assert, that if there were a Providence there would be no evils. For nothing, they affirm, can be less consistent with a Providence, than that in that world, on account of which the Deity is said to have created man, there should exist so great a number of calamities and evils. Chrysippus, in his fourth

tome ejusdem operis in libro uno ακεφαλον *."* Lactantius flourished in the fourth century; before the end of which St. Jerome wrote his Catalogue. But in the year 1712, Professor Pfaffius found a MS. at Turin, that had been complete, but by accident had since lost five chapters. To this edition our readers are indebted for the supplement; in consideration of which they are requested favourably to receive, or at least to pardon this little digression.

In some manuscripts we are given to understand, that this book was placed after the seventh.—This can be of no importance.—Many and perplexing are the disputes concerning Fate and Providence, among the ancient philosophers; each, perhaps, containing something to admire and approve, but resembling an unpolished gem, enveloped by extraneous matter, which obscured and defaced its beauty. The opinions of these sects will be found accurately detailed in Enfield's History of Philosophy.—On these subjects, ingenious and pleasing as the investigation of them may be, our best knowledge is the knowledge of ourselves, and our truest virtue resignation to the order of Providence.

> Hope humbly, then—with trembling pinions soar,
> Wait the great teacher Death, and God adore!
>
> In pride, in reasoning pride, our error lies,
> All quit their sphere, and rush into the skies.

---

* The common reading is ἀκεφάλω, but a Paris MS. 900 years old gives the reading which I have quoted.

*

book.

book concerning Providence, difputing againft thefe, obferves that nothing can be more abfurd or foolifh than their opinion, who think that there can be good, without the exiftence of evil. For as good is contrary to evil, and it is neceffary that both fhould exift, oppofite to each other, and as it were dependent upon mutual and oppofite exertions, fo there can be no oppofing thing exift, without its particular oppofite. For how could there be a fenfe of juftice, if there were no injuftice? or what indeed is juftice, but the abfence of injuftice? In like manner what can we imagine of fortitude, but as oppofed to pufillanimity? What of temperance, but from intemperance? What would prudence be, but for its oppofite imprudence? Why alfo fhould unwife men not require this, that there fhould exift truth, and not falfehood? In like manner exift good and evil, happinefs and mifery, pain and pleafure. Each, as Plato remarks, is confined to the other by contrary and oppofing vortices [2], fo that if you remove one you take away the other. This Chryfippus in the fame book

---

[2] *Vortices.*]—This doctrine is the diftinction of the Cartefian philofophy, where it was applied to explain the phænomena of the heavenly bodies. That it is inadequate to this, is what admits of mathematical proof. Thefe vortices exift in imagination only; the principle which actually and fatisfactorily explains thefe phænomena is known to have exiftence in nature, and that is gravity. Notes on the fubject of this chapter might be extended to an infinite length;

and

book examines, inveſtigates, and thinks it an important ſubjeċt of enquiry, whether the imperfeċtions of men are according to nature; that is, whether the ſame nature and Providence which formed this univerſe and the race of men, created alſo the defeċts and diſorders to which men are ſubjeċt. He thinks that it was not the firſt deſign of Providence to make men obnoxious to diſorders, for this never could be conſiſtent with the Author of nature, and the Creator of all good things. But as, he continues, he produced and formed many and great things, moſt convenient and uſeful, there are other kindred inconveniences, adhering to the things which he created. Theſe he ſays were not produced by nature, but by certain neceſſary conſequences, which he denominates κατα παρακολυθησιν.—Thus he remarks, when nature creates the bodies of men, a more ſubtle cauſe, and the very uſefulneſs of his work, required that the head ſhould be compoſed of certain very minute and very delicate bones; but another external inconvenience attached to this uſefulneſs in ſomewhat of more importance, that the head was leſs ſubſtantially defended, and was liable to be broken by blows and ſlight reſiſtances.—In like manner diſorders and ſickneſs are obtained whilſt health is produced. And thus it is, he remarked, that when, by the

and I ſhould certainly have indulged myſelf with ſome greater latitude, did I not fear to exceed the limits preſcribed me.

purpoſe

purpofe of nature, virtue is created. for man,
defects are alfo at the fame time produced by a
contrary affinity.

C H A P. II.[1]

*IIow the fame perfon proved the power and·neceffity
of Fate, and yet that we poffeffed a free will and
free agency.*

CHRYSIPPUS, the prince of the Stoics,
defines Fate, which the Greeks call
πεπρωμενη or ειμαρμενη, nearly in this manner:
Fate, fays he, is a certain immutable and eternal
                                                 feries

[1] All the ancient philofophers held different opinions
with refpect to fate or neceffity; which opinions are too
well known to be recapitulated here.—The definition of
fate here given by Chryfippus, is thus alluded to by Virgil,
Æn. iii. ver. 374.

Nam te majoribus ire per altum
Aufpiciis, manifefta fides; fic fata deum rex
Sortitur, *folvitque vices:* is vertitur ordo.

Many elegant and pertinent illuftrations of the fubjects
here difcuffed might be introduced from Pope's Effay on
Man; but as there is every where fuch a general fimilarity,
felection becomes difficult, and it feems better to refer the
reader generally to that poem; to the critical and philofo-
                                    phical

series and chain of things, moving and inter-weaving itself in a fixed and established order of events, with which it is fitted and connected. The very words of Chrysippus I have subjoined, as well as my memory would suffer me, that if any one shall think this my interpretation obscure, he may refer to the words themselves. In his fourth book on Providence he says, that Fate is a physical harmony of all things from eternity, each following the other, and that this combination still necessarily and invariably exists. The asserters of other systems and opinions object to this definition, thus: If Chrysippus, say they, thinks that all things are influenced and governed by Fate, and that the action and order of Fate cannot be affected or changed, the faults and errors of men ought not to be censured, nor imputed to them or their inclinations, but to a certain urgency and necessity which arises from Fate, which is the mistress and arbitress of all things, from whose agency whatever happens must of necessity happen. That therefore the punishment of crimes is unjustly appointed by the laws, if men

phical Commentary upon it, published by Dr. Warburton; as well as to Enfield's History of Philosophy.

The subject will, I think, allow me somewhat to enliven the chapter, by relating an anecdote of Zeno: He detected his slave in some act of theft, and ordered him to be flogged.—The fellow having in mind the dogmas of his master, exclaimed, It was fated that I should commit this theft.—And that you should be flogged, replied Zeno.

do

do not voluntarily commit, but are impelled to them by Fate. Againſt ſuch opinions Chryſippus argues with great ſubtlety and acutenefs. But the ſubſtance of all that he has replied on this ſubject is nearly this: Although it be ſo, ſays he, that all things are neceſſarily connected and compelled by Fate, yet the powers of our minds are no farther ſubject to this Fate, than as they have certain properties and qualities. If they are originally by nature formed well and uſefully, they tranſmit eaſily, and without injury, all the power which they externally derive from Fate. But if they be rough, and ignorant, and rude, ſupported by the props of no good arts, although impreſſed by little or no inconvenience of fatality, yet they are precipitated into frequent errors and diſorders, by their own voluntary un-amiablenefs and impetuoſity. And that this ſhould ſo happen is effected by that natural and neceſſary conſequence of things, which is called Fate. For it ſeems to be a fatality and conſe-quence in the order of things that vicious minds ſhould not be free from faults and errors. He gives an example of this, which ſeems equally pertinent and facetious. If, ſays he, you throw a cylindrical ſtone down a ſteep and inclined plane of the earth, you are the firſt cauſe and origin of its deſcent, but it is ſoon hurried on with in-creaſing velocity, not becauſe you do this, but be-cauſe the nature of its rotatory form effects this. Thus the order, and reaſon, and neceſſity of Fate

 influences

influences the general principles of caufes, but it is the peculiar will of each individual, and the conftitution of our minds, which regulates the force of our mental propenfities, and our confequent actions.

He then adds thefe words, agreeing with what I have faid:

"Therefore it is thus faid by the Pythagoreans: Know that men's fufferings are occafioned by themfelves.   As then each man's defects are occafioned by himfelf, and all fin and offend from their own propenfities, they are injured by their own free will and defign."

For this reafon he fays men who are bafe, audacious, and profligate, are not to be regarded or endured, who being convicted of turpitude and crime, fly to the neceffity of Fate, as to the afylum of fome temple, and affirm of their own enormous vices, that they are not to be imputed to their own paffions, but to Fate.   Homer, the moft wife and moft ancient of poets, has thus expreffed himfelf;

Perverfe mankind, whofe wills, created free,
Charge all their woes on abfolute decree;
All to the dooming gods their guilt tranflate,
And foilies are mifcall'd the crimes of Fate.

So alfo M. Cicero, in the book which he wrote on Fate, having faid that this queftion was moft obfcure and full of perplexity, affirms in thefe

words

words that Chryfippus the philofopher had not refolved it:

" Chryfippus, labouring and toiling to explain that all things happen by a fatality, and that this influences us, perplexes himfelf in this manner."

C H A P. III.

Story from Tubero of a ferpent of unufual fize.

TUBERO has written in his hiftory, that in the firft Punic War, Attilius Regulus the conful, being encamped in Africa, near the river Bagrada¹, had a great and fevere engagement with a fingle ferpent of extraordinary fiercenefs, whofe den

---

¹ *Bagrada.*]—There were feveral rivers called by this name.—The one here alluded to was in the vicinity of Utica. By Lucan and Silius Italicus, it is called the flow Bagrada.—This particular ferpent is alfo mentioned by Livy, Pliny, and Valerius Maximus. That there are enormous ferpents in Africa will admit of no doubt, but I believe ftill larger are met with in the interior parts of India; I have fomewhere read of travellers miftaking them, by their extraordinary magnitude, and when afleep, for the trunks of trees. It is afferted in the Philofophical Tranfactions, that in the kingdom of Congo ferpents have been found twenty-five feet in length, which will fwallow a fheep whole. Travellers alfo relate, that in the Brazils, ferpents have been found forty feet long.

was

was on that ſpot. That he ſuſtained the attack of the whole army, and was a long time oppoſed with the *balliſtæ* and *catapultæ* [2]; and that being killed, his ſkin, which was one hundred and twenty feet long, was ſent to Rome.

[2] *Balliſtæ and catapultæ.*]—Theſe were military engines, from which ſtones were projected. Modern writers generally expreſs balliſtæ with a ſingle *l*; but this is doubtleſs an error, as it is derived from the Greek word βαλλω, *jacio*, to caſt; or not improbably from βαλλιζω: concerning which word, ſee Athenæus, Book 8. c. 17. The Engliſh reader will hardly believe the fact recorded in this chapter; but it has neverthelefs exerciſed the acuteneſs and ſagacity of many critics and learned men. Dr. Shaw mentions it in his travels, and thinks it was a crocodile; but who ever heard of a crocodile one hundred and twenty feet long?—Mr. Daines Barrington diſbelieves it altogether, calling it an abſurd incredible circumſtance; to which opinion many will without reluctance accede.

Chap. IV.

The same Tubero's relation of the captivity of Re-
gulus [1]—Account given by Tuditanus of the same
Regulus.

WHAT is sufficiently notorious of Attilius
Regulus, I have very lately read in the
books of Tuditanus: That Regulus, being a
captive, in addition to what he said in the senate
at Rome, persuading them not to exchange
prisoners with the Carthaginians, declared this
also, that the Carthaginians had given him
poison not of immediate effect [2], but of such

[1] The story of Regulus, with its various circumstances, as
related by different historians, must be too well known to
justify my introduction of it more circumstantially here.

[2] *Not of immediate effect.*]—It has from very remote periods been told of the people of India and Africa, that they
are so well acquainted with the nature of poisons, as to be
able to procure death to any one at a longer or shorter period of time. Mead is of opinion, that this must be from the
fruits or inspissated juices of corrosive plants, which by producing ulcers in the bowels, may cause death to be slow and
lingering. That this idea of slow poisons was familiar in
the time of Shakespeare, appears from this passage in the
Tempest:

> Their great guilt,
> Like poison given to work a great time after,
> Now 'gins to bite the spirits.

kind

kind as to protract his death to a diftant period; intending him to live till the exchange fhould take place, and that afterwards, by the gradual operation of the poifon, his vital powers might be exhaufted. Tubero in his hiftory relates of the fame Regulus, that he returned to Carthage, and that he was tortured by the Carthaginians in a new and extraordinary manner. " They confined him," fays he, " in a dark and deep dungeon, and fome time afterwards, when the fun was in its meridian height, they fuddenly brought him out, expofed him to the adverfe ftrokes of the fun, and compelled him to fix his eyes on the firmament. They moved alfo his eyelids up and down, that he might not be able to fleep."

But Tuditanus relates that he was long prevented from fleeping, and fo deprived of life; and that when this was known at Rome, the moft noble of the Carthaginian prifoners were given up by the fenate to the children of Regulus, who confining them in an engine full of iron fpikes, there fuffered them to expire in torture, and from a fimilar want of fleep.

CHAP. V.

Miſtake of Alfenus[1] the lawyer, in the interpretation of ſome old words.

ALFENUS the lawyer, a follower of Servius Sulpicius, an attentive obſerver of antiquities, in his thirty-fourth book of Digeſts, and ſecond of Conjectures, ſays, in the treaty which was made betwixt the Romans and Carthaginians, it is written, that the latter were every year to pay the Romans a certain weight of ſilver, *puri puti*; and it was enquired what was meant by ſilver *purum putum*: I replied, ſaid he, that *purum putum* meant very pure, as we ſay *novum novicium*, and *proprium propicium*, as if willing to extend and amplify the ſignification of *novum* and *proprium*. On reading this, I was ſurprized that Alfenus ſhould think there was the ſame affinity betwixt *purum* and *putum*, as betwixt *novum* and *novicium*. If indeed it had been *puricium*, then it might have ſeemed to have been uſed like *novicium*. But this is wonderful, that he ſhould think *novicium* ſaid by way of amplifi-

---

[1] Alfenus is often quoted as of great authority on queſtions relating to civil law. He wrote forty books of Digeſts.

cation,

cation, when *novicium* is ufed not as *more new*, but becaufe it is faid and derived from *novum*, new. I agree therefore with thofe who think that *putum* is faid *à putando*; for which reafon they pronounce the firft fyllable fhort and not long, as Alfenus feems to have thought, who has confidered this as derived from *purum*. The ancients applied *putare* to the taking away and cutting off from any thing what was redundant [2], or unneceffary, or in the way, and the leaving what was ufeful and without defect. Thus trees and vines, and alfo arguments, are faid *putari*. As to the word *puto*, which I have ufed by way of explaining my opinion, it means nothing elfe, than that in a dubious and perplexing matter, *cutting off* and *amputating* the falfe opinions, we retain that which feems to be true, entire, and perfect. The filver therefore in the Carthaginian treaty was faid to be *putum*; that is, all were *exputatum*, lopped off, perfectly tried, and free from all foreign fubftance, and on this account without defect, and entirely pure from every blemifh. But the expreffion *purum putum* does not only occur in the Carthaginian treaty, but as in many other ancient books, fo alfo in a tragedy of En-

[2] *Redundant.*]—A vine pruner was denominated *putator*; as thus, in Virgil,

> Summumque *putator*,
> Haud dubitat terræ referens mandare cacumen.

See alfo Scaliger on this word.

nius,

nius, which is called Alexander, and in a satire of
M. Varro, named, " Old Men twice young."

Chap. VI.

*Virgil censured rashly and foolishly by Julius Hygi-
nus, because he called the wings of Dædalus
præpetes.—The meaning of* aves præpetes *explained.—What those birds were which Nigidius
calls* inferæ.

DÆDALUS ut fama est fugiens Minoïa
    regna,
Præpetibus pennis [1] ausus se credere cœlo.

[1] *Præpetibus pennis.*]—With swift wings.

Upon the word *præpes*, the grammarians have perplexed
themselves and others, with many subtle and protracted arguments. It is nearly synonymous with *celer* and *velox*; it
is so used by Virgil, and by all the writers of best authority.

According to Festus, the verb *præpetere* was anciently used
for *ante ire*, to go before.

The birds consulted by the augurs were in this manner
distinguished: They who gave omens by flight, were named
præpetes; they who gave omens by singing, were termed
oscines. The first were the eagle, vulture, and other birds
of that genus; the latter the raven, the crow, the owl, and
the cock.

Hyginus

Hyginus finds fault with these verses from Virgil, that *præpetibus pennis* is used with impropriety and ignorance. For those, says he, are called *præpetes aves* by the augurs, who either take their flight auspiciously, or fix themselves in proper places. He thought therefore that an augural term was not properly used in the flight of Dædalus, which had nothing to do with the ceremonies of the augurs. But Hyginus was exceedingly absurd, when he thought that he knew the meaning of *præpetes*, but that Virgil and Cn. Mattius, a learned man, did not know; who in in the seventh book of the Iliad, called Victory swift and *præpes*, in this verse,

Dum det vincenti præpes Victoria palmam.

But why did he not also blame Ennius, who in his Annals does not call the wings of Dædalus *præpetes*, but very differently; thus,

Quid
Brundusium pulchro præcinctum præpete portu?

And if he had considered the nature and power of the word, and not what the augurs had said alone, he would have forgiven poets the use of words not in their own peculiar signification, but with a licence of similitude and metathesis. For, since not only the birds which take their flight auspiciously, but also the proper and fortunate situations which they choose, are termed *præpetes*; he therefore called the wings of Dædalus *præpetes*, because he came from places in

which

which he feared danger, to others which were more fecure. For the augurs call alfo places *præpetes*; and Ennius has faid in his firft book of Annals;

Præpetibus hilares fefe pulchrifque locis dant.

But Nigidius Figulus, in his firft book of Private Augury, fays, that in oppofition to the *aves præpetes* are the *aves inferæ*; as thus, " The right differs from the left, the *præpes* from the *infera*." From which we may conjecture, that they were called *præpetes* from flying to a greater height; fince Nigidius fays, the *inferæ* differ from the *præpetes*. When I was a young man at Rome, at a time when I attended the grammarians, I heard Apollinaris Sulpicius, whom I more particularly preferred, when there was an enquiry concerning the office of augur, and mention was made of the *aves præpetes*, fay to Enucius Clarus, the præfect of the city, that the birds named *præpetes* feemed to him to be the fame with thofe which Homer named ταννπτερυγας; fince the augurs particularly regarded thofe which took their flight with broad and outftretched wings. He then repeated from Homer thefe lines:

But you order me to obey the birds with
    outftretched wings,
Which I mind not nor regard.

CHAP. VII.

Of Acca Larentia and Caia Tarratia. The origin of the priesthood of the Fratres Arvales.

THE names of Acca Larentia and Caia Tarratia, or as she is sometimes called Fufetia, are famous in ancient annals. To the one, after her death, but to the other whilst alive, the most distinguished honours were paid by the Roman people. The Horatian law proves that Tarratia was a Vestal virgin, which law was enacted on her account; and by it the greatest honours were paid her, among which, the power of giving her testimony was allowed her, she being the only woman permitted to be *testabilis*. This word occurs in the Horatian law. In the twelve tables we find *intestabilis*. IMPROBUS, INTESTABILIS, ESTO [1]. Moreover, if at the age of

forty

---

[1] *Intestabilis.*] Thus Horace says, as of a profligate and detestable character:

Is intestabilis et sacer esto.

Arnobius, in his tract Adversus Gentes, remarks, that cities of the greatest splendour and power were not ashamed to pay divine honours to prostitutes.

" In civitatibus maximis atque in potentioribus populis sacra publice fiunt scortis meritoriis quondam, atque in vul-

garem

forty [a] fhe thought proper to leave the priefthood and marry, fhe had the privilege given her of un-hallowing herfelf and taking a hufband, on account of her generous munificence, fhe having given the Campus Tiberinus, or Martius, to the Roman people. But Acca Larentia was a public proftitute, by which means fhe obtained a large fum of money. This woman by her will, as it appears in the Hiftory of Antias, made, as

garem libidinem proftitutis, nullus tremor indignationis in diis eft." See on this fubject alfo Lactantius, Macrobius, and Plutarch's Roman Queftions. By Plutarch, the ftory, which is not a very delicate one, is related at length.

The courtezan Leæna was alfo reverenced with divine honours by the Athenians; and here the lines of Pope prefent themfelves:

'Tis not the vice degrades her to a whore;
Let greatnefs own her, and fhe's mean no more.

See alfo Gibbon's account of Theodora, the wife of the emperor Juftinian. The proftitute, who in the prefence of innumerable fpectators had polluted the theatre of Conftantinople, was *adored* as a queen in the fame city, by grave magiftrates, orthodox bifhops, victorious generals, and captive monarchs. The lines of Pope above quoted are referred by Warburton to this Theodora in particular; but, as Gibbon obferves, it muft require Warburton's critical telefcope to fee this.

[a] *Age of forty.*]—Originally the vow of virginity taken by the Veftals was perpetual. The firft ten years they learned the facred rites; the next ten they practifed thefe; and the laft inftructed their juniors. It was very feldom that they availed themfelves of this permiffion to marry; if they did, it was thought highly unbecoming. See Dionyfius Halicarnaffenfis.

fome

some say, king Romulus, but according to others the Roman people, heirs of her effects. On this account public sacrifice was offered her by the Flamen Quirinalis, and a day of the public festivals was called after her name. But Sabinus Massurius, in his first book of Memorials, following some historians, says that Acca Larentia was the nurse of Romulus. This woman, says he, lost one of twelve male children by death; in his room Romulus gave himself as son to Acca Larentia, calling himself and the other brothers *Fratres Arvales* [3]. From this time there was a society of *Fratres Arvales*, twelve in number; of which priesthood the distinction is a garland of corn and white fillets.

[3] *Fratres Arvales*,] or rather *Fratres Ambarvales*. They offered sacrifice to Ceres and Bacchus, to obtain fertility to their lands.—They were called Ambarvales, because they carried the victim round the fields. See also Pliny, Book 18. c. 2. who relates the same story with his usual gravity.

CHAP.

C H A P. VIII.

Memorable anecdotes of Alexander and Publius Scipio.

APPION, a Greek, who was called Plifto-nices, was a man of agreeable and prompt elocution. When celebrating the praifes of king Alexander, he forbade, fays he, the wife of a conquered enemy, who was a woman of extraordinary beauty, to be introduced to his prefence [1], that he might not touch her, even with his eyes [2].

A pleafant

[1] *To his prefence.*]—On the contrary, Q. Curtius and Juftin both affirm, that the female relations of Darius were all introduced to the prefence of Alexander.

[2] *Might not touch her, even with his eyes.*]—Somewhat fimilar to this is the expreffion of Lear in our Shakefpeare:

> Might I but live to fee thee in my touch,
> I'd fay I'd eyes again.

Plutarch fays of Alexander, that on feeing the women of Perfia, he faid they were αλγηδονες ομματων, griefs of the eyes. But Herodotus makes the Perfians ufe this expreffion to Amyntas the Macedonian king. See my note at this paffage of the Greek hiftorian. Confult alfo the life of the emperor Julian, by the Abbé Bleterie, page 405–6. This eccentric character, in his laft and fatal expedition againft Perfia, took fome great city by ftorm. The Perfian women have ever been celebrated for their perfonal charms; and when his officers expreffed a wifh to prefent him with fome

female

A pleasant question may therefore be proposed, Who is to be reckoned the more continent, Publius Africanus the Elder, who having taken Carthage, a confiderable city in Spain, restored without violation to her father, a blooming virgin of remarkable beauty, the daughter of a noble Spaniard, who had been taken captive and brought to him; or Alexander [3], who refused to fee the wife and fifter of king Darius, captured in a mighty battle, who had been defcribed to him as very beautiful, and forbade them to be brought to his prefence?—But let thofe expatiate on both thefe fubjects concerning Alexander and Scipio, who have plenty of time, and words and genius for the employment. It will be enough for me

female captives of extraordinary beauty; that he might not yield to a paffion which has often triumphed over conquerors, and fometimes over philofophers, he refufed to fee them.

[3] *Or Alexander.*]—Bayle has a great deal to fay on this fubject, at the articles Abderame and Macedonia. Abderame was a Moorifh general, and by chance of war obtained poffeffion of the perfon of a widow lady of furprifing beauty, whom he treated with the greateft delicacy and generofity; an act, fays Bayle, which a Saracen writer would have extolled beyond the boafted continence of Alexander and Scipio. I would not diminifh the praife due to Alexander's felf-denial; but it is related of him, that he was by no means naturally of an amorous conftitution.—" If thou wert pure as fnow, thou fhalt not 'fcape calumny." Yet of Scipio, Valerius Maximus alfo relates, that in his early life he was a libertine.—Solutionis vitæ primos adolefcentiæ annos egiffe fertur.

to relate what is reported by hiftory. It is faid of this Scipio, I know not whether truly or otherwife, but it is related, that when a young man he was not immaculate; and it appears that thefe verfes were written by Cn. Nævius the poet againft him:

" He who often carried on great affairs with glory, whofe exploits yet live and flourifh, who alone is renowned among men, was by his father led away in his fhirt from his miftrefs."

I believe that thefe verfes induced Valerius Antias to exprefs himfelf concerning the morality of Scipio, in contradiction to all other writers; and to fay, that this captive maid was not reftored to her father, as we have faid above, but was detained by Scipio, and ufed by him for his amorous pleafures,

Chap. IX.[1]

A paſſage from the Annals of L. Piſo, intereſting in itſelf and agreeably related.

BECAUSE the thing ſeemed worthy of being recorded which L. Piſo in his third book of Annals affirms, that Cn. Flavius, a curule ædile, and ſon of Annius, did, and as this is told

---

[1] This chapter is of conſiderable importance, as it throws much light on ancient hiſtory. Upon the ſcribes of the ancients a volume might eaſily be written; they differed from each other conſiderably in rank, in the nature of their employments, and their conſequent views in the ſtate: generally ſpeaking, they were held in no great eſtimation.— They might not be admitted into the ſenate; and yet it appears from this chapter, that they were eligible to high and important offices. Cicero calls them an honourable body of men, in his fifth oration againſt Verres: " Quæ pars operis aut opportunitatis in ſcriba eſt......Ordo eſt honeſtus quis negat." Yet they were often in a ſervile condition, and generally found among the ſlaves of the great, diſtinguiſhed by no particular privileges. Their employment in this ſituation ſeems to have been that of librarian or ſecretary. We learn from the chapter before us, that it was uſual for them to appear in public with the inſtruments of their profeſſion.— Pliny calls his ſcribe or ſecretary, notarius: " Notarium voco—abit—rurſuſque revocatur, rurſuſque dimittitur."

When conſidered in a public capacity, their office ſeems to have nearly correſponded with that of our notary public.

†

by

by Pifo with much purity and elegance, I have tranfcribed the whole of the paffage.

" Cn. Flavius was the fon of a freedman, and by profeffion a fcribe. He appeared as a candidate for the curule ædilefhip at the time of election of ædiles, and was declared curule ædile by his tribe: but the ædile who held the comitia refufed to aceept him, not thinking it right that he who had been a fcribe fhould be curule ædile. Cn. Flavius, the fon of Annius, is faid to have thrown away his tablets, and renounced his profeffion of fcribe, and he was elected curule ædile. The fame Cn. Flavius, the fon of Annius, is faid to have made a vifit to his colleague when fick; and having entered into the inner apartment, many young noblemen who were fitting there treated him contemptuoufly. No one chofe to rife. At this Cn. Flavius, the fon of Annius, fmiled: he directed his ivory chair to be brought, and placed it at the entrance, fo that none of them could go out; and all of them reluctantly beheld him fitting in his chair of office."

C H A P.

Chap. X.

Story of Euclid the Socratic, by whose example the philosopher Taurus used to encourage his pupils to the earnest study of philosophy.

THE philosopher Taurus, a man in my memory of reputation in the Platonic sect, whilst he recommended the study of philosophy by many good and pertinent examples, particularly impressed on the minds of youth what he affirmed to have been frequently done by Euclid the Socratic.

The Athenians, says he, had decreed, that if any citizen of Megara [1] should be found to have

set

[1] *Of Megara.*]—See the Comedy of Errors.

> *Duke.* It hath in solemn synod been decreed,
> Both by the Syracusans and ourselves,
> To admit no traffic to our adverse towns;
> Nay more—
> If any born at Ephesus, be seen
> At any Syracusan marts or fairs,
> Again, if any Syracusan born
> Come to the bay of Ephesus, he dies.

Megara separated the territories of Athens from those of Corinth; it was consequently often involved in the hostilities of more powerful neighbours. It was at first governed by kings, but was finally subjected by the Athenians

§

to

ſet his foot in Athens, that man ſhould ſuffer death; ſo great a hatred did the Athenians entertain for their neighbours of Megara. Then Euclid, who was from the ſame place [2], of Megara, and who before reſided at Athens, and was a hearer of Socrates, after this decree had the public ſanction, at evening, as ſoon as it was dark, in a long female garb, and in a cloak of various colours, having his head in a hood, left his houſe at Megara to viſit Socrates at Athens, that at leaſt during ſome portion of the night he might enjoy his converſation and inſtruction. Early in the morning, diſguiſed in the ſame dreſs, he returned home, the diſtance being ſomething more than twenty miles. But now, continued he, we ſee philoſophers eagerly running of themſelves to the doors of young men who are rich, to give their leſſons; there they are obliged to ſit, ſhut up, till their pupils ſhall have ſlept off the laſt night's wine.

to their power. The philoſopher Euclid, mentioned in this chapter, founded at Megara a ſchool of philoſophy; the principles which he inculcated had a near reſemblance to the Platonic diſcipline. An anecdote of his amiable diſpoſition is recorded by Plutarch: His brother was offended with him, and exclaimed in a paſſion, " I will die if I have not revenge." " So will I," replied Euclid, " if I do not oblige you to love me again."—He was ſucceeded in his ſchool by Eubulus of Miletus.

[2] *From the ſame place.*]—Qui indidem Megaris, in the original; this is pointed out by Rutgerſius as an elegant imitation of Greek expreſſion, of which many examples are found in Cicero, Cornelius Nepos, Terence, and others.

C H A P.

Chap. XI.

Words of Quintus Metellus Numidicus, which it is a pleasure to remember, applicable to dignified stations and propriety of conduct.

SINCE it is unbecoming to contend in reproaches with very profligate men, and to retaliate ill words upon those who are vulgar and impudent, because you are so long like and equal to them, as you use and listen to their language; as much may be learned from an oration of Q. Metellus Numidicus [1], as from the books and precepts of philosophers. These are the words of Metellus against Cn. Manlius a tribune, by whom he had been insulted and reproached in very abusive terms before the people:

" And now, Romans, with respect to him, who thinks that he increases his own importance by declaring himself my enemy, but whom I neither receive as a friend nor fear as an enemy, I will not say another word against him. For I think him

---

[1] *Q. Metellus.*]—This was Quintus Cæcilius Metellus, who is often mentioned by Cicero in terms of the highest respect. He was an excellent magistrate, and a firm patriot. The Manlius whom he in this place so severely reprobates, was a friend to Catiline, for whose service he raised an army.

most

moſt unworthy of the praiſes of good men, neither is he a proper object for the reproaches
of the good; for if you name a fellow of this
deſcription at a time when you cannot puniſh
him, you treat him rather with honour than contempt."

Chap. XII.

*That neither " teſtamentum," as Servius Sulpicius
thought, nor " ſacellum," as Trebatius, are compounded. The former is derived from " teſtatio,"
the latter is a diminutive from " ſacrum."*

SERVIUS Sulpicius the lawyer, the moſt
learned man of his time, in his ſecond book
" On denouncing Sacred Rites [1]," aſſerts that
teſtamentum,

---

[1] *Denouncing Sacred Rites.*]—The heir was obliged to make
a declaration before the comitia curiata, that he would adopt
the ſacred rites which followed the inheritance; and this was
called, " deteſtatio ſacrorum." An inheritance not accompanied by this is called by Plautus, " hæreditas ſine ſacris."
This expreſſion Thornton properly enough, I ſuppoſe from
the authority of Feſtus, tranſlates, " An eſtate without an
incumbrance." Particular ſacrifices belonged to each Roman family, which neceſſarily involved a conſiderable expence.

An

teſtamentum, though I cannot tell why, is a compound word. He ſays it is compounded of *teſtatio* and *mens* ; what then ſhall we ſay of *calceamentum*, or *paludamentum*, or *pavimentum*, or *veſtimentum*, and a thouſand other words which are in a ſimilar manner extended? Shall we ſay that all theſe are compound? A falſe, but neither an inelegant nor prepoſterous ſignification of *mens* (mind) ſeems here to have intruded itſelf on Servius, or whoever elſe firſt made the aſſertion.

Indeed a ſimilar and equally pertinent idea occurred to C. Trebatius, in his ſecond book, " Of Religions." The *ſacellum* is a ſmall place with an altar, ſacred to a deity. He then adds, " I think *ſacellum* is compounded of the two words *ſacer* and *cella*, as *ſacra cella*." Thus Trebatius wrote ; but who knows not that *ſacellum* is a ſimple word, not compounded of *ſacer* and *cella*, but a diminutive of *ſacrum* ?

An anecdote on this ſubject is related by Livy, which ſeems to demand a place here.

The Fabian family were obliged at a certain time to offer ſacrifice on the Quirinal hill. When the Gauls were in poſſeſſion of the whole of Rome except the Capitol, Caius Fabius Dorſo, in a ſacred veſt, and having the ſacred utenſils in his hand, aſtoniſhed the enemy by his deſcending with undaunted intrepidity from the Capitoline hill. Without regarding their voices, geſtures, or menaces, he paſſed through their ranks, and came to the Quirinal mount. There, having with due ſolemnity offered the ſacrifice required, he again returned, and without moleſtation, to his friends ; the Gauls either venerating his piety, or overcome by his audacity.

CHAP.

Chap. XIII.

*Of certain questions discussed by Taurus the philoso-
pher at his table, and called symposiacs [1].*

THE following was generally done at Athens
by those who were more particularly intimate with the philosopher Taurus. When he
invited us to his house, that we might not come,
as he said, entirely free and without paying [2] any
thing, we subscribed to the supper not choice bits
of food, but some subtle questions. Every one
of us therefore went with his mind prepared to
propose some question; and when supper ended
conversation began. The questions proposed
were not severe and profound, but rather calculated to exercise acuteness; being facetious, trifling, and adapted to spirits moderately warmed

[1] *Symposiacs.*]—The literal meaning of this word is drinking together; from whence it came to mean disputations at
table, Plutarch having nine books of Questions so called.—
Such also is the work of Athenæus.

[2] *Without paying.*] — In the original, *asymbeli*. Thus, in
Terence, asymbolus ad cœnam venire, is to come to an entertainment without paying; the word is derived from α, *non*,
συν, *con*, and βαλλω, *jacio*. Anciently at every public entertainment each guest contributed his proportion, which was
called his συμβολη, or symbol. The word, as now used in our
language, bears a very different meaning.

with wine. Such, generally, as this ludicrous subtlety, which I shall mention. It was asked, When a dying man could be said to die; at the time he actually expired, or when he was on the point of expiring? When a person rising could be said to rise; when he actually stood, or when he was but just sitting? He who learned any art, at what time he became an artist; when he was really one, or when he was just not one? If you assert any one of these, you assert what is absurd and ridiculous; yet it will appear more absurd, if you assert both or allow neither. But when they said that all these quibbles were futile and absurd, Do not, interrupted Taurus, despise these altogether as a mere trifling sport. The gravest philosophers have enquired seriously concerning these things; and some have thought that the moment of dying was called and indeed really was that when life yet remained; others thought at this period no life existed, and they called actual death that which was the act of dying. So of other similar things [3], they have at different times defended different opinions. But our Plato, continued he, assigned this period neither to life

[3] *Similar things.*] — This delicate point of vibration between two things entirely opposite, yet closely approximating, is admirably described in the Ode to Indifference, by Mrs. Greville:

> Nor peace, nor ease, that heart can know,
>   Which, like the needle true,
> Turns at the touch of joy or woe,
>   But turning trembles too.

nor

nor death; which rule he also observed in all other disputes of a similar nature. For he saw indeed a contradiction each way, and that of two opposite things both could not separately be supported; and that the question was of the point of coherence betwixt two different things, namely life and death. For this reason he himself invented and expressed another new period as to the point of contact, which in a peculiar form of words he named " την εξαιφνης φυσιν [4];" and you will find him thus expressing himself in his book called Parmenides: " For this suddenness seems to express something like a transition from one to another."—Such were the contributions at the table of Taurus, and such as he himself used to say were the contents of his second course [5].

[4] της εξαιφνης φυσιν.]—A nature on a sudden, or a sudden nature.

[5] *Second course.*]—The contents of the second course among the Romans were called bellaria, and consisted of fruits and confectionary.

Chap. XIV.

*Three reasons assigned by philosophers for the punish-
ment of crimes. Why Plato has recorded only
two of them.*

IT is usually supposed that there are three proper reasons for punishing crimes; the one,
which is called νεθεσια (admonition), or κολασις,
or παραινεσις, when a rebuke is administered for
the sake of correction and improvement, that he
who has committed an accidental offence, may
become more regular and attentive. The second
is that, which they who distinguish nicely between these terms call τιμωρια (vengeance). This
mode of noticing an offence takes place when
the dignity and authority of him against whom it
is committed, is to be defended, lest the passing
by, the crime should give rise to contempt or a
diminution of respect, therefore they suppose this
word to signify the vindication of honour. The
third mode of punishment is called by the Greeks
παραδειγμα (example) and is applied when punishment is necessary for the sake of example, that
others may be deterred from similar offences
against the public by the dread of similar
punishment. Therefore did our ancestors also denominate the heaviest and most impor-

tant

tant punishments, examples [1]. When therefore there is either great hope, that he who has offended will without punishment voluntarily correct himself, or on the contrary there is no hope that he can be amended and corrected, or that it is not necessary to fear any loss of that dignity, against which he has offended, or the offence is of that kind, the example of which it is not necessary to impress with particular terror; in this case, and with respect to every such offence, there does not seem to exist the necessity of being eager to inflict punishment. These three modes of vengeance, other philosophers in various places, and our Taurus in the first book of his Commentaries on the Gorgias of Plato, has set down. But Plato himself has plainly said, that there only exist two causes for punishment. The one, which we have first mentioned, for correction; the other, which we have spoken of in the third place, to deter by example. These are the words of Plato:—" It is proper for every one who is punished, by him who punishes from a proper motive, that he should become better and receive advantage; or that he should be an example to others, that others, seeing him suffer, may from terror be rendered better."

In these lines it is evident that Plato used the word τιμωρία not, as I have before remarked some people have, but in its common and ge-

---

[1]. Thus we say in English *to make an example of a person?*

                                        neral

neral fenfe, for all kinds of punifhment. But whether, becaufe he paffed over as too infignificant and really contemptible, the inflicting punifhment to avenge the injured dignity of man; or rather that he omitted it as not being neceffary to the queftion he was difcuffing, as he was writing of punifhments which were to take place not in this life among men, but after death, this I leave to others to determine. [2]

[2] The fubject of crimes and punifhments is hardly to be exhaufted; and in all ages of mankind the graveft and wifeft philofophers have differed in their opinions and arguments concerning them. The ftate of fociety is conftantly changing in all places and at all periods; confequently that fyftem which may be wife at one epoch, may alfo be abfurd, inconfiftent, and inadequate in another. At one time feverity may be indifpenfably neceffary, at another, mildnefs becomes the trueft policy. To recapitulate the fentiments of thofe who have gone before us, or indeed of our cotemporaries, would be tedious, and perhaps, from my pen, uninterefting. I am happy to tranfcribe a fentence from Seneca concerning crimes and punifhments, to which I prefume the majority of mankind will without difficulty accede; it feems indeed to be the only unexceptionable bafis for every code of penal laws: " The end of punifhment is either to make him better who is punifhed, or that his example who is punifhed may make others better; or, laftly, that the bad being taken away, the good may live in greater fecurity."

Chap. XV.

Of the word quiefco; *whether the letter* e *ought to be made long or fhort.*

A FRIEND of mine, a man of ferious ftudy, and well verfed in the more elegant purfuits of learning, commonly ufed the word *quiefco* with the *e* fhort. Another friend of mine, who was very dextrous in the fubtleties of fcience, but too faftidious and nice with refpect to common expreffions, thought that he fpoke barbaroufly; faying, that he ought to have pronounced it long, and not fhort. _He obferved, that *quiefcit* ought to be pronounced as *calefcit, nitefcit, ftupefcit,* and many others of a fimilar kind. He added alfo, that *quies* was pronounced with the *e* long, and not fhort. But my friend remarked, with his accuftomed modefty and moderation, that if the Ælii [1], the Cineri [2], and the Santræ [3], thought it was to be fo pronounced, he would not comply

[1] *Ælius*]—is more than once mentioned by Gellius in terms of refpect, as a very learned man.

[2] *Cinerus.*]—I do not find this name in Nonius Marcellus, but he is again introduced by Gellius in the 16th book, and is mentioned by Macrobius.

[3] *Santræ.*]—Santra is a name which occurs in Marcellus, where he is reprefented as a writer on the antiquity of words.

with their opinion in contradiction to the univerſal uſage of the Latin tongue; nor would he be ſo particular in his language as to uſe harſh and uncommon expreſſions. He alſo wrote upon this ſubject in a kind of mock exerciſe; and demonſtrated that *quieſco* was not ſimilar to the words above mentioned, nor derived from *quies*; but that *quies* was derived from *quieſco*, and that this word had the manner and the origin of the Greek word εσχόν and εσκον, which is Ionice from the verb εσχω, ισχω. He proved then, by reaſons which were not unintereſting, that *quieſco* ought not to be pronounced with the *e* long.

C H A P. XVI.

The common word deprecor *applied by the poet Catullus in an unuſual but not improper manner. The meaning of this word, with examples from ancient writers.*

A CERTAIN perſon, who by an irregular and rude ſort of exerciſe, had aſſerted claims to the reputation of eloquence, but had not learned the true uſages of the Latin tongue, when we were one evening walking in the Ly=
ceum,

ceum, afforded us much mirth and amusement.
For as the word *deprecor* was placed with particular judgment in a poem of Catullus, he, not
knowing this, observed, that the lines were remarkably flat, which in my opinion are exceedingly beautiful. They are here added [1]:

Lesbia mi dicit semper male, nec tacet unquam
De me Lesbia; me despercam nisi amat,
Quo signo? quasi non totidem mox deprecor
  illi
Assidue: verum desperam nisi amo.

The good man [2] thought that *deprecor* was used
                                                in

[1] *Here added.*]—I have given in the text the original, as
it appears in the edition of Gronovius. It is undoubtedly
pointed wrong. It should be read thus:

Lesbia mi dicit semper male, nec tacet unquam
De me: Lesbia me desperam nisi amat, &c.

A friend thus translates the epigram,

So oft does Lesbia rail upon my name;
  Ah! may I perish but the maid's in love,
I know it—for I feel a kindred flame,
  And equal railings equal fondness prove.

This is elegant, and sufficiently explanatory of the poet's
meaning; but yet there is a point in the original which it has
not reached. Mr. Wilkes, in his elegant edition of Catullus,
has adopted the reading which I have given above. The
second line is sometimes read thus:

De me desperam me nisi Lesbia amat.

[2] *Good man.*]—Bonus homo; which expression is used in
a sense of ridicule or contempt. Thus, in English, the epithet *good* is often applied ludicrously; and we say, good

                                              man

in this paſſage, as it is generally applied by the vulgar, to ſignify, I earneſtly pray, entreat, and ſupplicate, where the prepoſition *de* is uſed intenſively. If it were ſo, the lines would be inanimate indeed; but the contrary is the fact. For the prepoſition *de*, as it is doubtful, conveys a double meaning in one and the ſame word; and *deprecor* is here applied by Catullus in the ſenſe of, I deteſt, execrate, put away, and abominate. It has a different meaning in Cicero's Oration for Sylla; where he ſays, " Quam multorum hic vitam a Sulla *deprecatus.*" Thus in his diſſuaſive from the Agrarian law: " Si quid deliquero, nullæ ſunt imagines quæ me a vobis deprecentur."

But it is not Catullus only who has thus uſed this word: the books of the ancients are full of this ſignification of it, from which I have ſelected one or two examples. Q. Ennius, in his Erectheus, has expreſſed himſelf not in a very different manner from Catullus:

Quibus nunc ærumna mea libertatem paro
Quibus ſervitutem mea miſeria *deprecor.*

Where it ſignifies to drive away, to remove either

man and good fellow, contemptuouſly. Good man is ſometimes uſed ſynonymouſly with huſband. See alſo Cardinal Wolſey's famous ſoliloquy in Shakſpeare:

The third day comes a froſt, a killing froſt;
And when he thinks, good eaſy man! full ſurely
His greatneſs is a ripening, nips his root,
And then he falls as I do.

by

by entreaty or by some other method. The same Ennius also, in his Ctesiphon:

> Ego quum meæ vitæ parcam, letum inimico
> *deprecor*.

Cicero in his sixth book De Republica, has thus expressed himself:

" Quod quidem eo fuit majus qui quum causa pari collegæ essent, non modo invidia pari non erant, sed etiam Claudii invidiam Gracchi caritas *deprecabatur*."

This also means, not that he earnestly intreated, but that he, as it were, drove from him, and averted envy. Thus the Greeks, by an affinity of expression, say παραιτημαι. In his Oration for A. Cæcina, Cicero also uses the word again:

" Quid huic homini facias? nonne concedas interdum ut excusatione summæ stultitiæ, summæ improbitatis odium *deprecetur*."
So in his second Oration against Verres;

" Nunc vero quid faciat Hortensius? avaritiæne crimina frugalitates laudibus *deprecetur*? an hominem flagitiosissimum, libidinosissimum nequissimumque defendet?"

Thus Catullus says, that he does the same as Lesbia; that he publicly spake ill of her, that he scorned, despised, and constantly detested her, and yet that he passionately loved her.

CHAP.

C H A P. XVII.

Who first instituted public libraries [1]. The number of books deposited in public libraries at Athens before the Persian invasion.

PISISTRATUS the tyrant is said to have been the first who supplied books of the liberal sciences at Athens for public use. Afterwards the Athenians themselves, with great care and pains, increased their number; but all this multitude of books, Xerxes, when he obtained possession of Athens, and burned the whole of the city except the citadel, seized and carried away

---

[1] *Public libraries.*]—That Pisistratus was the first who collected books, seems generally allowed by ancient writers. Before the Theban and Trojan wars we must not look even for books, much less for collections of books. It is singular that Pythagoras forbade his disciples to commit any thing to writing, with an exception, I believe, in favour of those who pursued mathematical studies.

In Greece were several famous libraries. Clearchus, who was a follower of Plato, founded a magnificent one in Heraclea. There was one in the island of Cnidos. The books of Athens were by Sylla removed to Rome. The public libraries of the Romans were filled with books, not of miscellaneous literature, but were rather political and sacred collections, consisting of what regarded their laws and the ceremonies of their religion. Their private libraries were very splendid and magnificent, as I have elsewhere described.   *

to Perſia. But king Seleucus, who was called Nicanor, many years afterwards, was careful that all of them ſhould be again carried back to Athens.

A prodigious number of books were in ſucceeding times collected by the Ptolemies [2] in Egypt, to the amount of near ſeven hundred thouſand volumes. But in the firſt Alexandrine war the whole library, during the plunder of the city, was deſtroyed by fire, not by any concerted deſign, but accidentally by the auxiliary ſoldiers.

[2] *The Ptolemies.*]—The Egyptian library was began by Ptolemy Philadelphus. It is worth relating of this prince, that when the Athenians were in great diſtreſs from a famine, he refuſed to furniſh them with proviſions till they ſhould firſt preſent him with the original works of their three celebrated tragedians. This library was accidentally burned by Cæſar's ſoldiers, but it was afterwards reſtored by Antony, who gave it to Cleopatra.

Nothing could be more honourable, or perhaps more uſeful to a nation, than a great national library. It may be ſaid, that in this country ſuch a library would be ſuperfluous, as there exiſt ſo many valuable and curious collections. This is true, but this is not enough.—I know that many ſuch collections exiſt among us, but I object that they are not ſufficiently eaſy of acceſs. The ingenuous pride and delicacy of a ſcholar, will often make him diffident of applying for books where alone they are to be had; particularly, which is often the caſe, when the loan of them is conſidered as a great perſonal obligation.

CHAP.

BOOK VII.

Chap. I.

Memorable facts of P. Scipio Africanus, taken from the Annals.

WHAT has been recorded in Greek history of Olympias, wife of king Philip, and mother of Alexander, has also been related of the mother of P. Scipio, first called Africanus. For C. Oppius [1], Julius Higinus, and others who have written on the life and actions of Africanus, affirm that his mother was for a long time supposed to be barren, and that Publius Scipio, to whom she had been married, despaired of having children. Afterwards, when in the absence of her husband, she slept alone in her own apartment, and usual bed, an immense serpent [2] was seen to

repose

[1] *C. Oppius.*]—C. Oppius was a biographer, and is quoted by Plutarch, Pliny, and others.

[2] *Immense serpent.*]—Many exalted characters have wished to circulate the opinion, that under the form of serpents, Jupiter or Apollo, or some other of the deities, were the authors of their being. In imitation of Alexander and Scipio,

Augustus

repofe near her, which (they who beheld it making a great noife, and being much terrified) glided
away

Auguftus Cæfar alfo was proud to have it believed, that in
the fhape of a ferpent Apollo enjoyed his mother Atia.—
The ftory is related at length by Suetonius; where alfo we
are told, that from the time of her conception there was impreffed on her body a fpot like a ferpent, which prevented
her from attending the public baths.

Sidonius Apollinaris thus fpeaks of this circumftance, as
it refpects Auguftus:

Magnus Alexander, nec non Auguftus, habentur
Concepti ferpente deo.

Dryden makes a happy ufe of this fabulous origin of
Alexander, in his Ode on St. Cecilia's day:

The fong began from Jove,
Who left his blifsful feats above,
Such is the power of mighty Love!
A dragon's fiery form belied the god:
Sublime on radiant fpires he trode,
When he to fair Olympia prefs'd,
And while he fought her fnowy breaft,
Then round her flender waift he curl'd,
And ftamp'd an image of himfelf, a fovereign of the world.

See alfo in Milton a beautiful allufion to thefe fables:

Pleafing was his fhape
And lovely, never fince of ferpent kind
Lovelier: not thofe that in Illyria chang'd,
Hermione and Cadmus, or the god .
In Epidaurus, nor to which transform'd
Ammonian Jove or Capitoline was feen;
He with Olympias, this with her who bore
Scipio, the heighth of Rome.

The ferpent, among the ancients, was univerfally confidered as the fymbol of good fortune. This perhaps is
enough,

away and could not be found. This was related by P. Scipio to the augurs; who replied, after performing sacrifice, that he would have children. Not many days after this serpent had been seen in her bed, the woman began to feel the usual symptoms of conception. In the tenth month she brought forth; and that Publius Scipio Africanus was then born, who conquered Hannibal and the Carthaginians in Africa, in the second Punic war. But he was much rather believed to be a man of divine merit from his actual exploits, than from this prodigy. Yet it is not impertinent to add, that the writers whom I have mentioned above have recorded, that this Scipio Africanus did very frequently, at the latter part of the night, before break of day, go to the Capitol, and command the chapel [3] of Jove to be opened; and that there he would remain a long time alone, as if consulting with Jupiter [4] concerning the repub-

enough, to say more would lead to a long discussion of serpent worship as practised by the Romans, the Greeks, the Phœnicians, and the Egyptians.

[3] *The chapel.*]—That is, the interior and more sacred part of the temple, where the image of the deity was deposited. The word in the original is *cellam.* Arnobius adversus Gentes uses *cellulas* in the same manner: Conclavia et cellulas fabricari.

[4] *As if consulting with Jupiter.*]—Thus also Numa Pompilius, in order to obtain greater influence with the people, pretended to have nightly communication with the nymph Egeria. To which tradition Juvenal thus alludes:

Madidamque Capenam
Hic ubi nocturnæ Numa constituebat amicæ.

lic,

lic. The porters alfo of the temple were greatly aftonifhed, that on his coming to the Capitol alone, and at that time, the dogs, who were always furious to other people, neither barked at nor molefted him.   The many admirable things which Scipio faid and did, feemed to ftrengthen and confirm the popular opinions concerning him. One of which was of this kind: He laid clofe fiege to a town in Spain, which was ftrong, well protected by its fituation, walls, and troops, and had alfo abundance of provifions; there were no hopes of his taking it; and on a certain day he fate in his camp adminiftering juftice, from a place whence the town was vifible at a diftance. Then one of the foldiers, whofe caufe was trying, ftanding near him, afked, as ufual, the day and place when his recognizance fhould appear [5]; Scipio, pointing with his hand to the citadel of the be- fieged town, " After two days," fays he, " they fhall appear yonder;" and fo it happened.   On the third day from the time when he ordered the fureties to appear the town was taken; and on that very day he adminiftered juftice in the cita- del of the place.

[5] *Recognizance fhould appear.*]—On the explanation of the legal terms here ufed by Gellius, confult Heineccius, page 592.

C H A P. II.[1]

Shameful error of Cæsellius Vindex, found in the book which he called " Ancient Readings."

WE find a difgraceful miftake in thefe very celebrated Commentaries of Ancient Readings of Cæfellius Vindex, a man who was indeed very accurate in moft inftances; which error has efcaped many, although, in order to reprehend Cæfellius, various things are calumnioufly hunted out[2]. Cæfellius has written, that Q. Ennius

nius

---

[1] The argument of this chapter has been objected to by fome, as a proof of great vanity and oftentation on the part of Gellius. H. Stephens undertakes his defence; which, if any defence were neceffary, will be found fufficient and fatisfactory. This vindication of Gellius by Stephens is written againft Ludovicus Vives in particular.

Gellius has made out his cafe clearly enough, and proved all that he afferted. We learn from this chapter the neceffity of never introducing falfe or partial quotations; by doing which truth itfelf may be injured, and the reputation of a man of genius difgraced.

Concerning Cæfellius Vindex, confult Book iii. Chap. 16.

[2] *Calumnioufly hunted out.*]—Whoever wifhes to fee this difingenuous fpirit of criticifm fuccefsfully expofed, with all the effect of wit and ridicule, will be amply fatisfied with Swift's digreffion concerning critics in his Tale of a Tub. " The proper employment of a true ancient genuine critic," fays Swift, " is to travel through this vaft world of writings;

nius, in his thirteenth book of Annals, ufed *cor* in the mafculine gender.   The words of Cæfellius are here added: " Ennius has ufed *cor*, as many other words, in the mafculine gender; for in the thirteenth book of Annals, he faid *quem cor*; he then fubjoins two verfes from Ennius:

Hannibal audaci cum pectore dehortatur
Ne bellum faciam: quem credidit effe meum cor?"

It is Antiochus king of Afia who fays this.   He is furprifed, and in aftonifhment, that Hannibal the Carthaginian fhould difcourage him, being inclined to make war upon the Romans.   But Cæfellius underftood thefe verfes as if Antiochus fhould fay, " Hannibal advifes me not to carry on war; which when he does, what fort of a heart does he fuppofe me to have? How foolifh does he fuppofe me to be, defiring to make me believe

to purfue and hunt thefe monftrous faults bred within them. To drag out the lurking errors, like Cacus from his den; to multiply them like hydra's heads, and rake them together like Augeas' dung, &c. &c.", Which paffage, by the way, bears a remarkable refemblance to one which occurs in a curious and fcarce little tract, De Charlataneria Eruditorum.

" Prima nobis prodeat grammaticorum ac criticorum gens afpera et ferox, qui cum pueros ad virgam obfequentes habuere in fcholis nulli eruditorum parcunt et in ipfum orbem Romanum Græciamque univerfam principatum quendam ambitiofe fibi vindicent. Sive enim Græcus, five Latinus fimplex preponatur, non tam id agunt ut fcite et appofite dicta evolvant ac nitori fuo reddant, quam ut nodum quærant in fcirpo at ad manufcriptos codices confugiant, variafque lectiones, nullo habito delectu cumulent; tum vero urere, fecare et nihil a virgula cenforia intactum relinquere."

this !" Thus Cæfellius : but the meaning of Ennius is very different; for there are not two but three verfes belonging to this affertion of Ennius, the third of which Cæfellius has not regarded :

Hannibal audaci cum pectore de me hortatur
Ne bellum faciam : quem credidit effe meum
    cor
Suaforem fummum et ftudiofum robore belli.

The fenfe and order of thefe words I believe to be this : " Hannibal, that moft bold and valiant man, whom I believed (for that is the meaning of *cor meum credidit*; as if he had faid, whom I, foolifh man, believed) to be a great advifer to war, diffuades and forbids me to make war." But probably Cæfellius, from this negligent difpofition of the words, read it *quem cor*, giving to *quem* an acute accent, as if it referred to *cor*, and not to Hannibal. But it does not efcape me, if any fhould be fo ftupid, that the *cor* of Cæfellius may be defended as mafculine, by reading the third verfe feparately and unconnected.—As if Antiochus were to exclaim, in a broken and abrupt mode of expreffion, *fummum fuaforem !* But they who fay this are unworthy of reply.

Chap. III.

Censure of Tullius Tiro, Cicero's freedman, on a speech of Marcus Cato, delivered in the senate for the Rhodians. The answer which I have made to that censure.

THE city of Rhodes [1] was celebrated for the convenience of its insular situation, the splendour of its works, its knowledge of navigation,

---

[1] *The city of Rhodes.*]—In my notes to Herodotus I have spoken at some length concerning the Rhodians, explaining their policy and their power.—The English reader may perhaps receive some benefit from consulting the place, Vol. III. page 260. The colossus of Rhodes is memorable as one of the seven wonders of the world, and notorious to every school-boy. Some few particulars concerning Rhodes, omitted in the note to which I allude, may not be unacceptable here. Cicero, in his Oration pro lege Manilia, testifies that, even within his remembrance, the Rhodians retained their national glory, and their naval skill. Consult also the fourteenth book of Strabo, who speaks of the Rhodians in terms of the highest commendation. According to Suidas, the Rhodians, from this circumstance of their colossus, were named Colassaeis: there were other colossi celebrated in ancient history; but this of Rhodes was far the most distinguished.— Learned men are not agreed about the etymology of the word Colossus. Some say it was so named from Coletus, an artist of Rhodes, who constructed this famous work: neither are writers better agreed about its height; it was probably of the height of about one hundred and twenty feet. Pliny says it was made by one Chares of Lindus, Book 34. chap. 7.

                    and

and naval victories. This city, though a friend and ally to the Roman people, was in friendship also with Perses, son of Philip king of Macedon, who was at war with Rome. The Rhodians endeavoured, by frequent embassies to Rome, to heal the difference betwixt them. But as this pacification could not be accomplished, addresses were often made by many Rhodians in their public assemblies, that if peace were not obtained, the Rhodians should assist the king against the Romans, though no public decree was passed on this matter. But when Perses was conquered and taken prisoner [2], the Rhodians were in great alarm, from the many things which had been done and said in their popular assemblies; and they sent ambassadors to Rome, who might palliate the temerity of some of their citizens, and clear them, as a body, from all imputation on their fi-

---

[2] *Prisoner.*]—In their treatment of this prince, the Romans by no means shewed their accustomed magnanimity. He was dragged in chains along the streets of Rome, to grace, or rather to disgrace the triumph of his conqueror. After repeated experience of the most severe and cruel treatment, he was permitted to expire in prison.—His eldest son, Alexander, was compelled to follow the mean occupation of a carpenter for a livelihood. He lived, however, to triumph so far over his ill fortune, as to obtain an honourable office in the Roman senate. The history of kings and princes who, like Perses, fell from their high estates to the abyss of misery, affords an useful but melancholy lesson.—See this subject of the vanity of human wishes happily illustrated by Juvenal, in his tenth satire, and by Dr. Johnson in his imitation of that poem.

delity.

delity. When the ambaffadors came to Rome, and were admitted into the fenate, and, after fpeaking in fupplicatory terms, had again departed, the queftion began to be put; and when part of the fenate complained of the Rhodians, and affirmed them to be ill-intentioned, and thought that war fhould be declared againft them, M. Cato arofe: He throughout afferted, that allies fo excellent and faithful, upon the plunder and poffeffion of whofe riches, not a few of the principal men were earneftly refolved, fhould be protected and preferved. He made that famous oration, which is feparately preferved, and is infcribed " Pro Rhodienfibus," and which is in the fifth book of Origins. Tiro Tullius, the freedman of M. Cicero, was a man of an elegant mind, and by no means ignorant of ancient literature. He was, from an early age, liberally inftructed, and employed by Cicero himfelf as an affiftant and companion in his ftudies. But indeed he prefumed farther than might be tolerated or forgiven. He wrote a letter to Q. Axius [1], the friend of his patron, with too great boldnefs and warmth, in which he feemed to himfelf to have criticifed this oration for the Rhodians with extreme acutenefs and fubtlety of judgment. From this epiftle I may perhaps be allowed to examine fome of his animadverfions, reprehending indeed Tiro with greater propri-

[1] *Axius.*] For Axius fome would in this place read Atticus.

ety,

ety, than he on this occasion observed towards Cato. The fault he first found was, that Cato ignorantly and absurdly, in his exordium, used a style of too much insolence, severity, and reproach, when he declared himself afraid, left the senate, from the joy and exultation of their successes, being unhinged in their minds, should act unwisely, and prove themselves but ill qualified properly to comprehend and deliberate. He remarks, " That patrons, at the beginning, who plead for the accused, ought to sooth and conciliate the judges ; and that, keeping their minds on the stretch of suspense and expectation, they should sooth them by modest and complimentary expressions, and not irritate them by insolent and imperious menaces." He then added the exordium, which was this :

" I know that with most men, happy, affluent, and prosperous affairs will usually elevate the mind, and increase and promote their pride and ferocity [4]; it is therefore of great concern

[4] *Ferocity.*] See this sentiment expressed with great force by Juvenal, in his sketch of the character of Sejanus. The passage to which I allude it is not impossible but Gray might have in mind when he wrote his Ode on the Prospect of Eton College—

> Ambition this shall teach to rise,
>   Then whirl the wretch from high,
> To bitter scorn a sacrifice,
>   And grinning infamy.

Consult also our Shakespeare's description of the character of Wolsey.

with

with me, as this matter has ſucceeded ſo fortunately, left any thing adverſe happen in our conſultation, to allay our good fortune; and that this
our exultation may not become too extravagant.
Adverſe affairs check themſelves[s], and teach
what is neceſſary to be done; thoſe which are
proſperous are apt, from the joy of them, to
thruſt people aſide from wiſe conſultation and
comprehenſion. I therefore the more ſtrenuouſly
adviſe that this matter be deferred for ſome days,
till, from ſuch exceſs of joy, we again become
maſters of ourſelves." Of what Cato next ſays,
he affirms:

" That they are a confeſſion, not a defence;
nor are they a removal or transferring of the
crime, but a participation of it with many others,
which has nothing to do with juſtification. Moreover," continues he, " he acknowledges, that the
Rhodians, who were accuſed of favouring and
wiſhing well to the king, in oppoſition to the Romans, were impelled to theſe ſentiments by views
of intereſt; left the Romans, by the conqueſt of
king Perſes, ſhould be elated to an extravagant
degree of pride and inſolence." He quotes the
words themſelves, which I ſubjoin; " I indeed
muſt confeſs that the Rhodians did not wiſh us

[s] *Check themſelves.*] In the original it is " domant ſe,"
literally tame themſelves; thus Gray calls adverſity the
tamer of the human breaſt.

to fight as we have fought, nor that we fhould overcome king Perfes; but I think alfo that many people and nations wifhed the fame; and I do not know whether fome of them might not be averfe to our fuccefs, not from a defire to fee us difgraced, but becaufe they apprehended that if there was no one whom we feared, and we had no limits to our will, they muft then be under our fole dominion, and in fervitude to us. I believe they were of this opinion, from a regard to their own liberty; nor did the Rhodians ever publicly affift Perfes. Reflect with how much greater circumfpection we act in our private characters, one among another. Each of us, if we think that any thing is imagined againft our intereft, oppofe it with all our force, that it may not take effect: but this people neverthelefs fubmitted."

With refpect to his cenfure of the introduction, Tiro ought to have known that the Rhodians were defended by Cato in the character of a fenator, of a man of confular and cenforial dignity, advifing what he deemed beft for the public, not merely as a patron [7] pleading the caufe of the accufed. One kind of exordium is proper to thofe who defend the accufed before judges, wifhing, by all poffi-

---

[7] *Not merely as a patron.*] The good fenfe of this reply will ftrike the flighteft obferver, and fully anfwers the objection and cavil of Tiro.

ble

ble means, to excite humanity and compaſſion; and another when the ſenate is conſulted concerning the commonwealth, by a man of ſuperior authority, indignant at the moſt unjuſt ſentiments of ſome, and with great ſerioufneſs and weight expreſſing his zeal for the public advantage, and his concern for the ſafety of their allies. It is properly and uſefully preſcribed in the ſchools of rhetoricians, that judges who ſit upon the lives of ſtrangers, in a cauſe not at all relating to themſelves, and from which no riſk, no emolument is to enſue to them, except the office of paſſing judgment, are to be ſoothed and conciliated to a mild and favourable opinion, and to the preſervation of thoſe who are accuſed before them. But when the common dignity, honour, and advantage of a nation is involved, and on this account advice is to be given, what ſhall be done hereafter, or whether the preſent proceedings ſhall not be deferred; then he who undertakes to render his hearers favourable and merciful, in exordiums of this kind, does no good, and uſes expreſſions not neceſſary for the purpoſe. The common intereſt and the common danger already prepare them to hearken to advice, and they are inclined of themſelves to require a benevolent ſpirit in him who gives it. But when he ſays that Cato allows that the Rhodians were unwilling that they ſhould have fought as they had fought, and that king Perſes ſhould be conquered by the Roman people; when he affirmed that theſe were the

ſentiments

sentiments not of the Rhodians only, but of many other nations, but that this availed nothing to justify or extenuate their crime, Tiro is, in the first instance, guilty of a great falshood. He gives the words of Cato, and calumniates him for words totally different. For Cato does not confess that the Rhodians were averse to the victory of the Roman people; but he confessed that he believed them to be so, which, doubtless, was an avowal of what he himself thought, and not an acknowledgment of the crime of the Rhodians. In which thing, it is my opinion, he is not only not to be censured, but worthy of praise and admiration, since he seemed to give his opinion against the Rhodians frankly and conscientiously, and by obtaining confidence to his candour, softened and conciliated what appeared to be hostile. They ought, therefore, from the reason of the thing, to be more dear and acceptable to the Roman people, who, when they might have been useful to the king, and desired to be so, yet actually contibuted nothing to his assistance. He afterwards adds these words from the same oration : " Shall we then suddenly forego these so great benefits, this valuable friendship, voluntarily and irregularly ? and what we say they were inclined to do, shall we make haste to do before them ?" This enthymeme [8], he says, is mean and vicious. For it may be replied, certainly we will anticipate

* *This enthymeme*] This in logic is an argument consisting of two propositions, the antecedent, and its consequence.

them,

them, for if we do not, we shall be oppressed, and shall fall into those snares against which we omitted to take previous caution. Lucilius, he adds, properly imputes this fault to the poet Euripides, because, when king Polyphontes said that he had killed his brother, because his brother had previously concerted his death, Merope, his brother's wife, reproved him in these lines :

> If, as thou say'st[9], my husband meant to slay
>   thee,
> Yet art thou bound to sheathe thy vengeful
>   blade
> Until that time arrive when he resolv'd
> To have accomplished his inhuman purpose.

But this, he remarks, is full of absurdity, to wish to do any thing with that design and purpose, that indeed you may never accomplish what you intend. But indeed Tiro did not reflect that in all kinds of precaution, the same rule did not apply ; and that the business and duties of human life, with respect to anticipation, delay, revenge, or caution, did not resemble the battles of gladiators ; for the fortune of gladiators prepared to engage, was of this kind, either to kill if they should conquer, or to die if they should yield[10]. But the life of
men

---

* *If, as thou say'st,*] I have given the version of Mr. Wod-hull.

[10] *Should yield.*] The preservation of a conquered gladia-tor did not depend upon his adversary, but on the caprice of the spectators, and was determined by a motion of the thumb.
When

men is not circumfcribed by fuch unjuft or infu-
perable neceffity, that you ought firft to commit
an injury, left, by not fo doing, you fhould endure
it ". So far was it from the humanity of the Roman people to anticipate, that they often neglected to avenge injuries committed againft themfelves. He afterwards afferts, that in this oration
Cato has ufed arguments both difingenuous and
too audacious, not at all proper for fuch a man
as he was, but full of art and deceit, refembling
the fallacies of Greek fophifts. For when,
fays he, it was objected to the Rhodians that they
wifhed to make war on the Roman people, he
did not pretend to deny it, but he required that
it fhould be forgiven, becaufe they had not done
it, although they greatly defired it; that he had
alfo introduced what the logicians call *epagoge* ",
which is indeed both infidious and fophiftical, not
fo much calculated for truth as for cavil, endeavouring to enforce and confirm by fallacious examples, that no one who wifhed to do ill could
juftly be punifhed, unlefs he had actually done

When the gladiator was overcome he lowered his arms; if
the fpectators wifhed his life to be faved, pollicem premebant,
they turned down their thumbs; if they wifhed him to be put
to death, pollicem vertebant, they turned up their thumbs.

" *Endure it*.] This is a generous and noble fentiment, and
worthy the more pure and chaftened fpirit of the gofpel.

" *Epagoge*.] That is, a comparifon of things or arguments refembling each other.

that which he wished to do [13]. The words of Cato in this oration are these:

" He who speaks with greatest acrimony against them, says this, that they desired to become enemies. And who is there among us, who as far as he himself is concerned, would think it right that any one should suffer punishment because it was proved that he desired to do ill? No one, I believe, for, as far as relates to myself, I certainly would not." Then a little afterwards he adds, " And I would ask, where is the law so severe as to assert, if any one shall desire to do this, let him be fined a thousand sesterces? If any one shall wish to have more than five hundred acres, let him be fined as much: if any one shall wish to have a greater number of cattle, let him be fined as much; but we all of us wish to have more than we already possess [14], and do so with impunity." Afterwards he adds, " But if it be not just that honour should be given to him who says he wished to do well, but really did not, shall it be injurious to the Rhodians, not that they acted ill, but that it is reported of them that they wished to do ill?"

[13] *Wished to do.*] Such, however, is the sublime morality of the gospel, which says of him who looketh with concupiscence on the wife of another, that he hath already committed the act of adultery in his heart.

[14] *Already possess.*] There are indeed very few who do not occasionally indulge a wish like this expressed by Horace:

Oh si angulus iste
Proximus accedet qui nunc deformat agellum.

By fuch arguments Tiro Tullius affirms that Cato ftrenuoufly contended that the Rhodians fhould not be punifhed, becaufe, though they defired to become the enemies of the Roman people, they really did not. It cannot, he allows, be contefted, that the facts were by no means parallel, to defire to have more than five hundred acres, which by a decree of the people was forbidden to colonifts, and to defire to make an unjuft and impious war on the Roman people; nor could it be denied that the one was deferving of reward, the other of punifhment. Services, fays he, which are promifed ought to be waited for, and certainly ought not to be rewarded till they are performed. But it is right to guard againft impending injuries, rather than expect them. It is the height of folly, he obferves, not to meet concerted injuries, but to wait and expect them; but when they are perpetrated and endured, then finally, when, being done they cannot be hindered, to punifh them. Thefe are the cold and infignificant objections which Tiro has brought againft Cato. But Cato has not introduced this epagoge naked, folitary, and defencelefs, but he has ftrengthened it by various means, and fupported it by many arguments; and becaufe he confulted not more for the Rhodians than for the commonwealth, he deemed nothing bafe that he faid and did in this matter, as he attempted to obtain the prefervation of allies by every kind of opinion: and firft he not unfkilfully accomplifh-

ed

ed this, which is neither forbidden by the law of nations nor the law of nature, but by the influence of laws issued to remedy any evil, or to obtain time, such as the number of cattle, the limits prescribed to land, and other similar things; in which things, what is forbidden by the law to be done, may not, according to the law, be done; but to desist to do this, if it be possible, is not dishonourable. And these things he insensibly compared and confounded with that which by itself it is not honest either to do or wish to do; then finally, lest the unsuitableness of the comparison should be obvious, he strengthens it by various modes of defence; nor does he give much importance to the trifling but thoroughly sifted censures of the will in things forbidden; which, in philosophic cases, are matters of dispute; but he exerts his whole force in this alone, that the cause of the Rhodians, whose friendship it was the interest of the republic to retain, should be considered either as just, or at least should be forgiven; in the mean time he affirms, that the Rhodians neither made war, nor desired to do so. He alledges also, that facts alone ought to be weighed and judged, but that the mere inclination, unsupported by any act, was neither obnoxious to the laws, nor to punishment. Sometimes, indeed, he seemingly concedes that they had offended, and he implores their pardon, and teaches that forgiveness is essential to human affairs. If they should refuse this pardon, he alarms them with fears of tumults in the commonwealth: on the contrary, if they should grant this pardon, he shews them that the magnanimity of the Roman people would be preserved. The imputation of pride, which at this time, among other things, was in the senate objected to the Rhodians, he turns off, and eludes by an admirable and almost divine mode of reply.—We will add the words of Cato, since Tiro has omitted them :

" They say that the Rhodians are haughty ; an imputation I would desire to avert from me and from my children. Let them be proud ; what is that to us ? shall we be angry that any are prouder than ourselves ?"

Nothing possibly could be introduced with more dignity and strength than this apostrophe against the haughtiest of mankind, who, loving pride in themselves, reprobated it in others. We may also observe in the whole of Cato's oration, that all the aids and implements of the rhetorical discipline were brought forwards, but by no means as in mock fights ', or in those carried on for amusement and pleasure ; the matter, I say, was not agitated with an excessive degree of refinement, discrimination, and order, but as it were in a doubtful engagement, when the troops being scattered, it is in various places fought with doubtful fortune. So in this cause, when the pride of the Rhodians had notoriously provoked universal hatred and envy, he used promiscuously every mode of protection and defence. Sometimes he commends them

---

' *Mock fights.*]—Simulachris præliorum. Thus in Virgil :

Bellique cient simulachra sub armis.

as having the greateft merit, fometimes he exculpates them as innocent, though he reprehends them for a lavifh wafte of their wealth and fortunes. Again he attempts to extenuate what they had done, as if they had really done wrong, then he points out their natural claims on the republic; finally, he reminds them of the clemency and generofity of their anceftors, and of the common good. All which things, if they could have been introduced with more perfpicuity, method, and harmony, certainly could not have been faid with more ftrength and energy. Tiro Tullius has therefore acted an unjuft part, having fingled out from the various qualities of fo rich an oration, happily connected with each other, a fmall and naked portion, as an object of his fatire; as if it were unworthy M. Cato to affert that the mere propenfity to faults not actually perpetrated ought not to be punifhed: but whoever will take in hand the entire oration of Cato, and carefully examine and perufe the letter of Tiro to Axius, will be able to form a more correct and fatisfactory judgment of the reply which I have made to Tullius Tiro. He will thus be enabled more accurately and more perfectly to correct and approve what I have advanced.

Chap. IV.

What sort of servants those were that Cælius Sabinus, the Civilian, says were exposed to sale with caps on [1]. The reason of this. What slaves were anciently sold, " sub coronâ," and the meaning of this phrase.

CÆLIUS SABINUS, the Civilian, has recorded that certain slaves were used to be exposed to sale, with caps upon their heads, and the seller of such slaves did not answer for them.—The reason

of

[1] *With caps.*]—The explanation of this is attended with some small difficulty.—Pileus, or the Cap, was the emblem of liberty, and we learn from Livy and Plautus, that when slaves were made free they were termed Pileati.—Slaves in general, when sold, had their heads bare. Were these slaves then, for whom the seller was not responsible, of a higher order, as being entitled to this distinction ? To me it seems probable that they were. When a slave was made free, his head was shaved, and he wore the cap of freedom. Thus Sosia says in Plautus :

So shall I directly
Cover my shorn crown with the cap of freedom.

Those also were called Servi Pileati, who preceded the funeral of their masters. If any person in his will gave liberty to any of his slaves, they immediately shaved their crowns, and walked in procession as freemen, with caps on their heads, before the funeral procession of their master. Slaves made free were called slaves ad pileum vocati, called to the cap. It will be seen that my opinion on this subject is different from

that

of which, according to him, was, that flaves of this defcription ought fo to be marked whilft on fale, that the buyers could not be miftaken or deceived, nor could the law of fale be perplexed. But it was immediately obvious what kind of flaves they were. "Thus," fays he, "anciently, flaves taken in war were brought forth wearing garlands, and therefore were faid to be fold fub corona. For as this garland was a fign of captives being fold, fo the cap indicated that flaves of that kind were to be fold, concerning whom the feller did not make himfelf refponfible to the purchafer."

But there is another explanation of this, why captives were faid to be fold " fub corona," becaufe foldiers, by way of fecurity, ftood round a number of captives expofed to fale, and this circle of foldiers was called corona. But that what I have before alledged is nearer the truth, we learn from Cato in his book De Re Militari. Thefe are Cato's words : " The people on their own account would rather crowned offer fupplication on account of good fuccefs, than, being crowned, be fold from ill fuccefs."

that given by Mr. Adams in page 35 of his Roman Antiquities. It may not be improper to add, that although the cap was an emblem of liberty, the Roman citizens did not wear it, they appeared in public with their heads uncovered; and therefore it is faid of Julius Cæfar, that he was exceedingly gratified by the permiffion to wear a crown of laurel, which concealed his baldnefs.

 C H A P.

Chap. V.

Remarkable story of Polus the player [1].

THERE was an actor in Greece of great celebrity, superior to the rest in the grace and harmony of his voice and action. His name it is said was Polus, and he acted in the tragedies of the more eminent poets, with great knowledge and accuracy. This Polus lost by death his only and beloved son. When he had sufficiently indulged his natural grief, he returned to his employment. Being at this time to act the Electra of Sophocles at Athens, it was his part to carry an urn as containing the bones of Orestes. The argument of the fable is so imagined, that Electra, who is presumed to carry the relics of her brother, laments and commiserates his end, who is believed to have died a violent death. Polus

[1] The actors of Greece, and of Athens in particular were held in extraordinary estimation. We accordingly find that they were occasionally employed on affairs of state, and sent on foreign embassies.—Thus we find, that in a solemn embassy sent from Athens to Philip of Macedon, there were players, and that he distinguished these with particular marks of kindness. On the Grecian theatre as well as on the Roman, the parts of women were performed by men, which custom also prevailed in the earlier periods of the English stage.

therefore,

therefore, clad in the mourning habit of Electra, took from the tomb the bones and urn of his son, and as if embracing Oreſtes, filled the place, not with the image and imitation, but with the ſighs and lamentations of unfeigned ſorrow. Therefore, when a fable ſeemed to be repreſented, real grief was diſplayed.

<hr>

CHAP. VI.

What Ariſtotle wrote on the natural defect of ſome of the ſenſes [1].

OF the five ſenſes which nature has given to animals, ſight, hearing, taſte, touch, and ſmell, called by the Greeks αισθησεις, ſome animals want one, ſome another, and are naturally produced either without ſight, ſmell, or hearing. But Ariſtotle affirms that no animal is born without

[1] Gellius is here guilty of a little lapſe of memory.—This quotation from Ariſtotle is not found in his tract on Memory, but in his treatiſe on Sleep and Watchfulneſs. Nature is very provident and very bountiful, for ſuch animals as are defective in any particular ſenſe, are notoriouſly excellent in thoſe which they poſſeſs.—We may truly ſay with Pope:

Whether with reaſon or with inſtinct bleſt,
Know all enjoy the power which ſuits them beſt.

the

the fenfe of tafte or touch.   The words from his book, " On Memory," are thefe: " Except the imperfect animals, all have touch and tafte."

C H A P. VII.

Whether the word affatim *fhould be pronounced like* admodum, *with the acute accent on the firft fyllable ; with certain obfervations on other words, not without their ingenuity.*

THE poet Annianus [1], befides his other agree-able accomplifhments, was very well fkilled in ancient literature and verbal criticifm ; he con-verfed alfo with a remarkable and learned grace-fulnefs.   He pronounced *affatim* as *admodum*, with the firft not the middle fyllable accented, and his opinion was that the ancients fo pronounced it.   He fays that in his hearing Probus, the grammarian, thus read thefe verfes in the Ciftellaria of Plau-tus :

[1] *Annianus.*]—This perfon's name again occurs in Book ix. c. 10.

Potin [2] es tu homo facinus facere ftrenuum,
Aliorum eft affatim qui faciant. Sane ego
Me volo fortem perhiberier virum.

The reafon of this accent he affirmed was, that *affa-tim* was not two diftinct parts of fpeech, but both parts were united in one word, as in this which we call *exadverfum,* he thought the fecond fyllable ought to be made acute, becaufe it was one and not two parts of fpeech, and that in Terence thefe two verfes ought to be read thus,

In quo [3] Hæc difcebat ludo, exadverfum loco
Tonftrina erat quædam.

He added alfo, that the prepofition *ad* was accented when it was ufed as we fay intenfively, as *adfabre,*

[2] *Potin.*]—This fragment is thus tranflated in Thornton's Plautus:

Are you a man that's fit to undertake
An enterprize of daring villainy?
  There are enough befides
Would undertake to do it.—I'm refolv'd
To fhew myfelf a man of courage.

Inftead of Ciftellaria, Gronovius recommends the reading of Clitellaria, from Clitellæ, which fignifies a pack-faddle.

[3] *In quo.*]—There was a barber's fhop oppofite the place where fhe went to fchool.

Barbers fhops at Athens and at Rome were reforted to by the idle and curious to difcufs the topics of the day, as not many years fince was cuftomary in this country.—I believe that it is ftill the cafe in country-towns and villages remote from the metropolis.

F 4

admodum,

admodum, and *adprobe*.   In other refpects alfo Annianus was very fenfible in his remarks.   But he thought that this particle *ad*, when ufed intenfively, ought to be acute; but this is not without exception, for we fay *adpotus* as well as *adprimus* and *adprimi*, in all which *ad* is ufed intenfively; nor is the particle *ad* properly pronounced with an acute accent.   But in *adprobus*, which fignifies *valde probus*, I cannot deny but that it ought to be made acute in the firft fyllable, Cæcilius, in his comedy which is called *Triumphus*, ufes this word.

Hierocles[4] hofpes eft mihi, adolefcens *adprobus*.

In thefe words, therefore, which we fay ought not to have the acute accent, is it that the fyllable which follows is long by nature, which does not admit the firft fyllable to be accented in words of more than two fyllables? L. Livius, in his Odyffey, ufes *adprimum*, with the firft fyllable long, in this verfe:

Ibi[5] denique vir fummus adprimus Patroclus. The fame Livius in his Odyffey fays *præmodum* like *admodum*.   Thus *parcentes præmodum*, which fignifies *fupra modum*, and it is ufed as it were *præter modum*, in which the firft fyllable ought to have the acute accent.

---

[4] *Hierocles*.]—Hierocles is my gueft, a moft deferving youth.

[5] *Ibi*.]—There alfo Patrocles a man in the firft degree illuftrious.

Chap. VIII.

Incredible story of a dolphin who loved a youth.

THAT dolphins are of a wanton and amorous nature, is declared as well by ancient hiftory [1] as by recent narratives. For in the time of the Cæfars [2], as Apion has related, in the fea of Puteoli, and fome ages before, off Naupactum, according to Theophraftus, certain dolphins were known and proved to be vehemently amorous. Neither were they thus attached to their own fpecies, but in a wonderful manner, and like human beings, felt a paffion for youths of an ingenuous appearance, whom they had feen in veffels or on the fhore. I have fubjoined the words of Apion [3], a learned man, from his fifth

book

[1] *Ancient hiftory.*]—See in the firft book of Herodotus the ftory of Arion, who was preferved by a dolphin, which feemed to receive delight from mufical founds.

[2] *Time of the Cæfars.*]—Pliny relates that this happened in the time of Auguftus Cæfar, who lived the century before Gellius.

[3] *Apion.*]—See Book v. chap. 14. the ftory of Androcles and the lion, related by this fame Apion; who appears to have been, in every fenfe of the word, a ftory-teller. This tale has a pertinent parallel in Shakefpeare, where Autolycus

produces

book on Egyptian Affairs, in which he relates the intimacy, fport, and actions of an amorous dolphin, and of a youth not difliking it, affirming that he and many others witneffed this:

" And I myfelf, near Dicæarchia, faw a dolphin who loved a youth, and who was obedient to his voice; for the fifh when fwimming, took the youth upon his back, and drew in his fins, that he might not wound him whom he loved: he then carried him, as if mounted on a horfe, to the diftance of two hundred ftadia. Rome and all Italy were collected to fee a fifh acting thus from love."

To this he adds what is no lefs wonderful.— " Afterwards," he continues, " this boy beloved by the dolphin died from fome difeafe: but the dolphin fwimming, in his ufual manner, frequently

produces a ballad for fale, " Of a fifh that appeared upon the coaft on Wednefday the fourfcore of April, forty thoufand fathom above water, and fung this ballad againft the hard hearts of maids.—It was thought fhe was a woman, and was turned into a cod fifh, for fhe would not exchange flefh with one that loved her.—This ballad is very pitiful, and as true."

See a fimilar ftory related by Pliny, Book ix. chap. 8. Some of the moft beautiful antiques which have been preferved reprefent Cupids riding on the backs of dolphins.

The reader will find fome whimifcal things on the paffion which fome animals have entertained for men in the thirteenth book of Athenæus.—We are there told of a cock which was enamoured of an eunuch, of a fheep in love with a child, of a peacock in love with a young woman, which died when fhe died; laftly, the fame author tells a tale of a dolphin entirely refembling the one recorded in the chapter before us.

to

to the fhore, when he faw that the boy, who ufed to meet him on the firft fhoal, did not appear, languifhed and died alfo[4]; and being found on the fhore by thofe who knew the circumftance, he was buried in the tomb of his favourite."

[4] *Died alfo.*]—Inftances will probably occur to the recol-lection of the reader, of dogs who on the death of their maf-ters have languifhed and died alfo.—The example of Argus in Homer, who expired from joy on feeing Ulyffes, muft doubtlefs be familiar.

> Thus near the gates, conferring as they drew,
> Argus, the dog, his ancient mafter knew;
> He, not unconfcious of the voice and tread,
> Lifts to the found his ear, and rears his head.
>   *   *   *   *   *   *   *   *
> He knew his lord,—he knew, and ftrove to meet,
> In vain he ftrove to crawl and kifs his feet;
> Yet all he could, his tail, his ears, his eyes,
> Salute his mafter, and confefs his joys.
>   *   *   *   *   *   *   *   *
> The dog, whom Fate had granted to behold
> His lord, when twenty tedious years had roll'd,
> Takes a laft look, and having feen him, dies;
> So clos'd for ever faithful Argus' eyes.

C H A P. IX.

Many ancient writers used pepofci, memordi, fpepondi, *and* cecurri, *not as afterwards with* o *or* u *in
the firft fyllable, but with* e, *according to the Greek
ufage. Moreover, many men, neither unlearned nor
vulgar, from the verb* defcendo *faid not* defcendi,
but defcendidi.

PEPOSCI, memordi, pepugi, cucurri,
feem to be proper[1], and now almoft all our
learned men ufe words of this kind. But Q.

---

[1] *To be proper.*]—What is noted in this chapter muft una-
voidably happen in all languages. Words which at one period are confidered as elegant and proper will, in the progrefs
of any language towards refinement, become obfolete and
vulgar: yet the public tafte is not in this refpect always
correct or juft; caprice and fafhion will often contradict and
fuperfede the judgment, and words and expreffions which
have both force and beauty will grow into difufe without
any adequate reafon. This is certainly true, in the Englifh
and other languages.—Words occur in Shakefpeare which
have admirable effect, but the ufe of which would now be
thought inelegant and improper. Here, however, the remark of Horace is pertinent:

> Quid autem
> Cæcilio Plautoque dabit Romanus, ademptum
> Virgilio, Varoque.

> Ita verborum vetus interit ætas
> Et juvenum ritu florent modo nata, vigentque.

> Ennius,

Ennius, in his Satires, wrote *memorderit* with an *e*, and not momorderit.—Thus he fays,

Meum non eft, at fi me canis memorderit.

So alfo Laberius[2] in his Galli—De integro patrimonio meo centum millia nummum *memordi*. The fame Laberius alfo, in his Colorator—Itaque levi pruna percoctus fimul fub dentes mulieris veni, bis ter *memordit*. So P. Nigidius, in his fecond book of Annals—Serpens fi *memordit*, gallina deligitur et opponitur. So Plautus, in his Aulularia—*Admemordit* hominem : But the fame Plautus, in his Trigemini, faid not *præmordiffe*, nor præmemordiffe, but præmorfiffe, as

Ni fugiffem medium credo præmorfiffet.

Atta[3] alfo, in his Conciliatrix—Urfum fe memordiffe autumat. Valerius Antias too, in his fortyfifth book of Annals, has faid *pepofci*, and not *popofci*.

Denique Licinius Tribunus Plebi perduellionis ei diem dixit et comitiis diem, a Q. Martio

---

[2] *Laberius, &c.*]—See Barthius, p. 400, where this play of Laberius is alfo quoted.

[3] *Atta.*]—This is Quinctius Atta the poet.—The name of Atta, according to Feftus, was ufually given to thofe who laboured under fome defect in their feet, which difabled them from walking.   This Atta is mentioned thus by Horace;

Recte necne crocum florefque perambulat Attæ
Fabula, fi dubitem : clament periiffe pudorem
Cuncti pene patres.

From this paffage we may conclude that the writings of Atta, who indeed lived in the Auguftan age, were very popular.

prætore

prætore *pepofcit*. *Pepugero* is alfo ufed by Atta, in his Ædelicia—Sed fi *pepugero* metuet. Probus has remarked, that Ælius Tubero, in his book written to C. Oppius, ufed *occecurrerit*, and has given his words—Si generalis fpecies *occecurrit*. The fame Probus has obferved, that Valerius Antias, in his twelfth book of Hiftories, has written *fpeponderant*. He gives the paffage thus— Tiberius Gracchus qui quæftor C. Mancino in Hifpaniæ fuerat et ceteri qui pacem *fpeponderant*; but the reafon of thefe words may feem to be this: As the Greeks, in one of the modifications of the præterite, namely the perfect præterite, often change into *e*, the fecond letter of the word, as γραφω γεγραφα, ποιω πεποιηκα, λαλω λελαληκα, κρατω κεκρατηκα, λυω λελυκα; fo alfo, mordeo memordi, pofco pepofci, tendo tetendi, tango tetigi, pungo pepugi, fpondeo fpepondi, curro cecurri, tollo tetuli. M. Tullius and C. Cæfar have ufed mordeo memordi, pungo pepugi, and fpondeo fpepondi. Moreover, I find that from the word fcindo, by fimilar reafoning, fefciderat is written, not fciderat. L. Attius, in his firft book of Sotadici [*], faid fefciderat. Thefe

---

[*] *Sotadici.*]—This name was given to obfcene poems, written in a particular metre.—They were fo called from their inventor, Sotades, a poet of Thrace. The peculiarity of the verfes was, that they might be read either way, without injury either to the metre or the fenfe, of which the following may ferve as a fpecimen:

Si bene te tua laus taxat, fua laute tenebis.

are

are his words: Non ergo aquila ita, uti prædicant *fcefciderat* pectus. Ennius [5] alfo, and Valerius Antias, in his feventy-fifth book of Hiftories, has written thus: Deinde furore locato ad forum *defcendidit*.   Laberius alfo, in his Catularius, faid

> Ego mirabar quomodo mammæ mihi *defcen-*
> *diderant*.

[5] *Ennius.*]—This paffage is evidently corrupt, and fome words without doubt are wanting.

CHAP. X.

Ufufcapio is an entire word, and ufed in the nomina-
tive cafe.   So alfo is pignorifcapio.

AS ufufcapio is ufed as an entire word, the letter *a* being made long, fo pignorifcapio is in like manner combined, and pronounced long.—Thefe are the words of Cato, in his firft book of Epiftolary Queftions:

" Pignorifcapio is a diftinct word of itfelf, on account of the military pay which the foldier was accuftomed to take from the pay-mafter tribune [1]."

From

[1] *Pay-mafter tribune.*]—This was an officer of inferior rank, and not improbably correfponding with the pay-mafter ferjeants

From which it is evident that we may fay *hanc capionem*, as *hanc captionem*, both with refpect to *ufus* and *pignus*.

C H·A P. XI.

The fignification of " levitas" and " nequitia" is not that which we ufually give them.

I UNDERSTAND that " levitas" is now generally ufed to fignify inconftancy and mutability, and " nequitia" for artifice and cunning. But they among the ancients who fpoke properly and correctly called thofe *leves* whom now we term vile, and worthy of no efteem : *levitas* accordingly was as *vilitas*, and *nequam* was applied to a man of no character or confequence, whom the Greeks call " an abandoned, loofe, worthlefs, immoral, or profligate perfon." He who wifhes for examples of thefe words, needs not go far, he will find them in Cicero's fecond Oration againft Antony. For when he was about to point out the extreme

ferjeants of our troops. Though their rank feems to have been inferior, yet the richer of the Plebeians were felected for this office. Their importance feems to have been fomewhat diminifhed by Auguftus, who added two hundred to their number, in order to judge caufes of more trifling moment.

meannefs

meanneſs of the life and conduct of Antony, that he lingered in taverns, that he drank late, that he walked with his face covered that he might not be known : reproaching him with theſe and other things, he ſays, *videte hominis levitatem* ; as if with this imputation he branded the man with all theſe marks of diſgrace. Afterwards, when he was heaping upon the ſame Antony other ſarcaſtical and opprobrious accuſations, he adds this at the concluſion : " *Oh hominem nequam* ; I can uſe no term more properly than this." But from the ſame place I think it expedient to add more of Cicero's words :

" Obſerve the levity of the man,—about the tenth hour [1] of the day he came to the Red Rocks, and concealed himſelf in a certain tavern : here, ſhutting himſelf up, he drank till night ; thence in his carriage he returned ſwiftly to the city, having his face covered [2]. The porter ſays, Who

---

[1] *Tenth hour.*]—That is, two hours before ſun-ſet.—*The Red Rocks* was a place betwixt Rome and Veii. See Livy, book the ſecond. Here fell the family of Fabii. It is now called *Grotta Roſſa.*

[2] *Face covered.*]—This expreſſion gives us an inſight into the private manners of the Romans. We learn that it was uſual for people of both ſexes, when they went abroad in the night, or upon any occaſion, when they did not chooſe to be known, to hide their faces. This was probably done, not by wearing any diſtinct veil, but merely by drawing their toga over the face. Thus in Juvenal, Meſſalina, when viſiting the brothels, is deſcribed as having her face concealed.

are you? A meffenger from Marcus. He is then introduced to the lady, for whofe fake he came, and gives her a letter. This fhe read with tears, for it was very amoroufly written: its fubftance was this, that in future he would have no connection with the actrefs: that he had taken all his love from one, and given it to the other. When the woman wept plentifully, the compaffionate man could not bear it, he revealed his face, and threw himfelf on her neck. *O hominem nequam* [3], for what epithet can I more properly apply? Therefore, that the woman might unexpectedly behold you as a hireling boy, you filled the city with nocturnal alarms, and fpread for many days a terror through Italy."

In like manner alfo Q. Claudius, in his firft book of Annals, called a luxurious life, and one licentious and profligate, *nequitiam*—" Perfuading a certain young man, named Lucanus, who was of the very firft rank, but who had wafted great wealth by luxury and *nequitia*."

M. Varro, in his book on the Latin tongue, fays, " That as from *non* and *volo*, *nolo* is made, fo from *ne* and *quicquam*, the middle fyllable being taken away, *nequam* is formed."

---

[3] *Nequam.*]—O worthlefs man! The word is combined from the two words *ne* and *quidquam*, as *nolo* is produced from *non* and *volo*.

The term *nequitia* feems generally to have implied a combination of luxury with voluptuoufnefs. It is perhaps moft frequently applied as expreffive of amorous extravagance.

P. Afri-

P. Africanus, fpeaking for himfelf before the Roman people, and concerning a fine, fays,

" All the evils, vices, and crimes which men commit, proceed from malice and profligacy. Which do you defend, malice, profligacy, or both? If you wifh to defend profligacy, you may: but you have wafted more wealth upon one profrtitute than you have given in to the cenfor as the value of the whole Sabine farm: who will wager a thoufand fefterces that this is not fo? But you have confumed more than a third part of your paternal inheritance on your vices: who will lay a thoufand fefterces that it is not fo? You will not then have profligacy, at leaft you will defend malice; but you willingly and deliberately have fworn in a precife form of words: who will venture a thoufand fefterces that this is not fo?"

                    CHAP.

Chap. XII.

Of the garments called chiridotæ—Publius Africanus reproved Sulpicius Gallus for wearing them.

IT was dishonourable[1] in Rome, and in all Latium, for a man to wear a vest which descended below his arms, to the extremity of his hands, near the fingers. Such vests our country-men

[1] The Romans, like all other nations, when a small and humble people, were remarkable for the simplicity of their dress and manners. But as their power encreased, and wealth multiplied, luxury stole in, and splendour and magnificence expelled neatness:—

> Banish'd from man's life, his happiest life,
> Simplicity and spotless innocence.

That these tunics with sleeves were at first reckoned effeminate, we learn from Cicero, and the passage from Virgil quoted in this chapter, which I subjoin at length from the 9th Æneid:

> Vobis picta croco et fulgenti murice vestis,
> Desidiæ cordi, juvat indulgere choreis,
> Et tunicæ manicas et habent redimicula mitræ,
> O vere Phrygiæ neque enim Phryges, &c.

Cicero also reproaches Catiline with exhibiting a like proof of degeneracy. These long sleeves, when first introduced, were plain and unadorned, but afterwards Julius Cæsar set the fashion of wearing them with fringes, probably in the manner of modern ruffles.

The

men call by a Greek name, Chirodotæ, and they
thought that a long and flowing garment was
proper for women only, protecting their arms
and legs from fight. The Romans at firſt were
cloathed without tunics, and with the toga only;
afterwards they wore cloſe and ſhort tunics below
the ſhoulders, which the Greeks call ἐξωμίδας.
P. Africanus, the ſon of Paulus, a man accom-
pliſhed in every good art and every virtue,
among other things with which he reproached
Sulpicius Gallus, an effeminate man, objected
this alſo, that he wore veſts which covered the
whole of his hands [*]. Theſe are Scipio's words;

The writing the above note has brought to my recollection a phraſe in our language, which ſeems no improper ſubject of enquiry in this place. When a perſon undertakes
any thing which is mean or contemptible, we often ſay he
has been upon a ſleevelefs buſineſs. It ſhould ſeem from
ſome paſſages in Shakeſpeare, and the writers before him,
that anciently in this country the ſleeve was a mark of gen-
tility. The ſimilitude of which circumſtance to the cuſtom
obſerved in ancient Rome, ſeems curious and remarkable.

[*] *Whole of his hands.*]—The uſe of gloves, or any cover-
ing for the hands, implies a conſiderable degree not only of
refinement but effeminacy. I have taken ſome pains to find
in what nation, and at what period, gloves were firſt introduced, but without ſucceſs: they were certainly in uſe in this
country at a very remote time, as appears from various paſſages in our oldeſt writers. It is a curious incident, though
it muſt be confeſſed not altogether pertinent to the ſubject
before us, that gloves were in this country worn in the hat,
from three very different occaſions—in memory of a friend,
as a favour from a miſtreſs, and as a mark of accepting a
challenge.

G 3

" For

" For he who every day perfumes himfelf, and dreffes by a looking-glafs, whofe eyebrows are fhaved, and who without a beard walks with thighs alfo bare; who at entertainments, being a young man, refting below his lover with his *tunica chirodota*; who is not only fond of drink but of men; can any one doubt but that he does what catamites do ?"

Virgil alfo reprobates vefts of this kind as effeminate and difgraceful.

Et tunicæ manicas et habent redimicula mitræ.

Quintus Ennius alfo feems to have called the Carthaginian youth *tunicatam*, reproachfully.

CHAP. XIII.

Whom M. Cato calls claſſicus, *whom* infra claſſem.

THE term *claſſici* [1] was applied, not to all thoſe who were *in claſſibus*, in the claſſes, but only to men of the firſt claſs, who were rated at a hundred and twenty thouſand pounds of braſs. The term *infra claſſem* was applied to all thoſe of the ſecond and under claſſes, who were rated at a ſum leſs than that mentioned above. I have curſorily noticed this, becauſe in the oration of M. Cato, in which he recommends the Voconian law [2], it is enquired what *claſſicus* is, and what *infra claſſem*.

[1] *Claſſici.*]—From this is derived our Engliſh word claſſic, which is applied preciſely with the ſame meaning. The authors of moſt diſtinguiſhed reputation in any language are denominated the claſſics in that language.

The term claſſici, it may be obſerved, was alſo applied by the Romans to the nautæ, remiges, or crew of a ſhip.

[2] *Voconian law.*]—This law is quoted by Cicero, in his ſecond Oration againſt Verres. The name of the author was Voconius, and its objeſt was to limit the fortunes that might be left to females. The law was annulled by Auguſtus.

 CHAP.

C H A P.　XIV.

Of the three kinds of eloquence, and of the three
philosophers sent on an embassy by the Athenians
to the Roman Senate.

BOTH in verse and prose there are three approved forms of speaking, called by the Greeks χαρακτηρις, and distinguished by the terms αδρον, ισχνον, μεσον. The first we call *copious* [1], the

---

[1] *Copious.*]—See the animadversions of H. Stephens, at this passage, in his edition of Gellius: αδρος, which is here interpreted copious, means also magnificent; ισχνος means not only graceful but acute; μεσος is not merely that which is middle, but that which is mixed and moderate.

Dr. Blair, in his Lectures on Rhetoric and Belles-Lettres, has entered very diffusely on the subject of style; and I refer the reader to him, rather than to any other modern writer, because he has made it more particularly his business to investigate this subject, and illustrate it by comparing modern with ancient writers.

This division of style is made also by Dionysius of Halicarnassus; he calls these three kinds the austere, the florid, and the middle.

A dissertation upon style would here be impertinent: perhaps, after all, it is absurd to lay down any precise rules for the formation of style.

Firſt follow nature, and your judgment frame
By her just standard, which is still the same;

Unerring

the next *graceful*, the third *middle*.   The copious
is that which comprehends dignity and grandeur;
the graceful is that which is becoming and neat;
the middle is partaker of both thefe.   To thefe
virtues of oratory there are an equal number of
kindred defects, which fallacioufly affume their
drefs and appearance.   Thus often the tumid
and the pompous pafs for the " copious," the
mean and the empty for the " graceful," the doubtful and the ambiguous for the " middle."   M.
Varro fays, that in the Latin tongue there are three
true and pertinent examples of thefe forms; namely, Pacuvius of the copious, Lucilius of the graceful, Terence of the middle[2].   But thefe three
modes

Unerring nature, ftill divinely bright,
One clear, unchang'd, and univerfal light,
Life, force, and beauty muft to all impart,
At once the fource, and end, and teft of art.

[2] *Terence of the middle.*]—The Fragments of Pacuvius are
found firft in H. Stephens Fragmenta Poetarum, afterwards
in Mattaire's Corpus Poetarum.   From thefe fragments we
cannot eafily be inclined to affent to the judgment here paffed on Pacuvius by Gellius; for indeed they feem to poffefs
neither elegance nor purity.   But we are certainly not qualified to judge; and when we confider what Quintilian fays, in
addition to the opinion of Gellius, we may with the lefs reluctance admit it to be true.   " 'Tragœdiæ fcriptores (I am
quoting Quintilian) Accius atque Pacuvius clariffimi, gravi-
tate fententiarum, verborum pondere, et auctoritate perfona-
rum;" than which an higher character cannot well be
given.

Of

modes of fpeaking are more anciently fpecified by Homer in three diftinct perfonages : Ulyffes [3] was magnificent and copious, Menelaus acute and concife, Neftor mixed and moderate. This threefold variety was alfo obfervable in three philofophers whom the Athenians fent on an embaffy to Rome and the Senate, to remit the fine impofed upon them on account of the plundering Oropus. This fine was almoft five hundred talents. Thefe philofophers were, Carneades of the Academy, Diogenes the Stoic, and Critolaus the Peripatetic ; and being admitted into the Se-

Of Lucilius, Quintilian remarks, that there are fome who prefer him to all other writers : " Non ejufdem modo operis auctoribus fed omnibus poetis præferre non dubitent." Horace, on the contrary, does not fpeak in terms of high refpect of Lucilius ; Horace thinks his ftyle heavy and dull. But Quintilian, giving his own opinion, fpeaks of him in thefe terms : " Eruditio in eo mira et libertas, atque inde acerbitas et abunde falis." Terence is too well known to require my fuffrage in his favour ; his great charm is fimplicity, his great defect want of point and energy.

[3] *Ulyffes, &c.*]—The different excellence of fpeaking, as poffeffed by thefe three eminent characters of antiquity, is thus defcribed by Aufonius :

> Prifcos ut et heroes olim
> Carmine Homeri commemoratos,
> Fando referres;
> Dulcem in paucis ut Plifthenidem
> Et torrentis ceu Dulichii
> Ninguida dicta;
> Et mellitæ nectare vocis
> Dulcia fatu verba canentem,
> Neftora regem.

5   nate,

nate, they employed C. Acilius, a senator, as their interpreter. But previously each of these, by way of displaying his abilities, had harangued in a numerous assembly. Then it is said that Rutilius and Polybius greatly admired the eloquence which was peculiar to each philosopher. They affirm that the oratory of Carneades was strong and rapid, that of Critolaus learned and polished, of Diogenes modest and temperate. But each of these forms, as I have before observed, when its ornaments are chaste and modest, is excellent, when daubed and painted it is contemptible.

CHAP. XV.

The severity with which thieves were punished by the ancients.—What Mutius Scævola has written on what is given or entrusted to the care of any one [1].

LABEO, in his second book on the Twelve Tables, has said, that among the ancients severe and extreme punishments were inflicted upon

[1] The penal laws of the Romans seem in many respects to have been borrowed of the Athenians, particularly in what related to theft. He who was taken in the act of theft during the night was punished with death. In the day-time also, if he had a weapon and presumed to defend himself, a thief was liable to the same penalty.

The right of the original proprietor to what had been stolen from him did not cease till after a period of thirty years, although in this interval the property should have passed through the hands of various masters.

To this Labeo, Gellius has been more than once indebted. See Book xx. chap. 1.

According to the Mosaic law, he who removed his neighbour's land-mark was accounted accursed; but we are not told whether it was distinguished between him who committed this crime from motives of wantonness and malice, and the man who had intentions of committing theft. It will not here be forgotten, that by the laws of Lycurgus theft was permitted, with the idea that encouraging boldness and dexterity was of greater service to the state than the purloining

a few

on thieves; and that Brutus ufed to fay that he was condemned as guilty of theft who led cattle aftray from the place where he was fent, or who had kept it longer than the diftance of his errand required. Q. Scævola, therefore, in his fixteeenth book on the Civil Law, has thefe words : " Who-ever applied to his own ufe. that which was en-trufted to his care, or, receiving any thing for a particular purpofe, applied it to a different one, was liable to the charge of theft."

a few trifles could be of detriment to individuals. In this, as in all other vices, there are doubtlefs gradations of guilt; and it may be faid properly with Horace,

> Nec vincet ratio hæc, tantundem ut peccat idemque
> Qui teneros cautes alieni fregerit horti,
> Et qui nocturnos divum facra legerit.

Or, in fewer words, ftealing a cabbage is not furely fo great a crime as facrilege.

Chap. XVI.

Passage from Marcus Varro's satire, called περι εδεσματων. Some verses of Euripides, in which he ridicules the extravagant appetite of luxurious men.

VARRO, in the satire which he wrote concerning things to be eaten, describes in some verses, written with much facetiousness and skill, the exquisite delicacies of food and entertainments [1]. He has produced and described in hexameters most of these things which these glut-
tons

---

[1] The luxury of entertainments among the ancients is most successfully ridiculed by Horace, in the second satire of the second book, which has been most ably paraphrased by Pope. Some of the best lines are these which follow; which do not seem in this place impertinent:

Now hear what blessings temperance can bring—
Thus said our friend, and what he said I sing—
First health; the stomach cramm'd from every dish,
A tomb of boil'd and roast, and flesh and fish,
Where bile, and wind, and phlegm, and acid jar,
And all the man is one intestine war;
Remembers oft the school-boy's simple fare,
The temperate sleeps, and spirits light as air.

Which two last lines it is not improbable but Gray might have in his mind when, describing a school-boy, he says,

The spirits pure, the slumbers light,
Which fly th' approach of morn.

Much

tons hunt for both by fea and land. The verfes to which I allude, whoever has leifure may find in the above-mentioned book. As well as I can remember, the kinds and names of eatables, and the places where thefe dainties, fuperior to all others, are found, which an inordinate gluttony has hunted out, and which Varro has in his fatire reprobated, are thefe which follow :

A peacock from Samos [2], a woodcock [3] from

Much alfo, which relates to the luxury and extravagance difplayed by the ancients in feafts, may be gathered from Athenæus.

[2] *Peacock from Samos.*]—The peacock was efteemed a great delicacy by the Romans. Horace thus ridicules it ;

Vix tamen eripiam pofito pavone velis, quin
Hoc potius quam gallina, tergere palatum
Corruptus vanis rerum, quia veheat auro
Rara avis et picta pandat fpectacula cauda.

Which Pope thus imitates :

I doubt our curious men
Will choofe *a pheafant* ftill before a hen;
Yet hens of Guinea full as gocd I hold,
Except you eat the feathers green and gold.

A great deal is faid concerning the peacock, and the eftimation in which it was anciently held, in the fourteenth book of Athenæus. The peacock was facred to Juno, and faid to have been firft produced in Samos, in the temple of that goddefs, and thence propagated through the world.

[3] *Woodcock.*]—This was another delicate article of food, as with us, and is highly commmended in Horace, Martial, and Athenæus. In this latter author, a fragment of Hipponax forbids the eating either of woodcock or hare.

Phrygia,

Phrygia, cranes [4] from Melos, a kid [5] from Ambracia, a tunny [6] from Chalcedon, a lamprey from Tarteſſus, codfiſh from Peſſinus, oyſters from Tarentum, cockles from Chios, and elops [7]

[4] *Cranes.*]—Theſe are alſo mentioned among the delicacies of the table by Horace and Pliny.

[5] *Kid.*]—The following paſſage from Athenæus requires a place here: " Many of the gueſts extolled in very high terms the lampreys and eels of Sicily, the bellies of dolphins taken near Cape Pachinus, *the kids of the iſle of Melos,* the mullets of Simothus; and, among other leſs important delicacies, oyſters from Cape Pelorus, pilchards from Liparos, creſſes from Thebes, and beet from Aſina."

Melos is now called Milo, or, according to Savary, Mile; it is deſcribed at great length by Tournefort, who alſo mentions the excellence of its kids:

" All the productions of the iſland are of incomparable excellence. Its partridges, quails, *kids,* and lambs, are in high eſtimation, yet extremely cheap."

Ambracia is a town of Epirus.

[6] *Tunny.*]—This was a younger fiſh of the tunny kind. See Pliny: " Limoſæ a luto pelamides incipiunt vocari, et cum annum exceſſere tempus, thynni."

See alſo Athenæus.

When it firſt begins to encreaſe in ſize the pelamys is called thynnus, in its next ſtate orcynus, in its largeſt it is a whale.

[7] *Elops.*—I am by no means able to diſcover what fiſh is here meant; it is neverthelcſs mentioned by various Latin writers. It is I believe ſometimes called acipenſer, which has been called in Engliſh a ſturgeon. See the Halieuticon of Ovid:

Et pretioſus helops noſtris incognitus undis.

In a fragment of Lucilius it is alſo called præclarus elops.

from

from Rhodes, char[8] from Cilicia, nuts from Thafus[9], palm from Ægypt[10], acorns of Hiberia[11].

But

[8] *Char.*]—This was a great favourite with the Roman
epicures; and it is related of Auguftus, that as this fifh was
not found in the Italian feas, he imported a great many from
the coafts of Afia Minor, giving orders that whoever, for
three years, fhould prefume to fifh for them fhould be drowned.

Confult, on the fubject of the fifhes of the ancients, the
feventh book of Athenæus, where, among other things, we
are told, on the authority of Seleucus of Tarfus, that the
fcarus is the only fifh which never fleeps: in Athenæus the
fcarus of Ephefus is recommended.

[9] *Nuts from Thafus.*]—Much is faid in the fecond book of
Athenæus, on the fubject of nuts, and the nuts of Perfia are
particularly recommended. Nux is by itfelf a generic name,
the fpecies of which is afcertained only by an epithet. It
is not eafy, therefore, to fay whether any or what particular
fpecies is to be underftood by the nuts of Thafus, the Perfian
nuts, &c. Nux by itfelf feems generally to mean a walnut-
tree, for the nuts ufed at weddings, and thrown among children, are known to have been walnuts.

[10] *Palm from Ægypt.*]—In oppofition to this, Strabo affirms, that the palms of Ægypt are mean and bad, except in the
Thebaid alone. Galen fays, that the fineft palms are produced in Judæa, in the vale of Jericho. In the 24th chapter
of Ecclefiafticus, the palm of Engaddi and the rofe of Jericho
are celebrated: " I was exalted like a palm-tree in Engaddi,
and as a rofe-plant in Jericho."

Upon this fubject of the palm-tree I have written before
at fome length, in my notes to the tranflation of Herodotus,
Vol. I. and to this work I beg leave to refer the reader.

[11] *Acorns of Hiberia.*]—Glans feems to have been ufed a-
mong the Romans in the fame fenfe that we ufe maft. Thus
the fruit of the beech is called glans: " Fagi glans nuclei fi-

But we shall think this industry of the appetite,
wandering about and searching for new and
unaccustomed juices, and hunting them in every
quarter of the earth, still more detestable, if we
have in mind the verses of Euripides. These
verses Chrysippus the philosopher frequently applied, as if a certain irritable lust of eating was
to be obtained, not for the necessary uses of life,
but through the luxuriousness of a mind loathing
what was to be easily got, from a certain wantonness of satiety. I subjoin the lines of Euripides [12]:

What can man need but these two things, the
    fruits
Which Ceres yields, and the refreshing spring,
                             Ever

milis," says Pliny. But, strictly speaking, it means only such
fruits as contain only one seed, which is covered at the lower
part with a husk, and is naked at the upper part: thus the
fruit of an oak, which we commonly call an acorn, is properly a glans. " Glandem," says Pliny, " quæ proprie intelligi-
tur, ferunt robur, quercus, esculus, cerrus, ilex suber."

Martyn.

The acorn then was doubtless the production of some
species of oak; but it seems difficult to imagine in what manner it could possibly be prepared to gratify the palate of a
Roman, in the luxurious times of that empire.

Iberia is mentioned by Horace as being fruitful in poisons:

Herbasque quas Iolcos, atque Iberia
Mittit venenorum ferax.

[12] *Lines of Euripides.*]—This is a fragment of the Æo-
lus of Euripides; and I have used the translation of Wodhull.

Concerning

Ever at hand, by bounteous nature given
To nourish us? We from the plenty rise
Dissatisfied, and yielding to the allurements
Of luxury, search out for other viands.

Concerning the articles of food enumerated in this chapter, the following circumstances may properly enough be added:

Apicius says, " Isicia de pavo primum locum habent." The real meaning of isicium it may not be easy to determine; from its etymology it probably means a kind of sausage.

The same Apicius describes with what sauce the attagena should be dressed and eaten.

The grus was understood to be what an Englishman would term very hearty food, it was put upon the table with a great variety and multitude of sauces, and was decorated, as is with us sometimes customary to send up pheasants. " Gruem," says Apicius, " lavas, ornas et includis in olla." Includere in olla, signifies to pot any thing.

See in Apicius, Book viii. chap. 6. various directions for dressing a kid or lamb.

The pelamys was also considered as strong food, and required a long time and considerable pains to make it tender.

The murena was always esteemed as one of the greatest delicacies of the table: Columella says, " Jam celebres erant deliciæ popinales cum a mari deferrentur vivaria quorum studiosissimi velut ante devictarum gentium Numantinus et Isauricus: ita Sergius orata et Licinius murena captorum piscium lætabantur vocabulis."

The fish asellus, according to Varro, was so named from its resemblance in colour to an ass. - The asellus is probably what we call a haddock.

Athenæus relates, that when the emperor Trajan was carrying on war against the Parthians, and at a great distance from the sea, he was delighted and surprised at receiving some fresh oysters from Apicius.

C HAP.

Chap. XVII.

Conversation with an ignorant and insolent grammarian, on the meaning of the word obnoxius—*Origin of this word.* [1]

I ENQUIRED at Rome of a certain grammarian, of the firſt celebrity as a teacher, not indeed for the ſake of trying him, but really from a deſire of knowledge, what was the meaning of the word *obnoxius*, and what was the nature and origin of the word. He, looking at me, as if ridiculing the trifling inſignificance of the queſtion,—"You aſk," ſays he, "a very obſcure queſtion, and what requires great pains to inveſtigate. Who is ſo ignorant of the Latin tongue as not to know that he is called *obnoxius*, who in any reſpect can be incommoded and injured by him to whom he is ſaid to be *obnoxius*, and has any one conſcious *ſuæ noxæ*, that is of his fault? But rather," he continued, " put aſide theſe trifles, and introduce ſomewhat worthy of inveſtigation and argument." On this, I, being moved, thought

---

[1] It is obvious that the word *obnoxius* is uſed by the beſt Latin writers in a variety of ſenſes; and it muſt be acknowledged, as Quintus Carolus obſerves, that Gellius in this chapter has not thrown much more light upon the ſubject than the grammarian whom he points out to ridicule.

that

that I ought to diffemble, as with a foolifh fellow—" With refpect to other things, moft learned Sir, which are more abftrufe and profound, if I fhall want to learn and know them, when occafion fhall require, I fhall doubtlefs come to you for inftruction; but as I have often ufed the word *obnoxius*, and knew not its proper meaning, I have enquired and learned from you, what indeed not only I, as it feems to you, did not comprehend, but it fhould feem that Plautus alfo, a man of the firft eminence for his knowledge of verbal nicety and elegance in the Latin tongue, did not know what *obnoxius* meant. There is a verfe in his Stichus [2], of this kind:

Nunc ego hercle perii plane, *non obnoxie;*

which by no means accords with the interpretation you have given me; for Plautus has brought together, as oppofite to one another, the two words *plane* and *obnoxie,* which is very remote from your explanation." But this grammarian foolifhly enough, and as if *obnoxius* and *obnoxie* differed, not only in declenfion but in effect and meaning, " I," faid he, " obferved, what *obnoxius* was, and not *obnoxie.*" Then I, aftonifhed at the

---

[2] *Stichus.*]—A comedy called Stichus.

The tranflators of Plautus have not noticed the contraft betwixt *plane* and *obnoxie* in this quotation, but have rendered it—" I am a dead man, plain, out of doubt." The meaning of *obnoxie,* according to the commentators on this paffage, is, I am a dead man, and my fate is not fubject to any one's will.

ignorance

ignorance of this conceited man, replied, " We will paſs over then, if you pleaſe, that Plautus has uſed the word *obnoxie*, if you think this foreign from the purpoſe. We will alſo not mention what Salluſt has ſaid in his Catiline, Minari etiam ferro, ni ſibi *obnoxia* foret, but you ſhall explain to me what is more common and familiar. Theſe verſes from Virgil are very well known :

Nam neque tunc[3] aſtris acies obtuſa videri
Nec fratris radiis *obnoxia* ſurgere luna.

Which you ſay is *conſcium ſuæ culpæ*. Virgil alſo, in another place, uſes this word very differently from your opinion, thus—

Juvat arva videre[4]
Non raſtris hominum, non ulli *obnoxia* curæ.

For care is generally beneficial to fields and not injurious, which is your explanation of *obnoxius*.

[3] *Nam neque tunc, &c.*]—Thus rendered by Martyn:
" For then the light of the ſtars does not ſeem dim, nor does the moon ſeem to riſe as if indebted to her brother's beams."

And thus by Dryden—

The ſtars ſhine *ſmarter*, and the moon adorns,
As with unborrow'd beams, her ſharpen'd horns.

[4] *Juvat arva, &c.*]—Thus rendered by Martyn—
" It is delightful to ſee fields that are not obliged to harrows, or any care of man."

Thus by Dryden—

But much more pleaſing are theſe fields to ſee,
That need not ploughs nor human induſtry.

How

How too can that which Ennius has written in his Phænice agree with what you say :

> Sed virum [5] vera virtute vivere animatum ad-
>   decet,
> Fortiterque *innoxium* vacare adverfum ad-
>   verfarios ;
> Ea liberta' eft, qui pectus purum et firmum
>   geftitat,
> Aliæ res obnoxiofæ nocte in obfcura latent."

But he, hefitating, and like one perplexed, replies, " I have not time now, when I have, you fhall come and fee me again, and fhall know what Virgil, Salluft, Plautus, and Ennius meant by this word;" faying this, the ftupid fellow departed. If any one fhall choofe to examine, not only the origin of the word, but alfo its meaning and variety, let him refer to this paffage, which I tranfcribe from the Afinaria of Plautus:

> Maxumas [6] opimitates gaudio effertiffimas

---

[5] *Sed virum.*]—Thefe lines may perhaps be thus tranflated
It becomes a man of fpirit to live with real courage, and an innocent man to bear up boldly againft his adverfaries. He who has an upright and courageous heart has this liberty, other viler things are concealed in darknefs.

[6] *Maxumas.*]—Thus rendered by the tranflators of Plautus—

> Plenty of good things he and I fhall heap
> Upon his mafters, both the fon and father,
> Who for this kindnefs ever will remain
> Bound to us in the ftricteft bands.

                    Suis

> Suis heris ille una mecum pariet gnatoque et
>   patri,
> Adeo ut ætatem ambo ambobus nobis sint *ob-*
>   *noxii*
> Nostro devincti beneficio.

With respect to the definition which this grammarian gave, this, in a word of such various application, seems to have marked one use of it only; which agrees indeed with the signification given it by Cæcilius in his Chrysius. This is the passage:

> Quamquam ego [7] mercede huc conductus tua
> Advenio, ne tibi me esse ob eam rem *obnoxium*
> Reare: audibis male si male dixis mihi.

[7] *Quamquam ego.*]—" Although I came here expecting to be paid by you, you must not on that account think that I am wholly subject to you. If you speak ill of me, you will be ill spoken of in return."

The word *obnoxious* also, in English, is used in different senses. We call any one offending *obnoxious*, both as he is unworthy in himself, and subject to punishment.

Chap. XVIII.[*]

*Religious obfervance of an oath among the Romans—
Of the ten captives whom Hannibal fent to Rome,
taking from them an oath to return.*

THAT an oath was held to be facred and inviolable among the Romans, appears from
their manners, and from many laws; and what I
am going to relate is alfo no fmall proof of it. After the battle of Cannæ, Hannibal, the Carthaginian general, fent ten prifoners, felected from
our countrymen, to Rome, and commanded and
agreed with them, that if the Roman people ap-

[*] On the fubject of this chapter fee Gellius again, Book xx.
chap. i.

Mr. Gibbon, fpeaking of the integrity of the ancient Romans, thus expreffes himfelf:

" The goddefs of faith *(of human and focial faith)* was
worfhipped not only in her temples but in the lives of the Romans; and if that nation was deficient in the more amiable
qualities of benevolence and generofity, they aftonifhed the
Greeks by their fincere and fimple performance of the moft
burthenfome engagements."—The ftory of Regulus will here
prefent itfelf to the reader; and many examples of the ftrict
adherence of the Romans to their engagements, may be
found in Valerius Maximus, Book vi. The form of the
folemn oath among the Romans I have given in Vol. I. p.
80. With refpect to the evafion here recorded, there can
be but one opinion—it is an example of meannefs and perfi-
dy.

proved

proved it, there should be an exchange of prisoners, and that for those, which either should happen to have more than the other, a pound of silver should be paid. Before they went, he compelled them to take an oath to return to the Carthaginian camp, if the Romans would not exchange prisoners. The ten captives came to Rome; they explained in the senate the message of the Carthaginian commander. The exchange was not agreeable. The parents, relations, and friends of the captives embraced them; assured them they were now effectually restored to their country, that their situation was independent and secure, and entreated them by no means to think of returning to the enemy. Then eight of them replied, that this restoration to their country was by no means just, since they were bound by an oath to return; and immediately, according to this oath, they went back to Hannibal. The other two remained in Rome, asserting that they were free, and delivered from the obligation of their oath, since, when they had left the enemy's camp, they had, with a deceitful intention, returned on the same day, as if on some accidental occasion, and so, having satisfied their oath, they departed free from its obligation. But this their fraudulent evasion was deemed so base, that they were despised and reproached by the common people, and the censors afterwards branded them with disgraceful marks of every kind, since they had not done that, which they had sworn to do.

do.   Cornelius Nepos, in his fifth book of Examples, has also recorded that many of the senate were of opinion, that they who refused to return should be taken into custody and sent back to Hannibal; but this opinion was set aside, as not agreeable to the majority.   But those men who did not return to Hannibal became so very odious and infamous, that, being wearied of life, they destroyed themselves.

Chap. XIX.

History taken from the Annals concerning Tiberius Sempronius Gracchus, father of· the Gracchi, tribune of the people; with the form of words used by the tribunes in their decrees.

THERE is recorded a noble, generous and magnanimous action of Tiberius Sempronius Gracchus. It is as follows: Caius Minucius Augurinus, a tribune of the people, imposed a fine upon L. Scipio Asiaticus, brother of P. Scipio Africanus the elder; and on this account called upon him to produce his securities. Scipio Africanus, in the name of his brother, appealed to the college of tribunes, entreating them to defend a man of consular rank, who had triumphed, from the violence of their colleague. Eight of the tribunes, after investigating the matter, made a decree, the words of which I have added, as they appear written in the monuments of the Annals:

QUOD . P. SCIPIO . AFRICANUS[1] . POSTULAVIT . PRO . L. SCIPIONE . ASIATICO . FRATRE . QUUM . CONTRA .

[1] *Quod P. Scipio Africanus.*]—I thus translate the decree—Publius Scipio Africanus, in the name of his brother Lucius Scipio Asiaticus, has represented, that the tribune of the people, contrary to the laws and customs of our ancestors,

CONTRA . LEGES . CONTRA . Q. MOREM . MAJORUM .
TRIBUNUS . PLEBEI . HOMINIBUS . ACCITIS . PER .
VIM . INAUSPICATO . SENTENTIAM . DE . EO . TULE-
RIT . MULTAM . Q. NULLO . EXEMPLO . IRROGARIT .
PRÆDES . Q. OB . EAM . REM . DARE . COGAT . AUT .
SI . NON . DET . IN . VINCULA . DUCI . JUBEAT . UT .
EUM . A . COLLEGÆ . VI . PROHIBEAMUS . ET . QUOD .
CONTRA . COLLEGA . POSTULAVIT . NE . SIBI . IN-
TERCEDAMUS . QUO . MINUS . SUAPTE . POTESTA-
TE . UTI . LICEAT . DE . EA . RE . NOSTRUM . SENTEN-

anceftors, having by undue means collected a multitude
together, has impofed a fine upon him, for which there
exifts no precedent. He has exacted fecurities from him;
on his refufal to produce which, he has commanded that he
fhould be imprifoned. He has entreated our protection
from the violence of our colleague; who, on the contrary,
has entreated that we fhould not interfere with his exercife
of his juft authority.

The opinion given on this fubject in common by us all,
is this—If Lucius Cornelius Scipio Afiaticus will give to
our colleague the fecurities required, we will intercede to
prevent his being committed to prifon.—If he fhall refufe to
give the fecurities required, we will by no means obftruct our
colleague in the exercife of his authority."

The fame fact is related in Livy, Book xxxviii. c. 60.
and every thing which the Roman law involves, illuftrative
of the queftion here difcuffed, is to be feen in Heineccius, p.
677, 678, and 679.

The ftory of Scipio was this—He was reported to have
been bribed by Antiochus to grant him favourable terms of
peace at the fum of fix thoufand pounds weight of gold, and
four hundred and eighty thoufand pounds weight of filver.
He was called upon by the tribune to account for this, or
fubmit to fuch penalties as his official authority enabled him
to impofe.

TIA .

TIA . OMNIUM . DATA . EST . SI . L. CORNELIUS .
SCIPIO . ASIATICUS . COLLEGÆ . ARBITRATU .
PRÆDES . DABIT . COLLEGÆ . NE . ÆUM . IN . VINCU-
LA . DUCAT . INTERCEDEMUS . SI . EJUS . ARBI-
TRATU . PRÆDES . NON . DABIT . QUO . MINUS . COL-
LEGA . SUA . POTESTATE . UTATUR . NON . INTER-
CEDEMUS.

After this decree, when Augurinus, the tribune of the people, commanded L. Scipio, not giving securities, to be seized and led to prison, Tiberius Sempronius Gracchus, a tribune of the people, and father of Tiberius and Caius Gracchus, who, from various disputes respecting the commonwealth, was a violent enemy to P. Scipio Africanus, publicly avowed that no reconciliation had taken place betwixt him and P. Africanus. He then thus recited a decree from his tablet. The words of which were these:

CUM . L. CORNELIUS . SCIPIO .[2] ASIATICUS .
TRIUMPHANS . HOSTIUM . DUCES . IN . CARCEREM .
CONJECTAVERIT.

[2] *Cum Lucius C. Scipio.*—In English thus: " Lucius Cornelius Scipio Asiaticus having obtained the honour of a triumph, and thrown the leaders of the enemy into prison, it seemed inconsistent with the dignity of the republic to commit a general of the Roman people to that place where the leaders of the enemies had been by him confined. Therefore I use my interposition to save Lucius Cornelius Scipio Asiaticus from the violence of my colleague."

The interposition of Gracchus availed but only for the present moment. The invidious business was afterwards resumed; and though it appeared that all the effects and pro-

CONJECTAVERIT . ALIENUM . VIDETUR . ESSE . DIG-
NITATE . REIPUBLICÆ . IN . EUM . LOCUM . IMPERA-
TOREM . POPULI . ROMANI . DUCI . IN . QUEM .
LOCUM . AB . EO . CONJECTI . SUNT . DUCES . HOS-
TIUM . ITA . Q. L. CORNELIUM . SCIPIONEM .
ASIATICUM . A . COLLEGÆ . VI . PROHIBEO.

But Valerius Antias, contrary to this record of
the decrees, and againſt the authority of the Ancient Annals, has affirmed, that this interceſſion
made by Tiberius Gracchus in favour of Scipio
Aſiaticus, was after the death of Scipio Africanus: He adds, that no fine was impoſed upon
Scipio; but that, being condemned for peculation
with reſpect to the money of Antiochus, on his
not giving ſecurity, he was ordered to be ſent
to priſon, from which he was delivered by the
interceſſion of Gracchus.

perty of Scipio were not of ſufficient value to ſatisfy the fine
which had been impoſed, yet every thing he had was ſold.
A ſtriking proof how tranſient is the gale of public favour,
though obtained, as in the caſe before us, by real and important ſervices.

Chap. XX.

That Virgil, becaufe he was refufed water by the inhabitants of Nola, erafed the word " Nola" from his verfe, and inferted " Ora;" with other pleafant obfervations on the harmonious found of letters.

I HAVE found in fome commentaries, that thefe verfes were originally recited and edited by Virgil thus,

> Talem ' dives arat Capúa et vicina Vefevo
> Nola jugo.

Afterwards Virgil requefted of the people of Nola permiffion to introduce water into his neighbouring farm. The Nolani would not grant the favour which was afked; the poet being offended, erafed the name of their city from his poem, as if it were the fame as erafing it from the memory of man. He changed Nola into Ora, and fo left it.

> ——et vicina Vefevo
> Ora jugo.

* *Talem.*]—Such a foil is ploughed about rich Capua, and the country of Nola, which lies near mount Vefuvius.

This probably is like many other old ftories, for it is very evident that Gellius gives it no great degree of credit.

I am

I am at no pains to prove whether this be true or falſe ; but it certainly cannot be doubted, but that Ora is more agreeable, and more harmonious to the ear than Nola. For the ſame vowel ending the ſyllable of the former verſe, and beginning the verſe which follows, together form a combination of ſound, which is at the ſame time full and harmonious. Many examples of this kind of harmony may be found in the beſt poets, which appear to be the effect not of accident but art; but they occur far more frequently in Homer than in any other. In one paſſage, theſe as it were disjointed ſounds he brings together in many words :

'Η δ' ἑτέρη θερεϊ προρέει εἰκυῖα· χαλάζη
'Η χιόνη ψυχρῇ ἤ εξ ὕδατος κρυσταλλῳ.

Thus alſo in another place——

Λᾶαν ἄνω ωθεσκε ποτὶ λόφον.

Catullus in like manner, the moſt elegant of poets, ſays,

> 'Miniſter [a] vetuli puer Falerni
> Inger, mi calices amariores,

Ut

[a] *Miniſter, &c.*]—The lines from Catullus I inſert at length.

> Miniſter vetuli puer Falerni
> Inger, mi calices amariores,
> Ut lex Poſtumiæ jubet magiſtræ,
> Ebrioſa acina ebrioſioris ;
> At vos quo lubet hinc abite lymphæ,
> Vini pernicies, et ad ſeveros
> Migrate: hic merus eſt Thyonianus.

> Ut lex Poftumiæ jubet magiftræ,
> Ebriofa acina ebriofioris.

When he might have faid both *ebriofus*, and, what is more common, have ufed *acinum* in the neuter gender. But being partial to this harmony of the Homeric disjunction, he ufed *ebriofa*, from the fimilar agreement of the vowel immediately following. They who think that Catullus wrote *ebrios*, or *ebriofos*, for this latter abfurd reading has alfo appeared, have met with books doubtlefs compofed from very corrupt copies.

Thus imperfectly attempted in Englifh—

> Boy, who the rofy bowl doft pafs,
> Fill up to me the largeft glafs,
> The largeft glafs, and oldeft wine,
> The laws of drinking give as mine:
> Still muft my ever-thirfty lip
> From large and flowing bumpers fip.
> Ye limpid ftreams, where'er ye flow,
> Far hence to water-drinkers go,
> Go to the dull and the fedate,
> And fly the god whofe bowers you hate.

CHAP.

CHAP. XXI.

Why quoad vivet *and* quoad morietur *exprefs the fame point of time, though the expreffion is taken from two contrary facts*[1].

WHEN the terms *quoad vivet* and *quoad morietur* are ufed, they appear to be expreffive of two contrary things, but both terms indicate one and the fame point of time. In like manner when it is faid *quoad fenatus habebitur*, and *quoad fenatus dimittetur*, although the words *haberi* and *dimitti* are oppofite, yet one and the fame thing is expreffed by both. For when two periods of time are oppofite to each other, and yet fo approximate that the termination of the one is confounded with the beginning of the other, it is of no confequence whether the confine be demonftrated by the extremity of the former, or the beginning of the latter.

[1] The fame mode of expreffion prevails in our own and probably in all other languages. " Whilft I live and till I die," though the mode of expreffion is taken from the two contraries of life and death, communicate the fame idea.

CHAP.

C. H A P. XXII.

That the censors' were accuſtomed to take away their horſes from ſuch knights as were too fat and corpulent.—Enquiry made whether this is done with diſgrace of the knights, or without any diminution of their dignity.

THE cenſors were accuſtomed to take away the horſe from a man too fat and corpulent, thinking ſuch ill calculated to perform the duty of a knight, with the weight of ſo large a body. But this was no puniſhment, as ſome ſuppoſe, but they were ſuſpended without ignominy from their duty: yet Cato, in the oration which he wrote, De ſacrificio commiſſo, alledges this matter in the form of an accuſation, ſo as to make it appear to have been ignominious. If

* The power of the cenſors has been ſpoken of in various places. And this ſeems very properly to have been exerciſed on the equites or knights, whoſe duty it was to ſerve on horſeback; yet the term of eques or knight was not given indiſcriminately to all thoſe who ſerved on horſeback. The cenſor choſe a certain number into the equeſtrian order; he gave them, when he did this, a gold ring and a horſe, which was paid for by the public. He conſequently was juſtified in reprobating the miſuſe or neglect of that, which was in fact the public property.

you

you take it thus, it may be prefumed that he did not appear entirely blamelefs, or free from indolence, whofe body had luxurioufly fwelled to fo inordinate a fize [2].

[2] An old Latin epigram mentions, among the qualities of a good man, a diligent care not to become too fat.

Jufto trutinæ fe examine pendit
Ne quid hiet, ne quid protuberet, angulus æquis
Partibus ut coeat, nil ut deliret amuffis, &c.

See Burman's Latin Anthology, vol. ii. 417.

B O O K VIII.[1]

C H A P. I.

Whether the phrase hesterna noctu[2] *is proper or not.—What is the grammatical tradition concerning these words.—The decemviri[3], in the Twelve Tables, used* nox *for* noctu.

C H A P.

[1] We have in this book one of those lamentable chasms which modern ingenuity cannot supply. It seems singular enough, that the heads of the chapters only should remain to us; but these are of sufficient importance to make us sincerely regret the loss we have sustained in the original chapters to which they belong.

It is reasonable to presume, that many peculiarities of the Latin tongue were here explained by Gellius, many beauties pointed out, and many circumstances of the private and domestic manners of the Romans familiarly and agreeably discussed.

[2] *Hesterna noctu.*]—See Macrobius, L. i. Saturnal. c. 4. This author, who was accustomed to borrow, without much ceremony of acknowledgment, from Gellius, may perhaps, in some degree, supply the loss of this chapter.

[3] *Decemviri.*]—See Macrobius, in the place before quoted; " Decemviri in Duodecim Tabulis inusitate nox pro noctu dixerunt.

dixerunt.` Verba hæc funt: SEI, NOX FURTIM FACTUM ESIT SEI IM ACCISIT IOURE CAISUS ESTO. The meaning of which decree is, if an act of theft be committed in the night, and the thief be killed, he is lawfully killed. Here *nox* is evidently ufed for *noctu*. Theft by the Mofaic law was punifhed by a fine ; and it was not till fome confiderable degree of refinement prevailed in fociety, that the crime of theft was punifhed by death. Some admirable remarks upon the punifhment which ought to be inflicted for theft, are to be found in the Marquis Beccaria; Blackftone alfo has fome excellent obfervations on this fubject, from which it may be concluded that he was no friend to extreme and fanguinary punifhments.

Mr. Gibbon, with great juftice, reprobates the feverity of the Twelve Tables :

" The Twelve Tables afford a more decifive proof of the national fpirit, fince they were framed by the wifeft of the fenate, and accepted by the free voice of the people ; yet thefe laws, like the ftatutes of Draco, are written in characters of blood."

The French, after their revolution, profeffed to enact a penal code that was to give a great example to mankind of mildnefs and philanthropy. But fuch is the verfatile character of that people, that on the firft folemn occafion which prefented itfelf, they violated their own principles by the unexampled and unprovoked barbarity, with which they treated their unhappy fovereign.

CHAP. II.[1]

Ten words pointed out to me by Favorinus, which, though used by the Greeks, are spurious and barbarous—Ten likewise which I pointed out to him of common and popular use among the Latins, but which are not properly Latin, nor to be found in old books.

[1] The loss of this chapter is seriously to be regretted. In every language new words are continually introduced, which, rejected at first by the learned as vicious or inelegant, become finally sanctified by use, and in time perhaps are quoted as authority for the very language which they were at first imagined to debase.

CHAP.

CHAP. III.

The manner in which Peregrinus [1] the philosopher, in my hearing, severely rebuked a Roman youth of equestrian rank, for standing in his presence [2] in a careless manner, and yawning repeatedly.

CHAP.

[1] *Peregrinus.*]—This Peregrinus is spoken of at some length by Gellius in his 12th book. For a particular account of him see Lucian and Philostratus. He was born in the 236th Olympiad. He affected to imitate Hercules in his death, and threw himself into a funeral pile, in the presence of innumerable spectators. His statue, which was erected at Paros, a city of the Hellespont, was reported to utter oracles: see Athenagoras. From the variety of characters he assumed, and parts he played, this man was surnamed Proteus. Although the inhabitants of Parium, where he was born, erected a statue in his honour, it is notorious that he was driven into banishment for crimes at which humanity shudders. It is no less singular than true, that by his dissimulation and hypocrisy, after professing himself a christian, he arrived at the highest eminence in the christian church. Perhaps a more eccentric character never existed upon earth; but as the applause paid to acts of uncommon effrontery, cunning and boldness, is fleeting and transient, posterity has paid a proper tribute to morality and virtue, by branding his memory with the infamy and abhorrence it so justly deserves.

[2] *Standing in his presence.*]—I have before had occasion to speak of the veneration which was paid by the ancients to those, whose office or whose age commanded t. Gellius, in another place, relates an anecdote of a man who was fined by the censors for yawning in his presence.

Gronovius

Gronovius imagines, that of this chapter he has reason to believe, that he has discovered a fragment in Nonius Marcellus, at the article *hallucinare*. The fragment is as follows:

" Et assiduo oscitantem vidit atque illius quidem delicatissimas mentis et corporis hallucinationes."

The conjecture of Gronovius may probably be right.

CHAP. IV.[1]

Herodotus, the most celebrated historian, falsely asserts, that the pine-tree alone, of all trees, when cut down, never puts forth shoots from the same root.—The same person, concerning rain-water and snow, has assumed for granted, what has not been sufficiently explored.

[1] The passage to which there is here an allusion, is in the 37th chapter of the sixth book of Herodotus.

The expression of being destroyed as a pine became proverbial, and was applied to utter destruction without the possibility of recovery. What Herodotus says of the pine is true also of various other trees, which, as Bentley, in his Dissertation on Phalaris, remarks, all perish by lopping.

The other passage in Herodotus is, as Wesseling conjectures, in his Dissertatio Herodotea, in the 22d chapter of the 2d book. In this place the historian remarks, that it is a kind of law of nature, that it should rain five days after a fall of snow.

The place in Herodotus is probably corrupt; and if this book of Gellius had remained entire, we should perhaps have had a very difficult passage perfectly illustrated.

CHAP. V.

The meaning of cœlum ſtare pulvere *in Virgil, and how Lucilius has uſed* pectus ſentibus ſtare. [1]

[1] The paſſage from Virgil is this,

> Et ſævus campis magis ac magis horror
> Crebreſcit, propiuſque malum eſt, jam pulvere cœ-
> lum
> Stare vident.

Dryden has not rendered the paſſage with ſufficient ſtrength:

> Meantime the war approaches to the tents,
> Th' alarm grows hotter, and the noiſe augments;
> The driving duſt proclaims the danger near.

The driving duſt is by no means what Virgil intended to expreſs by cœlum ſtare pulvere. The air was in a manner rendered thick and immoveable by the condenſed duſt.

See Nonius Marcellus, at the article *ſtare*, where alſo it is not improbable but ſome fragment from this loſt chapter may have been introduced.

CHHP. VI.[*]

When, after trifling difputes, a reconciliation takes place, mutual expoftulations can do no good.—Dif-courfe of Taurus on this fubject, with a paffage taken from the writings of Theopbraftus.—Cice-ro's opinion, de amore amicitiæ, in his own words.

[*] The affertion in the beginning of this article doubtlefs avows an excellent moral truth.

On the fubject of this loft chapter fee Gellius, Book i. chap. 3. De amore amicitiæ, means concerning the love of friendfhip, that is, the particular fpecies of love or affection which friendfhip excites.

Chap. VII.

Observations on the nature and power of memory ', from the book of Ariſtotle entitled περι μνημης.— Certain examples therein read or heard of concerning its extraordinary ſtrength or deficiency.

C H A P.

' The power of the memory preſents an inexhauſtible ſubjeɛt; and innumerable inſtances of the excellence of this faculty in ſome men would fill a volume. It is very happily defined by Cicero thus,—" Memoria certe non modo philoſophiam ſed omnis vitæ uſum, omneſque artes, una maxime continet."

The poſition of Montaigne is certainly very diſputable. He affirms that a ſtrong memory is commonly coupled with infirm judgment. The converſe of which ſtrange propoſition was ſingularly true, as it related to himſelf, who was remarkably deficient in this quality. He tells, in his Eſſays, that his ſtudy was in a remote corner of his houſe, and that if he wanted to conſult any book, or write any thing down, when he was ſitting in ſome other apartment, he was obliged to truſt the memory of others. He could never remember the names of his ſervants, and was inclined to believe, that if he lived to be old' he ſhould forget his own name.

The moſt extraordinary example of the power of memory in this, or perhaps in any country, was the celebrated Jedediah Buxton. He was able, by his memory alone, to anſwer the moſt difficult arithmetical queſtions that could be propoſed; of which the following are a few ſpecimens:

He was aſked, in a field 351 yards long and 261 yards wide, how many acres there were. In eleven minutes he replied, 18 acres, 3 roods, 28 perches, and 14 remained.

A ſecond

A fecond queftion put to him was, Suppofe found moves 1142 feet in one fecond of time, how long after the firing of a cannon could the fame be heard at the diftance of five miles ? In about a quarter of an hour he replied, 23 feconds, 7 thirds, and 46 remained.

A third queftion was, If I fet 3584 plants in rows four feet afunder, and the plants feven feet apart in a rectangular piece of ground, how much land will the plants take up ? In half an hour he faid, two acres, one rood, eight perches, and a half.

The following was the hardeft queftion ever propofed to him :

What dimenfions muft I give my joiner to make a cubical corn-bin, that fhall hold juft a quarter of malt, Winchefter meafure?

In an hour's time he replied, It would be a little more than $25\frac{3}{4}$ inches on a fide, and that 26 inches would be too much. —All which anfwers are as true and correct as poffible.

C H A P.

CHAP. VIII.

That I have been accustomed to interpret, and have endeavoured to render faithfully in Latin, certain passages [1] from Plato.

[1] *Passages.*]—In the edition of Gronovius and many others, the original is *locos*, but it is sometimes read *jocos*, which means *jests*. It may be observed, that in the earlier editions of Gellius, the reader will find nineteen books of Gellius, without the heads of the chapters of the eighth book, nor I do know when these heads were first discovered and printed.

CHAP. IX.

Theophraſtus, the moſt elegant philoſopher of his age, when about to addreſs a few words to the people of Athens, from an emotion of baſhfulneſs, became ſilent[1].—The ſame thing happened to Demoſthenes, when ſpeaking to king Philip.

CHAP.

The ſame amiable diffidence is related of ſome of the more celebrated characters of antiquity, and in particular of Marcus Craſſus and Cicero.

Demoſthenes was ſent with nine other ambaſſadors to Philip of Macedon, to treat with him concerning a peace ; and I cannot do better than give the anecdote which is here alluded to, in the words of Dr. Leland, from his Hiſtory of the Life and Reign of Philip.

Demoſthenes was the youngeſt, and conſequently the laſt to ſpeak. He now ſtood before a prince whom he was conſcious he had frequently ſpoken of, with the greateſt ſeverity, and who he knew was thoroughly informed of every thing ſaid or done at Athens. He was to contend with a complete maſter in his own art: and the reputation of the great Athenian orator, who was ever lancing the bolts of his eloquence againſt the king, muſt have raiſed a ſolemn attention in the court: even the ambaſſadors themſelves were curious to hear thoſe irreſiſtible remonſtrances which the orator is ſaid to have promiſed with the greateſt confidence, and which Philip and his courtiers were by this time warned to expect. All was ſuſpenſe and eager curioſity, and every man now waited in ſilence for ſome extraordinary inſtance of force and dignity in ſpeaking: but he who had ſo frequently braved

all

all the tumult and oppofition of an Athenian affembly, was
in this new fcene in an inftant difconcerted and confounded.
He began in a manner utterly unworthy of his reputation,
obfcure, ungraceful, and hefitating : his terror and embar-
raffment ftill encreafed, and fcarcely had he uttered a few broken and interrupted fentences, when his powers totally failed
him, and he ftood before the affembly utterly unable to proceed. Philip faw his diftrefs, and with all imaginable polite-
nefs endeavoured to relieve it. He told him, with that con-
defcenfion and good-nature which he knew fo well to affect,
that at his court he need be under no apprehenfions: he was
not now before an affembly of his countrymen, where he
might expect fome fatal confequences if his hearers were not
pleafed : he begged he would take time to recollect himfelf,
and purfue his intended difcourfe. Demofthenes attempted
to proceed, but his confufion ftill continued: he appeared ftill
embarraffed, and was foon obliged to be again filent.—The
ambaffadors were then ordered to withdraw.

Chap. X.

A dispute I had at Eleusis¹ with a certain conceited grammarian, who was ignorant of the tenses of verbs, and the common exercises of a school-boy; but who ostentatiously proposed intricate questions, and bugbears to catch the minds of the vulgar.

¹ *Eleusis.*]—This was a town of Attica, and dedicated, or rather consecrated, to the Goddess Ceres. It is still better known from the celebration of the Eleusinian mysteries.

Chap. XI.

The facetious reply of Socrates¹ to his wife Xantippe, requesting him to be somewhat more liberal in giving an entertainment at the feast of Bacchus.

¹ I have somewhere seen an anecdote of Socrates and Xantippe, which may possibly be the same as was recorded in this chapter. Socrates had invited some men, who were known to be rich, to sup with him, and Xantippe was offended with the mean and scanty preparation: " Never mind," said Socrates, " if they are temperate they will by no means despise a frugal entertainment; if they shall be profligate and extravagant,
they

they will be beneath our notice and efteem. Some people," he continued, " live merely that they may eat, whilft I eat only that I may live." This was faid to have happened at the feaft of the Dionyfia, a feaft celebrated in honour of Bacchus; at which time people were fomewhat more profufe in treating their friends.

C H A P. XII.

The meaning of the phrafe plerique [1] omnes *in the old books, and that thefe words feem borrowed from the Greeks.*

[1] Plerique, confidered feparately by itfelf, may be underftood to mean ferme omnes, or almoft all ; but when omnes is added to plerique, it feems to have the fenfe of immo omnes : thus in Englifh it may be interpreted, *almoft all*, nay quite *all*.

C H A P. XIII.

The word quopſones[1], *which the Africans uſe, is a Greek and not a Carthaginian word.*

[1] Moſt of the older editions read this word Qupſones. Scaliger, in ſome manuſcript, found it written Eupſones, which he altered to Eudones, from the Punic word Haudoni, which means, Hail, maſter! and perhaps, therefore, continues Gronovius, the Africans uſed Eudones for Adonis. Notwithſtanding, therefore, what Gellius imagines, Eudones is probably a Syriac word. See the remainder of the note of Gronovius.

C H A P. XIV.

A very pleaſant diſpute of the philoſopher Favorinus, with a certain intemperate opponent, arguing on the ambiguity of words.—Certain words applied in an unuſual manner, from the poet Nævius, and from Cnæus Gellius[1].—Origin of words inveſtigated by Publius Nigidius.

[1] The older editions read Cneius Gallus; and Gronovius ſenſibly remarks, that in all probability it ought to be Cæcilius.

CHAP. XV.

*The manner in which the poet Laberius[1] was igno-
miniously treated by Caius Cæsar.—Verses by the
same Laberius on this subject.*

[1] This Laberius has been before mentioned, and the reader has been told to expect the verses of the prologue which
Laberius spoke on the occasion, when he suffered the indig-
nity to which allusion is here made. I insert the original,
with the translation by a friend:

Necessitas, cujus cursus transversi impetum
Voluerunt multi effugere, pauci potuerunt,
Quo me detrusit pœne extremis sensibus?
Quem nulla ambitio, nulla unquam largitio,
Nullus timor, vis nulla, nulla auctoritas
Movere potuit in juventa de statu;
Ecce in senecta ut facile labefecit loco
Viri excellentis mente clemente edita
Submissa placide, blandiloquens oratio.
Etenim ipsi Di negare cui nihil potuerunt
Hominem me denegare quis posset pati?
Ergo bis tricenis annis actis sine nota,
Eques Romanus lare egressus meo
Domum revertar mimus; nimirum hoc die
Uno plus vixi mihi quam vivendum fuit,
Fortuna immoderata in bono æque atque in malo,
Si tibi erat libitum litterarum laudibus
Floris cacumen nostræ famæ frangere;
Cur cum vigebam membris præviridantibus,
Satis facere populo et tali cum poteram viro
Non flexibilem me concurvasti ut carperes

K 3

Nunc

Nunc me quo dejicis? quid ad fcenam affero
Decorem formæ, an dignitatem corporis,
Animi virtutem, an vocis jucundæ fonum?
Ut hedera ferpens vires arboreas necat,
Ita me vetuftas, amplexu annorum, enecat.
Sepulcri fimilis, nihil nifi nomen retineo.

In Englifh.

Oh thou, the iffue of whofe tranfverfe courfe,
Neceffity! the few alone can fhun,
Low haft thou laid me in the wane of life——.
While nor ambition, nor the fordid bribe,
Nor fear, nor force, nor fway of fovereign pow'r,
Could in my youth betray me from my ftate;
Behold, in weak old age, how eafily
The powerful eloquence of yon great man,
Mild and perfuafive, fteals me from my rank.
For could it be that I could e'er deny
His power, whom nought the Gods themfelves refufe?
Forth from my houfe I came, a Roman knight,
That threefcore years had pafs'd unftain'd by crime,
And homeward I fhall now return, a player.
I feel that I have liv'd one day too long.
Fortune, in each extreme of good or ill
Unable to preferve a temp'rate fway,
If with this fcenic literary wreath
Thou would'ft break down my yet unhonour'd brow,
Why, when the vigour and the ftrength of youth
Could more have aided me to yield content
To Roman audiences, and this great man,
Didft thou not bend my lefs unpliant ftem?
Now whither doft thou caft me? To the ftage!
What profit can I bring? that have nor fhape
Nor dignity, nor fpirit left, nor voice?
The creeping ivy clafps and kills the tree.
So falls Laberius in th' embrace of age,
And, like a tomb, bears but the name of man.

BOOK IX.[1]

CHAP. I.

The reason why Quintus Claudius Quadrigarius, in the nineteenth Book of his Annals, has observed, that a mark was struck with greater effect and certainty, when the projection was to take place upwards, than if it were downwards.

QUINTUS CLAUDIUS, in his nineteenth Book of Annals, describing the siege of a town by Metellus the proconsul, and

the

---

[1] The books of Gellius have at different periods been differently arranged. In some manuscripts the book before us has been called the eighth book.

The assertion which is here made certainly comes in a very questionable shape, and is perhaps altogether untrue Perhaps the converse may be the fact, and that they who project any thing from an eminence must do it with more force and greater certainty. The force of gravity acts constantly in opposition to any thing projected upwards, which if it does not render the hitting the mark more precarious, must certainly diminish the momentum or the aggregate of the velocity, and the quantity of matter of the thing projected.

K 4

The

the refiftance which was made by the citizens from the walls, has thus expreffed himfelf:

" The archers and flingers, on both fides, dif-perfe their weapons with great ardour, and extra-ordinary courage. But there is this difference, whether you projeٰ an arrow or a ftone up-wards or downwards; neither can be projeٰted downwards with certainty, but both of them with great effeٰt upwards. Therefore the foldiers of Metellus were much lefs wounded, and, what was

of

The flingers of the ancients were remarkably expert, and well they might, if what Vegetius relates be true, that they were accuftomed to this exercife from their earlieft infancy, and that mothers would not fuffer their children to have their meals, unlefs they could hit fuch objeٰs as were pointed out to them. It was ufual to wind the fling once round the head before they projeٰted its contents; this was obvioufly to throw with greater force; but the pofition of a perfon in an inferior fituation, who has to throw any thing at a mark above him from a fling, feems very inconvenient for this mo-tion.

Virgil, defcribing Mezentius about to throw from a fling, reprefents him as winding the fling three times round his head:

Pofitis Mezentius haftis,
Ipfe ter adduٰta circum caput egit habena,
Et media adverfi liquefaٰto tempora plumbo
Diffidit, ac multa porreٰtum extendit arena.

Thus rendered by Dryden—

The Thufcan king
Laid by the lance, and took him to the fling;

Thrice

of greater confequence, eafily defended themfelves from the battlements of the enemy."

I enquired of Antonius Julianus, the rhetorician, how this that Quadrigarius afferted came to
pafs, that a blow was much more effectual and
certain, if a ftone or an arrow were hurled upwards than downwards, when the throwing of
any thing from an eminence downwards was more
natural and eafy, than to throw from a lower
fituation upwards. Then Julianus, approving
of my enquiry, replied—

" What is here faid of an arrow or a ftone, is
equally true of almoft every miffile weapon. It
is certainly eafier, as you obferve, to throw any
thing downwards; if your object be only to throw
and not hit; but if the manner and force of
the projection is to be moderated and directed,

> Thrice whirl'd the thong around his head, and threw
> The heated lead, half melted as it flew,
> It pierc'd his hollow temples and his brain,
> 'The youth came tumbling down, and fpurn'd the
>   plain.*

The ufe of arrows and flings in battle was fuperfeded by
the invention of gun-powder, and was difcontinued almoft
immediately after that period.

* This circumftance of the lead becoming warm from the fwiftnefs of its rotatory motion, is mentioned frequently by the Latin
poets. See Ovid.

> Non fecus exarfit quam cum balearica plumbum
> Funda jacit, volat illud et incardefcit eundo
> Et quos non habuit fub nubibus invenit ignes.

then

then if you throw downwards, the force and pre-cifion of him who throws is interrupted both by his own precipitatenefs, and the weight of the weapon which is projected. But if you throw at any thing above, and the hand and eyes be pre-pared to hit an elevated object, the care that is taken will carry the weapon to the object at which it is aimed."

It was nearly in thefe terms that Julianus con-verfed with me on the words of Claudius; but what the fame Claudius fays, they eafily defended themfelves from the enemy's battlement, it is to be obferved, that he has ufed the word *defendebant*, not as it is generally applied, but with great pro-priety and pure Latinity. For the words *defen-dere* and *offendere* are oppofite to each other; the one fignifies *incurrere in aliquid*, to meet any thing, the other to repel, which is the thing in-tended by Q. Claudius in this paffage.

CHAP. II.

The words in which Herodes Atticus reproved one who, with the dress and habit, falsely assumed the title and manner of a philosopher.

IN my presence, a certain man, with a long cloak [1] and hair, and with a beard reaching to his girdle, approached Herodes Atticus, a man of consular rank, eminent for his amiable

[1] *Long cloak.*]—The affected austerity of manner and mean dress which distinguished the old philosophers, was a subject which frequently exercised the talents of the comic writers of Greece and Rome. The man here mentioned was probably a Cynic, to which sect the remark above more particularly applies. An entertaining description of one of these philosophers is found in Alciphron, and is to this effect:

" He saw one of those people who, from their behaviour, are called Cynics, and, in imitation of him, soon exceeded the extravagance of his master. The appearance he makes is hideous and disgusting; he shakes his uncombed locks, his look is ferocious; as to his dress, he goes half naked, having a little wallet hanging before him, and a staff of wild olive in his hands. He wears no shoes, is very filthy, and totally unmanageable, &c." See also the Hermotimus of Lucian; and Alciphron, in another place, thus speaks of Epicurus— " He is an unwholesome, filthy wretch, wrapped up in cloth made of hair instead of wool." The character of Apemantus is well represented by Shakspeare, in his play of Timon of Athens.

amiable difpofition, and his accomplifhments in Grecian eloquence, and requefted money to be given him for bread. Herodes on this afked him who he was? he, with an angry tone and frowning countenance, replied, he was a philofopher; and expreffed his furprize that he fhould be afked who he was, when his appearance declared it. " I perceive," returned Herodes, " the beard and the cloak, but I do not fee the philofopher; but I befeech you to tell us with good-humour, by the ufe of what arguments we fhould be able to know you to be a philofopher." On this, fome of thofe who were prefent with Herodes affirmed, that this was a ftrolling fellow, of no character, a frequenter of the meaneft brothels; and that unlefs he got what he afked, it was his cuftom to be impudent and abufive. " Let us," interrupted Herodes, " give this man fomething, whoever he may be, confidering our own characters, and not his;" and he ordered money enough to be given him to procure bread for thirty days. Then, looking upon us who were near him,

Athens. This perfonage, fpeaking of the drefs which Timon now wore, affecting to imitate him, fays,

If thou didft put this four cold habit on
To caftigate thy pride, 'twere well.—

See alfo Horace. Ep. 2. B. 2. This poet, fpeaking of the affected peculiarities of this race of men, mentions, among other things, their folemn filence—

Statua taciturnior exit
Plerumque et rifu populum quatit.

" Mufonius,"

"Mufonius," fays he, "gave to a beggar of this kind, pretending to be a philofopher, a thoufand fefterces; and when many people obferved, that he was a profligate fellow, of the vileft character, who deferved nothing at all, they affirm that Mufonius replied with a fmile, ' therefore he deferves money[1].' But this it is," he continued, "which affects me with real grief and vexation, that thefe very vile and contemptible creatures ufurp a moft venerable name[2], and are called philofophers.

[1] *Deferves money.*]—Meaning, without doubt, that money is in itfelf fo contemptible a thing as to be beneath the attention of men of wifdom, and followers of true philofophy:

Thus much of gold will make black white, foul fair,
Wrong right, bafe noble, old young, coward valiant.
How, you gods, why this—what this, you gods—why this
Will lug your priefts and fervants from your fides,
Pluck ftout men's pillows from below their heads.
This yellow flave
Will knit and break religions, blefs the accurfed,
Make the hoar leprofy ador'd, place thieves,
And give them title, knee, and approbation
With fenators on the bench; this is it
That makes the wappen'd widow wed again,
She whom the fpital-houfe and ulcerous fores
Would caft the gorge at, this embalms and fpices
To the April day again.

SHAKSPEARE.

[2] *Venerable name.*]—See a facetious dialogue in Erafmus, on the abufe of names—De rebus et vocabulis.

" Jam fi quis nobis adeffet dialecticus qui fcite definiret quid fit rex, quid epifcopus, quid magiftratus, quid philofophus, fortaffis et hic invenerimus qui mallent nomen quam rem."

But

But my anceftors, the Athenians, enacted by a public decree, that none of fervile condition fhould ever bear the names of the two valiant youths, Harmodius and Ariftogiton, who, to accomplifh the reftoration of liberty, attacked the life of the tyrant Hippias, deeming it impious that names devoted to their country's liberty fhould be contaminated by the contagion of fervitude. Why then do we allow the moft illuftrious character of philofophy to grow vile among the worft of mankind? I find too," he added, "by a fimilar example of a contrary kind, that the ancient Romans determined that the prænomens of certain patricians, who had deferved ill of their country, and for this reafon had incurred the penalty of death, fhould not be borne by any other patrician of that family, that their very names might feem to be degraded, and to expire along with them.

C H A P. III.

The letter of King Philip [1] *to Ariſtotle the philoſopher,
on the birth of Alexander.*

PHILIP, ſon of Amyntas, king of Macedonia, by whoſe valour and exertions the
Macedonians, increaſing their opulence and dominions, began to have ſovereignty over various
nations, and whoſe power and arms the celebrated orations of Demoſthenes declare to have been
formidable to the whole of Greece ; this Philip,
though at all times occupied and exerciſed in the
toils and triumphs of war, never neglected the
liberal purſuits of literature, and the ſtudies of
humanity. He did and uttered many things with
equal facetiouſneſs and urbanity.   There are ſaid

---

[1] *Philip.*]—For every thing relating to the life of this extraordinary perſonage, I beg leave to refer the reader to
Leland's work, the exordium of which ſeems pertinent in
this place.—" The founder of the Macedonian greatneſs was
by no means of the number of thoſe princes who were aſ-
ſiſted by the advantages of an illuſtrious country, who inherit-
ed the opulence and force of ſplendid and extenſive dominions, or were ſtrengthened by the acquiſitions, and animated
by the atchievements of a long train of renowned anceſtry.
To his own abilities alone did Philip owe his elevation, and
appears equally great, and equally the object of admiration,
in ſurmounting the difficulties attending on his infant power,
as in his maturer and more extenſive fortune."

to

to have been volumes of his letters full of elegance, grace, and wisdom: such is that in which he related to Aristotle the philosopher the birth of his son Alexander[2]. This letter, as it seems to be an inducement for care and diligence in the education of children, I have thought proper to transcribe, that it may impress the minds of parents. It may be interpreted nearly in this manner:

" Philip sends health to Aristotle—Know that a son is born to me ; I therefore thank the gods, not so much because he is born, but that he happened to be born during your life—I hope, that being instructed and brought up by you, he may prove worthy both of me and the conduct of affairs."

[2] *Birth of his son Alexander.*]—This day was also memorable for an event which demonstrates that there is no excess of folly or extravagance to which the human mind may not be transported, when warmed by enthusiasm. On this day Erostratus set fire to the temple of Diana at Ephesus, from the strange idea of rendering his name immortal. It is related by Plutarch, in his life of Alexander, that the priests of the goddess ran frantic through the streets of Ephesus, exclaiming, that on this day something was produced which would cause the destruction of Asia. This was of course made to apply to the birth of Alexander.

CHAP. IV.

*Of the prodigies and miracles of barbarous nations;
of their horrid and destructive fascinations—and
of women who were suddenly turned into men.*

AS we were returning from Greece to Italy, we touched at Brundusium [1], and going on shore, we wandered about that celebrated harbour, which Q. Ennius has named *Præpes*, a word somewhat remote indeed, but very apposite— we saw some bundles of books exposed for sale, to which I ran with eagerness. They were Greek books, full of prodigies and fables; of things unheard of and incredible, and old writers of no mean authority—Aristeas [2] of Proconnesus,

[1] *Brundusium.*]—From this celebrated harbour the Romans usually embarked to go to Greece. It was in this place, now called Brindisi, that Virgil died.

[2] *Aristeas.*]—This Aristeas was a poet; and a long account of him may be found in the fourth book of Herodotus. Two fragments of his works remain, one in Longinus, the other in Tzetzes.

Ifigonus[3] of Nicæa, Ctefias[4], Oneficritus[5], Polyftephanus[6], and Hegefias[7]. The volumes, from
their long expofure, were very filthy, and in their
outward appearance as bad as poffible. I approached, however, and enquired the price: induced by their wonderful and unexpected cheap-
nefs, I bought a great many books for very little
money; and in the two following nights I took a
curfory perufal of them all. In my progrefs I
made fome felections, and noted many wonderful things, which few, if any, of our writers have
handled. I have inferted them in thefe commentaries, that whoever fhall read them may not

[3] *Ifigonus.*]—This perfon is fpoken of by Pliny, in the
2d Chapter of the 7th book of his Natural Hiftory. Perhaps no other account of him remains than what appears in
that author.

[4] *Ctefias.*]—This man was an hiftorian, and wrote many
things contradicting the affertions of Herodotus. He probably lived in the time of the younger Cyrus. The Biblio-
theca of Photius contains the particulars of this author's
works, with fome remarks on his ftyle and abilities.

[5] *Oneficritus.*]—Arrian, Strabo, and Plutarch, feverally
make mention of this writer, who was the companion, and
who, in a diffufe metaphorical ftyle, wrote the exploits of
Alexander the Great.

[6] *Polyftephanus,*]—was an hiftorian, and is mentioned in
terms of refpect by the Scholiaft to Apollonius Rhodius.

[7] *Hegefias.*]—It is related of this philofopher, that he
painted the calamities of life in fo very forcible a manner,
that many of his hearers were induced to put an end to their
lives. See Cicero, Tufculan Queftions, Book i.

be

be altogether ignorant, and one who has never
been a hearer of such things. In these books
were passages such as these:—

That the Scythians who are most remote,
and who live as it were at the very pole,
fed on human flesh, and supported themselves by such nutriment, and were called Anthropophagi[8]: that there were also men beneath
the same climate having one eye in the middle of
the forehead, and called Arimaspi[9], with which

[8] *Anthropophagi.*]—Of whom Herodotus speaks in his
Melpomene. See a curious and entertaining chapter on the
subject of cannibals in Montaigne's Essays. There is also
a passage on this subject in the fifteenth Satire of Juvenal, not
unworthy attention.

[9] *Arimaspi.*]—These people are also mentioned by Herodotus, Melpomene, chap. 13. See also the Prometheus
vinctus of Æschylus—

> ———avoid
> The Arimaspian troops, whose frowning foreheads
> Glare with one blazing eye.

These Arimaspians are introduced by Lucan, in his third
book: he says, they bound their hair with gold.

> ———Auroque ligatas
> Substringens Arimaspe comas.

Other authors represent, that there were continual wars
betwixt the gryphons and Arimaspians, for this gold, of
which fable Milton makes an elegant use:

> As when a gryphon through the wilderness,
> With winged course, o'er hill or moory dale
> Pursues the Arimaspian, who by stealth
> Had from his wakeful custody purloin'd
> The guarded gold———

L 2

countenances

countenances the poets defcribe the Cyclops: that there were alfo men near the fame diftrict of extraordinary fwiftnefs, having the direction of their feet reverfed, and not as other men, pointing forwards. They related alfo, how it had been handed down from tradition, that in a certain remote part of the earth, which is called Albania, men were produced whofe hair was grey in childhood, and who, faw more clearly by night than by day : that it was faid and believed of the Sauromatæ, who live at a great diftance beyond the Boryfthenes, that they only took food on every third day, abftaining on that which intervened. I alfo found written in the fame books, what I afterwards read in the feventh book of the Natural Hiftory of the Elder Pliny, that in Africa were certain families of men, who had the power of fafcination in their fpeech [10]; who, if by chance they

[10] *Fafcination in their fpeech.*]—To this idea Virgil without doubt alludes in his feventh Eclogue—

> Aut fi ultra placitum laudarit, baccare frontem
> Cingite ne vati noceat mala lingua futuro.

La Cerda fays, that it was ufual with the antients, when they praifed any thing, to add præ-fafcino, that is, fine fafcino, meaning they had no evil intentions, no thought of fafcination. The baccar was fuppofed to counteract the effects of magic. The idea that a power of fafcination exifted in the eyes was more prevalent, and certainly more plaufible. See Virgil's third Eclogue—

> Nefcio quis teneros oculus mihi fafcinat agnos.

> I cannot tell what eye fafcinates my tender lambs.

The

they extrvagantly praifed beautiful trees, plentiful crops, lovely infants, excellent horfes, cattle which were fat and well fed, all of thefe fuddenly died from this and no other caufe. It was related in thefe fame books, that a mortal fafcination fometimes exifts in the eyes; and it is faid that there are men in Illyrium, who kill by their fight thofe whom they look at for any time, with anger; and that thefe, of whom there are both male and

The fame Pliny alfo makes mention of a people diftinguifhed by peculiarities certainly not lefs wonderful than any which are here defcribed—they were propagated without women :—

"Gens fola et in toto orbe præter cæteras mira fine ulla fœmina omni venere abdicata, fine pecunia, focia palmarum. Ita per feculorum millia incredibile dictu gens æterna eft in qua nemo nafcitur. Tam fœcunda illis aliorum vitæ pœnitentia eft."

Which fentence Mr. Gibbon thus paraphrafes :

"The philofophic eye of Pliny had furveyed with aftonifhment a folitary people, who dwelt among the palm-trees, near the Dead Sea, who fubfifted without money, who were propagated without women, and who derived from the difguft and repentance of mankind a perpetual fupply of voluntary affociates." See alfo Robinfon's Difquifition concerning Ancient India.

But unfortunately Megafthenes was fo fond of the marvellous, that he mingled with the truths which he related, many extravagant fictions; and to him may be traced up the fabulous tales of men with ears fo large that they could wrap themfelves up in them; of others with a fingle eye, without mouths, without nofes, with long feet and toes turned backwards; of people only three fpans in height; of wild men with heads in the fhape of a wedge; of ants as large as foxes, that dug up gold, and many other things no lefs wonderful.

female,

female, who have this deadly power of fight, have two pupils " in each eye. That there are alfo, in the mountains of India, men-who have heads, and who bark like dogs ", and who fupport themfelves by hunting birds and wild beafts: as alfo, what is no lefs wonderful, there are, in the extreme parts of the Eaft, men, called Monocoli, who go hopping on one leg with the moft wonderful fwiftnefs; and that there are fome who have no heads, whofe eyes are in their fhoulders. But it exceeeds all bounds of wonder, what thefe fame writers affirm, that there is a nation in the extremity of India, having their bodies fledged, and with the plumage of birds, who eat no kind of food, but live by inhaling by their noftrils the perfume of flowers: that not far from thefe are the Pigmies, the talleft of whom are not more than two feet and a quarter. I read thefe and many other things of the fame kind, but in tranfcribing them I was difgufted by the ufeleffnefs of fuch writings, not at all contributing to the ornament or comfort of life. Yet I think it not

" *Two pupils.*]—Ovid has applied this idea very happily, in fome verfes, where he execrates a bawd for inftructing his miftrefs in meretricious arts.

> Hanc ego nocturnas verfam volitare per umbras
> Sufpicor, et pluma corpus anile regi,
> Sufpicor, et fama eft oculis quoque pupula duplex
> Fulminat, et gemino lumen ab orbe venit.

" *Like dogs.*]—See Herodotus, Book iv. chap. 191. to which paffage, with my note upon it, I beg leave to refer the reader.

improper,

improper, in this chapter of miracles, to transcribe what Pliny the Elder, a man who, in his own times, was of high authority, both for talents and dignity, has in his seventh book of Natural History recorded, not as what he had heard or read, but what he had himself known and seen. The passage which is added below is in the words of Pliny, taken from the above-mentioned book, which indeed make the popular tale of Cænis and Cæneus in the old poets neither incredible nor ridiculous.

"That women," he says, "have been changed into men" is not fabulous. We find, in the Annals, in the consulship of Q. Licinius Crassus, and Caius Caffius Longinus, that at Caffinum a girl became a boy, in the house of its parents, and by command of the augurs was transported to a desert island. Licinius Mucianus has related that he himself saw at Argos one Arescontes, whose name had been Arescusa, and who had been married, but who afterwards had a beard, became a man, and took a wife: and that at Smyrna also he had seen a boy of this description. I myself, in Africa, saw Lucius Cofficus, a citizen

---

[1] *Into men.*]—The following extract, without any comment, is from Montaigne: "Myself passing by Vitry le François, a town in Champagne, saw a man, the bishop of Soissons had in confirmation, called German, whom all the inhabitants of the place had known to be a girl, till two-and-twenty years of age called Mary"—It was by straining himself in a leap, it seems, that this wonderful change took place.

of

of Thyſdrum, who became a man on the day of his marriage, and was alive when I wrote this."

The ſame Pliny, in the ſame book, has alſo theſe words : " There are men born who have the marks of each ſex, whom we call herma- phrodites : formerly they were called Androgyni, and reckoned prodigies [4], now they are conſider- ed as objects of delight.

[4] *Prodigies.*]—When any of theſe monſtrous births hap- pened, the child, by order of the Aruſpices, was anciently ordered to be thrown into the ſea.

CHAP. V.

Different opinions of eminent philofophers concerning the nature of pleafure.—Words of Hierocles the philofopher, in which he oppofes the decrees of Epicurus.

THE ancient philofophers have avowed different opinions concerning pleafure. Epicurus afferts, that pleafure is the chief good, and he defines it thus, " a firm conftitution of body." Antifthenes, the Socratic, calls it the greateft evil. His expreffion is this—" I would rather be mad, than purfue pleafure."

Speufippus, and all the old academy, fay that pleafure and pain are two evils oppofing one another; that is good which is intermediate betwixt both. Zeno thought pleafure a thing indifferent, that is neutral, neither good nor evil, which he himfelf named, by a Greek word, αδιαφορον. Critolaus, the Peripatetic, affirms, that pleafure is an evil, and produces of itfelf many other evils, injuries, floth, oblivion, and ftupidity. Above all thefe, Plato has difputed concerning pleafure in fo many and various ways, that all thefe fentiments I have mentioned before, feem to have iffued from the fources of his arguments. For he ufes every one of them, as the nature of pleafure

itfelf,

itfelf, which is multiplied, allows, and as the reafon of the caufes which he inveftigates, and of the
things which he would demonftrate, requires. But
our countryman Taurus, as often as mention was
made of Epicurus, had in his mouth, and on his
lips, thefe words of Hierocles the Stoic [*], a man
of

---

[*] *Thefe words of Hierocles the Stoic.*]—Enfield's valuable Hiftory of Philofophy will fatisfy and inftruct the Englifh reader
on the fubject of the fummum bonum, or chief good, as difcuffed by the ancient philofophers. The Greek faying of Hierocles at the conclufion of the chapter, has ftrangely perplexed
the commentators on Gellius. It remained for our Bentley to
remove all obfcurity from the paffage, by an alteration fo fimple that it is wonderful it fhould not fooner have occurred;
and fo fatisfactory as to exclude all further controverfy. I
cannot do better than give the reader Bentley's own words:
" Now that I am fpeaking of προνοια, I cannot omit a very
elegant faying of Hierocles the Stoic, which, as A. Gellius tells
us, the Platonic philofopher Taurus had always in his mouth
when Epicurus was mentioned, Ηδονη τελος πορνης δογμα, ουκ
εστιν πορνεια ουδεν πορνης δογμα; which being manifeftly corrupted, our moft excellent bifhop Pearfon corrects it thus, Ηδονη
τελος· πορνης δογμα· ουκ εστι προνοια ουδεν· πορνης δογμα: That is,
" Pleafure is the fummum bonum, a ftrumpet's tenet. Providence is nothing, a ftrumpet's tenet."—Now the emenda-
tion in the main is true and good, for πορνεια is with great
fagacity changed by him into προνοια, which is the bafis of
the whole fentence. But yet there is fomething harfh in
the fyntax that his Lordfhip has made there, ουκ εστι προνοια
ουδεν, for the author, if he had ufed ουδεν, would have faid
προνοια ουδεν εστι. Befides, that the fame anfwer, πορνης δογμα,
coming twice, makes the faying a little too flat, and fcarce
worthy to be ufed by Taurus fo frequently; nor is it true that
all ftrumpets deny Providence. I am perfuaded that the
true

of great dignity and worth, " Let pleafure be the end, is the tenet of a harlot; but that there is no Providence, is not the tenet even of an harlot."

true reading is thus: Ἡδονὴ τέλος· πόρνης δόγμα· ουκ εστὶ πρόνοια· ουδε πόρνης δόγμα. Now it is impoffible in our language to exprefs this faying with the fame brevity and turn that the original has, but the meaning of it is, " Pleafure is the fummum bonum,—a ftrumpet's tenet. There is no Providence —a tenet too bad even for a ftrumpet." Bentley on Phalaris.

Pope, in his Ethic Epiftles, thus comments on the opinions of the ancient philofophers on happinefs:—.

> Afk of the learn'd the way; the learn'd are blind;
> This bids to ferve, and that to fhun mankind;
> Some place the blifs in action, fome in eafe,
> Thefe call it pleafure, and contentment thefe;
> Who thus define it, fay they more or lefs
> Than this, that happinefs is happinefs?
> One grants his pleafure is but reft from pain,
> One doubts of all, one owns ev'n virtue vain.

See Bifhop Warburton's remarks on the above paffage in anfwer to Croufaz.

CHAP. VI.

How the frequentative verb from ago *is to be pronounced in the first vowel* [1].

FROM *ago, egi,* come the verbs which the grammarians call frequentative, *actito, acti-tavi.* I have heard some, and these not unlearned men, pronounce these as if the first vowel was short: and they give as a reason that in the principal verb *ago* the first vowel is so pronounced. Why then from the verbs *edo* and *ungo,* in which verbs the first letter is pronounced short, do we make the first letter of their frequentatives *esito* and *unctito* long; and on the contrary we make the first letter of *dictito,* which comes from *dico,* short? Are therefore *actito* and *actitavi* to be long?

Since frequentatives are almost without exception pronounced, with respect to the first vowel,

[1] This is without doubt one of the chapters in Gellius which cannot be supposed materially to interest the English reader, but, with many other chapters, it is of use to prove that the Romans must unquestionably have had a mode, and that a very delicate one, of varying the pronunciation of words, some of which, to us, appear perfectly unequivocal. In such a word as *actito,* or *unctito,* the first vowel is obviously long by position, nor is it easy to vary its pronunciation, so that it might be imagined a short syllable.

Quando veteres dicunt syllabam esse brevem quæ positione fit longa, intelligi hoc debet de solo vocalis sono, non de syllaba; sic prima in *dictito* brevis, ut A. Gellius ait, lib. ix. cap. 6. quasi dicas etsi dicatur *deico,* tamen ejus frequentativum non sonare *deictito,* sed *di-ctito.*—Vossius de Arte Grammatica, l. ii. c. 12. See also what he says, l. i. c. 12. about *unctito, actito,* &c.

8

as the participles of the preterite of the verbs from which they are derived are pronounced, on the fame fyllable, as *lego, lectus, lectito*; fo *ungo, unctus, unctito*; *fcribo, fcriptus, fcriptito*; *moveo, motus, motito*; *pendeo, penfus, penfito*; *edo, efus, efito*; but we fay *dico, dictus, dictito*; *gero, geftus, geftito*; *veto, vectus, vectito*; *rapio, raptus, raptito*; *capio, captus, captito*; *facio, factus, factito*.   So alfo *actito* is to be pronounced long in the firft fyllable, fince it comes from *ago, actus*.

CHAP. VII.

Of the change of leaves * *on the olive-tree on the
first day of winter and summer. Of musical
strings sounding at that time without being struck.*

IT has been popularly written and believed,
that the leaves of olive-trees undergo a
change on the first day of the winter or summer
solstice; and that part of them which was beneath
and out of sight became uppermost, visible to
the eye, and exposed to the sun; which I myself,
more than once, being desirous to observe, have
seen actually take place.

* *Change of leaves.*]—Assertions made in this unequivocal
form must certainly have been the result of some observation,
however erroneous. Of the science of botany the ancients without doubt knew a great deal more than we are inclined to allow; but this remark of Gellius, with respect to the olive, is
unquestionably a mistake. Some leaves, as for instance those of
the aspin and the poplar, which are subject to a constant and
tremulous motion, might, from being in a greater degree affected by the equinoctial winds, deceive the eye; and there are
also other leaves, as those of the hyacinth, campanula, &c.
which can perform their functions in any situation. But the
olive is a sturdy and inflexible plant, and if the leaves were,
by any operation, placed with the lower parts above, the fibres
must be wounded, and the leaves die. Here is therefore
some greater mistake than my knowledge of the subject will
enable me to explain.

But

But what is said of musical strings [2] is more uncommon and wonderful, which thing many other learned men, and in particular Suetonius Tranquillus, in his book of Ludicrous History, affirms, has been sufficiently proved, and indeed is unequivocally certain, that some chords of musical instruments, on the day of the winter solstice, being struck with the fingers, others will sound.

[2] *Musical strings.*]—With the usual inaccuracy of the ancients in matters of experiment, we have an effect of musical strings here mentioned as belonging to a particular season, which would doubtless have taken place at any other time, though perhaps better in some kinds of weather than in others. From the concise manner in which the fact is mentioned, it is rather doubtful what might be intended; but as we know of no sympathetic sounds except those produced by the vibration of strings in unison, or octave, to the string which is struck, we may conclude that this was what Suetonius wrote of. As the instruments of the ancients had no great compass of notes, it probably was meant that a string struck on one lyre would produce sound in another; which certainly is true, but this effect would have taken place at any part of the year, had it been tried. We cannot suppose any thing so subtle to be intended as the third sounds of Romieu and Tartini, the production of which depends upon holding out the sounds of two notes at once, in a way that could not have been practised on the ancient *fides*. This, however, or any other effect we can conceive of such a nature, would have happened in all seasons.

Chap. VIII.

He who has much muſt neceſſarily want much.—
The opinion of Favorinus the philoſopher on this
ſubject expreſſed with elegant brevity [1]*.*

IT is certainly true what wiſe men, from
their obſervation of the uſe of things, have
ſaid, that he who has much muſt want much,

and

[1] That this chapter contains a great moral truth, nobody
will attempt to deny; and a multitude of paſſages might be
cited, both from Greek and Latin writers, to prove that the
idea and expreſſion was proverbial.

Gronovius thinks, and with great probability, that in this
place Favorinus alludes to the celebrated Lucullus, whoſe
enormous wealth was a frequent ſubject of admiration with
the poets and writers of his time.

> Chlamydes, Lucullus, ut aiunt,
> Si poſſet centum ſcenæ præbere rogatus,
> Qui poſſum tot ait; tamen et quænam et quos habebo
> Mittam, poſt paulo ſcribit ſibi millia quinque
> Eſſe domi Chlamydum, partem vel tolleret omnes.

Pope, perhaps, in his imitation of Horace, has been leſ
ſuccefsful, with reſpect to this brilliant paſſage, than in other
places: he contents himſelf with ſaying,

> This wealth brave Timon glorioufly confounds;
> Aſk'd for a groat, he gives a thouſand pounds.

Perhaps in any other writer than Pope it would have been
obſerved, that the firſt line is far from perſpicuous; for i

may

and that great indigence arifes not from great want, but great abundance. For many things are wanted to preferve the many things which you have. Whoever, therefore, having much, wifhes to take care, and fee before-hand that he may not want or be defective in any thing, has need of lofs and not of gain, and muft have lefs that he may want lefs. I remember this fentiment uttered by Favorinus, amidft the loudeft applaufes, and conveyed in thefe very few words:

" He who has ten thoufand or five thoufand garments, muft inevitably want more. Wanting therefore fomething more than I poffefs, if I take away from what I have, I may content myfelf with the remainder."

may be afked, what is meant by Timon confounding his wealth? The idea of Horace is very different, and lucid as the light itfelf: he reprefents an individual as being fo exceedingly rich, that he does not know the extent of his riches. The quotation from Favorinus, as it ftands in the edition of Gronovius, is not fatisfactory. But all difficulty feems immediately to be removed, if inftead of οἷς γαρ ιχω we read οἷς γ' αρ ιχω.

Chap. IX.

Manner of transferring Greek sentiments into Latin compositions.—Of those verses of Homer which Virgil has been thought to have imitated well and elegantly, or the contrary.

WHEN elegant sentiments are to be imitated and translated from Greek poems, we are not, it is said, always to endeavour to place every word [1] according to the order in which they originally stand; for many things lose their beauty when, in a translation, they are distorted as it were by unnatural violence. Virgil has therefore demonstrated both skill and

---

[1] *To place every word.*]—A similar sentiment is expressed by Lord Bolingbroke, in his Letters on History, which I have before had occasion to quote. To translate servilely into modern language an ancient author, phrase by phrase, and word by word, is preposterous, &c.

From an ingenious publication, entitled, An Essay on the Principles of Translation, I extract the following account of a perfect translation: " I would therefore," says this writer, " describe a good translation to be that in which the merit of the original work is so completely transfused into another language, as to be as distinctly apprehended, and as strongly felt, by a native of the country to which that language belongs, as it is by those who speak the language of the original work."

judgment,

judgment, when, defiring to transfer paſſages from Homer, Heſiod, Apollonius, Parthenius, Calli-machus, or Theocritus, he has omitted ſome things, and borrowed others. Thus, when very lately at table the Bucolics of Theocritus and Virgil were read together, we perceived that Virgil had omitted what in the Greek is indeed very delightful, but which neither can nor ought to be tranſlated. But what he has ſubſtituted in place of what he omitted, is perhaps more agree-able and pertinent.

Βαλλει και μαλοισι τον αιπολον ἁ Κλεαρίϛα[a]
Τας αιγας παρελωντα και αδυ τι ποππυλιασδει.

Malo me Galatea petit, laſciva puella,
Et fugit ad ſalices et ſe cupit ante videri.

[a] Theſe lines of Theocritus are thus tranſlated by Mr. Polwhele:

Oft Cleariſta pelts with apples *criſp*
Her ſwain, and in a whiſper loves to liſp.

But this is inadequate, and leaves out a material circum-ſtance. The literal meaning is, Cleariſta throws apples at the goat-herd *as he drives his goats along*, whiſpering ſome-thing kind at the time.

Virgil's lines are thus rendered by Dryden,

My Phyllis me with pelted apples plies,
Then tripping to the woods the wanton hies,
And wiſhes to be ſeen before ſhe flies.

A ſimilar idea is beautifully expreſſed by Horace—

Nunc et latentes proditor intimo
Gratus puellæ riſus ab angulo.

We

We obſerved alſo that in another paſſage he had carefully omitted what in the Greek verſe is moſt delightful—

> Τιτυρ εμιν το καλον πεφιλαμενε, βοσκε τας αιγας [3]
> Και ποτι ταν κραναν αγε Τιτυρε · και Τον ενορχαν
> Τον Λιβυκον Κυακωνα φυλασσεο μη το κορυψη.

How could he have expreſſed το καλον πεφιλαμενε, which words indeed defy tranſlation, but have a certain native ſweetneſs? This therefore he omitted, tranſferring the reſt with much pleaſantry; except that what Theocritus calls ενορχαν he calls *caprum*. According to Varro that in Latin is *caper* which has been caſtrated,—

> Tityre, dum redeo, brevis eſt via, paſce ca-
> pellas
> Et potum paſtas age, Tityre, et inter agen-
> dum
> Occurſare capro, cornu ſerit ille, caveto.

[3] The Greek lines of Theocritus are thus rendered by Mr. Polwhele.

> Tityrus, guide them to their wonted rill;
> Yet, whether ſtream or paſturage be thy care,
> That Lybian ram with butting head beware.

The correſpondent verſes in the ninth Eclogue of Virgil, Dryden thus tranſlates—

> Oh Tityrus, tend my herd, and ſee them fed,
> To morning paſtures, evening waters led,
> And ware the Lybian ridgil's butting head.

Ridgil is a word of rare occurrence. In another place Dryden uſes ridgling—it means a ram half caſtrated. Lord Lauderdale, in his verſion of Virgil, has the ſame word.

And

And now I am on this subject of transferring passages from one language to another, I remember hearing from the scholars of Valerius Probus, a learned man, and very expert in comprehending, and properly estimating the writings of the ancients, that he was used to say, that Virgil had in no instance imitated Homer with less success than in these charming verses, in which Homer describes Nausicaa:

Οιη δ' Αρτεμις εισι κατ' αρεος ιοχεαιρα, [4]
Η κατα Τηυγετον περιμηκετον, η Ερυμανθον
Τερπομενη καπροισι και ωκειης ελαφοισι,
Τη δε θ' αμα νυμφαι, κπραι Διος αιγιοχοιο
Αγρονομοι παιζυσι, γεγηθε δε τε φρενα Λητώ
Πασαων δ' υπερ ηγε καρη εχει ηδε μετωπα.
Ρεια δ' αριγνωτη πελεται καλαι δε τε πασαι.

Qualis

---

[4] I use Pope's translation of these lines from Homer:

> As when o'er Erymanth Diana roves,
> Or wide Täygetus refounding groves,
> A filver train the huntrefs queen furrounds,
> Her rattling quiver from her fhoulder founds;
> Fierce in the fport, along the mountain's brow
> They bay the boar, or chafe the bounding roe;
> High o'er the lawn, with more majeftic pace,
> Above the nymphs fhe treads with ftately grace;
> Diftinguifh'd excellence the goddefs proves,
> Exults Latona as the virgin moves:
> With equal grace Naufîcaa trod the plain,
> And fhone tranfcendent o'er the beauteous train.

M 3

Thefe

Qualis in Eurotæ ripis aut per juga Cynthi
Exercet Diana choros: quam mille fecutæ
Hinc atque hinc glomerantur Oreades, illa
    pharetram

These of Virgil are thus rendered by Dryden—

> Such on Eurotas banks, or Cynthus height,
> Diana feems, and fo fhe charms the fight.
> When in the dance the graceful goddefs leads
> The quire of nymphs, and overtops their heads,
> Known by her quiver and her lofty mein,
> She walks majeftic, and fhe looks their queen.

It may not be improper to infert here the anfwer of Scaliger to this criticifm of Gellius, which, however, will not fatisfy every reader. I tranfcribe the note from Pope's own edition of his Homer.

Scaliger obferves, that the perfons, not the places, are intended to be reprefented by both poets; otherwife Homer himfelf is blameable, for Naufcaa is not fporting on a mountain, but a plain, and has neither bow nor quiver, like Diana. Neither is there any weight in the objection concerning the gravity of the gait of Dido, for neither is Naufcaa defcribed in the act of hunting, but dancing. And as for the word *pertentant*, it is a metaphor taken from muficians and mufical inftruments, it denotes a ftrong degree of joy. *Per* bears an intenfive fenfe, and takes in the perfection of joy. As to the quiver, it was an enfign of the goddefs, as αργυρoτοξος was of Apollo, and is applied to her upon all occafions indifferently, not only by Virgil but more frequently by Homer. Laftly, μια δι, &c. is fuperfluous, for the joy of Latona compleats the whole; and Homer has already faid, γεγηθι δι, &c.

Upon which Pope remarks, that there is ftill a greater correfpondence to the fubject intended to be illuftrated in Homer than in Virgil, which indeed feems fufficiently obvious, without adding any thing further on the fubject.

Fert

Fert humero, gradienſque deas ſupereminet
omnes,
Latonæ tacitum pertentant gaudia pectus.

They obſerved, firſt, that it appeared to Probus, that in Homer the virgin Nauſicaa, ſporting
among her fellow nymphs in a ſolitary place, is
properly and conſiſtently compared with Diana
hunting on the ſummits of the mountains among
the rural goddeſſes : but Virgil has been by no
means conſiſtent; for as Dido is in the midſt of a
city, walking among the Tyrian princes, with a
ſerious gait and geſture, as he himſelf ſays, ſuper-
intending the labours of her people and her future empire, he can from thence take no ſimilitude
adapted to the ſports and huntings of Diana.
Homer afterwards ingeniouſly and directly places
the pleaſures and purſuits of Diana in hunting.
But Virgil, not having ſaid any thing concerning
the hunting of the goddeſs, only makes her carry
her quiver on her ſhoulder as a fatigue and a bur-
den. And they added, that Probus particularly
expreſſed his ſurprize at Virgil's doing this, becauſe the Diana of Homer enjoys a real and un-
affected delight, and one which entered deeply
into the very receſſes of her ſoul; for what elſe
can mean γεγηθε δε τε φρενα Λητω? which Virgil
deſiring to imitate, has repreſented a ſtupid, trifling, precarious pleaſure, affecting only the ſur-
face of the heart; for he could no otherwiſe underſtand the term *pertentant*. Beſides all this,

M 4

Virgil

Virgil appears to have omitted the flower of the paſſage, having taken no notice of this verſe of Homer—

Ρεια δε αριγνωτη πελεται· καλαι δε τε πασαι.

Since no greater or more expreſſive praiſe of beauty could poſſibly be introduced, than that ſhe alone excelled where all were fair ; ſhe alone was eaſily diſtinguiſhed from the reſt.

CHAP.

CHAP. X.

That Annæus Cornutus has injured, by an unjust and odious calumny, those lines of Virgil wherein he, with modest reserve, speaks of the matrimonial intercourse betwixt Venus and Vulcan.

ANNIANUS the poet, and many others also of similar pursuits in literature, have commended with great and repeated praise the verses of Virgil, in which he describes the conjugal union of Vulcan and Venus. Having to represent what the laws of nature require to be concealed, he involved it in a modest application of words. He says thus—

———Ea verba locutus [a]
Optatos dedit amplexus : placidumque petivit
Conjugis infusus gremio per membra soporem.

They

---

[a] *Ea verba, &c.*]—Thus rendered by Dryden—

Trembling he spoke, and, eager of her charms,
He snatch'd the willing goddess to his arms;
Till in her lap infus'd he lay, possess'd
Of full desire, and sunk to pleasing rest.

Similar to the expression in the original of conjugis infusus gremio, is that in the second Georgic—

Fœcundis imbribus æther
Conjugis in gremium lætæ descendit, &c.

They thought it lefs difficult, in defcribing a thing of this kind, to ufe words demonftrating it by one or more fhort and fimple fign, as Homer has faid, παρθενικης ζωνην, και λεκτροιο θεσμον, and ιςγα φιλοτησια.

Τω μεν αρ εν τρητοισι κατευνασθεν λεχεεσσιν.

But no other perfon has reprefented this facred myftery of chafte enjoyment in fo many plain, yet not obfcene [2], but pure and honeft terms. But Annæus Cornutus, a man in other refpects neither unlearned, nor abfurd, in the fecond book which he wrote on the Figures of Speech, has violated the whole of this highly to be commended modefty, by a prepofterous and odious examination. For, having approved this kind of figure, and allowed the verfes to be compofed with fufficient circumfpection, he fays that he has ufed the word *membra* fomewhat indifcreetly.

See a curious chapter in the Adverfaria of Gataker upon λογοι σεμνοι, where, among other things, he fays, " Ita nec verba nuda claraque fermo patitur pudicus ubi facti mentionem erigit caufæ jufta neceffitas." See alfo Plutarch de Præceptis Conjug. The Annotations alfo of Quintus Carolus on this chapter are worth confulting.

[2] *Not obfcene.*]—In the original, verbis prætextatis, the origin of which is differently explained by learned men. The fame expreffion occurs in Suetonius. See the Life of Vefpafian. Erat enim dicacitatis plurimæ, et fic fcurrilis ac fordidæ, ut ne prætextatis quidem verbis abftineret.

CHAP.

CHAP. XI.

Of Valerius Corvinus, and why called Corvinus. [1]

NONE of our beft writers have fpoken diffe-rently of M. Valerius, than that he was called Corvinus from the aid given him in battle by a raven. This really wonderful incident is thus related in the books of Annals:

" A youth fo defcended [2] was, in the conful-fhip of L. Furius and Claudius Appius, made a military tribune. At this time large bodies of the Gauls had taken poffeffion of the plains of Pomp-tinum [3], and the forces were drawn out by the con-fuls, who were not without alarm at the power and number of the enemy. Then the leader of the Gauls, of vaft and gigantic ftature, his arms glit-tering with gold, advanced with a rapid ftep, and

[1] This ftory of Corvinus is to be found in Livy, and is alfo related by Valerius Maximus.

[2] *So defcended.*]—The reader will obferve that this is the continuance of a ftory.

[3] *Pomptinum,*]—is written varioufly, Pomtinus and Po-metinus. This place was, in the time of Juvenal, the refort of robbers.

Interdum et ferro fubitus graffator agit rem,
Armato quoties tuta cuftode tenentur,
Et Pontina palus et Gallinaria pinus.

wielding

wielding in his hand a fpear. Looking round him, with an air of haughtinefs and contempt, he challenged from the whole Roman army any one to come forth and encounter him. Then Valerius the tribune, the reft hefitating [*] from fear or fhame, firft demanding leave of the confuls to engage this vain boafter, went forth with an undaunted yet modeft ftep to meet him.—They met, and, after a fhort paufe, commenced an attack ;—but here a divine interpofition was vifible. Suddenly a raven flew and refted on the helmet of the tribune, and thence began to attack the face and eyes of his opponent. It leaped upon him, and greatly haraffed him, tearing him with his claws, and obftructing his fight with his wings; and having fatisfied his rage, flew back to the helmet of the tribune. Thus the tribune, in the fight of both armies, by the force of his own valour, and the affiftance of the bird, conquered

[*] *The reft.*]—Thus Homer defcribes the effect of Hector's challenge on the Grecian army—

> The fierce defiance Greece aftonifh'd heard,
> Blufh'd to refufe, and to acccept it fear'd.

Such alfo was the impreffion made by the challenge of Goliath : " When Saul and all Ifrael heard thefe words of the Philiftine, they were difmayed and greatly afraid."

When Argantes in Taffo challenges the nobles in the camp of Godfrey, they are reprefented as being indignant, but not afraid.

> The challenge gan he then at large expofe,
> With mighty threats, high terms, and glorious words.
> On every fide an angry murmur rofe.

the

and flew the daring leader of the enemy; and from this circumftance he obtained the cogno- men of *Corvinus.* This happened in the four hundred and fifth year from the building of the city. To this Corvinus the divine Auguftus erected a ftatue in his own forum [s], upon the head of which ftatue is a raven, commemorating the incident and battle above defcribed."

[s] *In his own forum.*]—The forum of Auguftus is reckon- ed by Pliny among the moft magnificent ornaments of Rome. Till the time of Auguftus there were but three forums at Rome, the Roman, Julian, and that of Auguftus, more were afterwards added. They muft have made a fplendid appearance, for they were furrounded by porticoes, and adorned with marble columns and ftatues.

Chap. XII.

Of words which are used with two opposite significations. [1]

AS the term *formidolosus* is applied both to him who fears, and to him who is feared; *invidiosus* to him who envies, and to him who is envied; *suspiciosus* to him who suspects, and to him who is suspected; *ambitiosus* to him who solicits a vote, and to him whose vote is solicited; as *gratiosus* to him who gives, and to him who receives thanks; *laboriosus* to him who labours, and to that which is laboured upon; and as many other words of this kind may be applied both ways, so *infestus* is also used in an ambiguous sense: for he is called *infestus* who offers injury to any one, and so is he also over whom the injury is suspended. But what I had asserted before by

[1] The circumstance noticed in this chapter is perhaps common to all languages: in our own particularly, the word *fearful*, corresponding to the Latin *formidolosus*, is used in both senses. We say it is a *fearful*, for it is a *dreadful* thing; and we also say of a timorous person that he is very *fearful*. Shakspeare says—

And in a time,
When *fearful* wars point at me.

We say a *suspicious person* also for one likely to excite suspicion, as well as for one whose disposition inclines him to feel it.

no means wants examples. So also many call an enemy or opponent *infestum*. But the other assertion is less known, and more obscure; for who in general would apply the term *infestus* to him, to whom another was *infestus* (an enemy)? But many of the ancient writers did this; and M. Tullius, in the oration which he wrote for Cn. Plancus, has thus used this word:

" Dolebam Judices et acerbe ferebam si hujus salus ob eam ipsam causam esset *infestior* quod is meam salutem, atque vitam sua benivolentia præsidio, custodiaque texisset."

We enquired therefore concerning the origin and reason of the word, and found it thus explained by Nigidius:

" *Infestum* is so called *a festinando* [2], for he who presses upon any one, and eagerly urges him, and studies and makes haste to injure him; or, on the contrary, if any one's peril or ruin is eagerly hastened, both are said to be *infestus*, from the urgency and imminence of the mischief which is either about to be committed or endured."

If any one shall wish to see an example for *suspiciosus* above-mentioned, or of *formidolosus*, in the less common sense, concerning the former

---

[2] *A festinando.*]—I question whether this derivation will satisfy many readers. It is certainly far-fetched. Vossius would derive it immediately from *festus*. The etymology here given by Nigidius is adopted by Nonius Marcellus.

word

word he may find this paſſage in M. Cato, " de Re Floria [3]."

" Sed niſi qui palam corpore pecuniam quæreret, aut ſe lenoni locaviſſet et ſi *fabuloſus* et *ſuſpicioſus* fuiſſet, vim in corpus liberum non æquum cenſuere afferri."

Here Cato uſes the word *ſuſpicioſus* for one *ſuſpected*, not for one who ſuſpects.

Salluſt, in his Catiline, thus uſes *formidoloſus* for one who is feared—

" Igitur talibus viris non labos inſolitus, non locus ullus aſper aut arduus erat, non armatus hoſtis *formidoloſus*."

Thus alſo C. Calvus, in his poems, uſes *laborioſus*, not in the common acceptation, for him who labours, but for that which is laboured upon. He ſays—

Durum rus fugis et *laborioſum*.

In the ſame manner Laberius alſo, in his Siſters—

Œcaſtor multum *ſomniculoſum*.

And Cinna, in his poems—

Somniculoſum ut Pœnus aſpidem Pſyllus.

The words *metus* and *injuria* alſo, with ſome

---

[3] *Re Floria.*]—It is ſufficiently known, that in the ceremonies obſerved at Rome in honour of the goddeſs Flora, many obſcenities were practiſed ; againſt theſe Cato wrote a book. Lactantius and Arnobius both of them reprobated with becoming ſeverity theſe feſtivals ; and indeed every thing was then practiſed offenſive to delicacy and good morals. Ovid calls this goddeſs Floris.

others of this kind, may so be applied both ways, for *metus hostium* is proper, both when enemies fear, and are feared. Therefore Sallust, in his first history, says, *metum Pompeii*, not that Pompey was afraid, which is the more common sense, but that he was feared. These are Sallust's words: " Id bellum excitabat *metus* Pompeii victoris Hiempsalem in regnum restituentis." Thus also in another place,—" Postquam remoto *metu* Punico simultates exercere vacuum fuit."

We also apply *injuriæ* to those who suffer, and those who commit injury, examples of which may easily be found. The following expression also in Virgil has this same form of signification, to be interpreted either way—

Et vulnere tardus Ulyssei—

speaking of the wound, not which Ulysses had received, but inflicted. *Nescius* is also applied to him who is unknown, and to him who knows not. Only that *qui nescit* is the more frequent acceptation of this word, *quod nescitur* not so. *Ignarus* may in like manner be applied both ways; and means not only he who is ignorant, but who is unknown. Plautus, in his Rudens, says—

Quæ in locis *nesciis nescia* spe sumus.

And Sallust—

More humanæ cupidinis *ignara* visundi.

And Virgil—

Ignarum Laurens habet ora Mimanta.

Chap. XIII.

*A passage from the History of Claudius Quadriga-
rius, where he describes the engagement of Manlius Torquatus, a noble youth, and an enemy of
Gaul, who gave a general challenge.*

TITUS MANLIUS was a person of
high rank, and of the first degree of nobility; he afterwards received the cognomen of
Torquatus. We have been informed that the
cause of this cognomen was a chain, a golden
spoil which he took away from an enemy whom
he flew, and afterwards wore. Who the enemy
was, of how great and formidable stature, how
audacious the challenge, and in what kind of
battle they fought, Quintus Claudius, in his first
book of Annals, has described with much purity
and elegance, and in the simple and unadorned
sweetness of ancient language. When Favorinus
the philosopher read the passage from this book,
he used to say that his mind was affected with
no less serious emotion, than if he had seen the
combatants engaged before him.—I have added
the words of Claudius, in which this battle is
described:

" At

" At this period a Gaul, entirely unprotected,
except with his shield and two swords [1], advanced, wearing a chain and bracelets : he was fuperior to the reft in ftrength, in fize, in vigour,
and in courage. In the very height of the battle,
when both fides were fighting with the greateft
ardour, he made a motion with his hand [2] that
the

[1] *Shield and two fwords.*]—The fhields of the Germans
and Gauls were very large, their fwords very long and
heavy. One of thefe fwords was probably a dagger. The
Turks, befides their fword, have commonly a dagger ftuck
in their girdle. The moft fublime defcription of a battle
betwixt two warriors, is that of Milton, in his fixth book,
where Satan is reprefented as oppofed to Michael :—

        Who, though with the tongue
Of angels, can relate, or to what things
Liken on earth confpicuous, that may lift
Human imagination to fuch height
Of godlike power? for likeft gods they feem'd,
Stood they or mov'd, in ftature, motion, arms,
Fit to decide the empire of great heaven.
Now wav'd their fiery fwords, and in the air
Made horrid circles; two broad funs their fhields
Blaz'd oppofite, while expectation ftood
In horror: from each hand with fpeed retir'd,
Where erft was thickeft fight, th' angelic throng,
And left large field, unfafe within the wind
Of fuch commotion, &c. &c.

[2] *Motion with his hand.*]—It is not eafy to conceive how,
in the clamour and tumult of a great battle, in which multi-
tudes were engaged, this could be effected. Homer defcribes

                    Hector

the battle should ceafe on both fides. A cef-fation enfued; immediately filence being obtained he cried with a loud voice, that if any one would fight with him, he was to come forth. On account of his ftature and ferocious appearance, nobody anfwered. The Gaul then began to exprefs fcorn and contempt[3]. A perfon named Manlius, of illuftrious rank, was fuddenly ftruck with grief that fo great a difgrace fhould happen to his country, and that of fo numerous an army, no one fhould accept the challenge. He, I fay, on this advanced, nor would fuffer the Roman valour to be bafely contaminated by a Gaul; armed with the fhield of a foot foldier, and a Spanifh fword, he accordingly met him. This meeting on the bridge, in the prefence of both armies, infpired univerfal awe. As I before faid, they met in arms: the Gaul, according to the manner of his country, putting forth his fhield, advanced with a kind of fong[4]. Manlius, relying on

Hector as fufpending the battle by a motion of his fpear, that is, with regard to his own troops,—

> The challenge Hector heard with joy;
> Then with his fpear reftrain'd the youth of Troy,
> Held by the midft athwart, and near the foe
> Advanc'd, with fteps majeftically flow.

[3] *Contempt.*]—See Chapter XI.

[4] *With a fong.*]—I have defcribed, in my notes to Herodotus, the different modes in which the ancients advanced to combat. The modern Gauls, it feems, affect to advance to battle with a fong; and the Marfeillois hymn has been the fignal of many a fanguinary fcene.

his

his courage rather than skill, struck shield to shield, and disconcerted the position of the Gaul. When the Gaul a second time endeavoured to place himself in a similar position, a second time Manlius struck shield to shield, and again obliged the Gaul to shift his ground. Thus placing himself as it were beneath the sword of the Gaul, he stabbed him in the breast with his Spanish blade. He then, by the force of his right shoulder, continued the blow, nor did he remit his effort till he had overthrown him, not suffering the Gaul to have the opportunity of a stroke. When he had overcome him he cut off his head [5], took his chain, and placed it, stained with blood, round his own neck; from which incident, both he and his descendants bore the cognomen of Torquatus." From this Titus Manlius, whose battle Quadrigarius has here described, all severe and imperious orders were called Manlian [6], since afterwards,

[5] *Cut off his head.*]—It seems in a manner the natural impulse of a fierce and barbarous people to cut off the heads of their enemies, partly to satisfy revenge, and partly to carry away as a trophy. This we accordingly find to have been done; and hence, among the Indians of America, rose the custom of scalping. It was found cumbrous and inconvenient to carry away a number of heads, for it must have been a constant impediment to flight, and indeed to activity. Convenience, therefore, suggested the idea of taking away only the scalp, an operation which the Indians perform with extraordinary skill and facility.

[6] *Manlian.*]—Manliana imperia became a proverbial expression. The fact here alluded to is recorded in the

eighth

afterwards, when he was conful in a war againft the Latins, he commanded his fon to be beheaded, who being fent by him to reconnoitre, with orders not to fight, had killed an enemy who had challenged him.

eighth book of Livy; and the hiftorian, after relating the ftory, makes an obfervation which equally becomes him as a philofopher and a man of humanity. The example, fays he, was doubtlefs falutary with regard to pofterity, but at the period when it was perpetrated it could not fail to make the character of the conful odious. Valerius Maximus relates the fame anecdote, adding, that when Manlius returned to Rome, none of the young men would go to meet him; in fuch deteftation was he held by all the Roman youth, who among themfelves gave him the name of Imperiofus.

C H A P.

Chap. XIV.

The same Quadrigarius asserts, that hujus facies, *in the genitive case, is proper and good Latin; with other observations on the declensions of similar words.*

THE expression made use of by Quadrigarius in the preceding chapter, *Propter magnitudinem atque immanitatem facies*, I have taken pains to discover in some of our old writers, and I find that he has authority for it : for many of the ancients thus declined *facies, hæc facies, hujus facies*; which now, in grammatical propriety, is written *faciei*. But I have found some corrupted books, in which *faciei* is used; the word *facies* written before being obliterated. I remember also, that in the library of Tiburtus [1], in this same book of Quadrigarius, I have found both words used, *facies* and *faciei*. But *facies* was used in the text, and *facii*, with a double *i*, written in the margin; and it appeared to us that this was entirely consistent with ancient usage. For as they said *hic dies* and *hujus dii*, so also from *hæc fames*

[1] *Tiburtus.*]—See our author again, Book xix. c. 5. where he says this library was in the temple of Hercules.

they

they ufe *hujus fami*. Q. Ennius, in his fixteenth Annal, has ufed *dies* for *diei*, in this verfe:

Poftremæ longinqua dies confecerit ætas.

Cæfellius alfo affirms, that in the oration which Cicero made for P. Seftius [2], he wrote *dies* inftead of *diei*. After confiderable pains, and the careful examination of many old copies, I find it actually written as Cæfellius affirms. Thefe are the words of M. Tully: *Equites vero daturos illius* dies *horas*. It is this fact which induces me the more readily to give credit to thofe who have afferted, that they had feen a manufcript in Virgil's own hand, in which it is thus written:

Libra *dies* [3], fomnique pares ubi fecerit horas.

That

---

[2] *Seftius.*]—In Cicero it is read Sextius; but Seftius is found in many manufcripts.

[3] *Libra dies,* &c.]

When Libra has made the hours of the day and fleep equal. The note of Martyn at this paffage of Virgil is fo curious that I infert it here.

" Here Virgil exemplifies his precept relating to aftronomy. The time which he mentions for fowing barley, is from the autumnal equinox to the winter folftice. This perhaps may feem ftrange to an Englifh reader; it being our cuftom to fow it in the fpring. But it is certain, that in warmer climates they fow it at the latter end of the year; whence it happens that their barley-harveft is confiderably fooner than their wheat-harveft. Thus we find, in the book of Exodus, that the flax and the barley were deftroyed by the hail, becaufe the barley was in the ear and the flax was in feed; but the wheat and the rye efcaped, becaufe they were not yet come up."

This

That is, *Libra diei somnique.* But as in this paffage Virgil feems to have written *dies*; fo there
is no doubt, but that in this verfe he has written
dii for *diei:*

> Munera, lætitiamque *dii* —

which thofe who are lefs learned read *dei*,
from a kind of difguft arifing from want of ufe.
So alfo by the ancients it was declined, *dies, dii*;
as *fames, fami*; *pernicies, pernicii*; *progenies, pro-
genii*; *luxuries, luxurii*; and *acies, acii.* M. Cato,
in the oration which he made on the Carthaginian war, wrote thus: *Pueri atque mulieres extru-
debantur fami caufa.* Lucilius, in his fifteenth
book, fays: *Rugofum atque fami plenum.* Sefenna,
in his fixth book of Hiftories, has this expreffion:
Romanos inferendæ pernicii caufa veniffe. Pacuvius,
in his Paulus;

> Pater fupreme, noftræ *progenii* patris.

Cn. Matius in his 21ft Iliad:

> Altera pars *acii* vitaffent fluminis undas.

The fame Matius, in his 23d book:

> An maneat *fpecii* fimulachrum in muto filentum.

C. Gracchus *De legibus promulgatis*, fays, *Ea luxurii caufa* aiunt inftitui. In the fame book, in

---

This paffage from Virgil is minutely imitated by Lùcan:

> Tempus erat quo Libra pares examinat horas,
> Non uno plus æqua dies, noftique rependit
> Lux minor hybernæ verni folatia damni.

another

another place, *Non est ea luxuries, quæ necessario parentur vitæ causa*; from which it appears, that he has made *luxurii* the genitive case from *luxuries*. Marcus Tullius also, in the oration where he defends Sex. Roscius, has written *pernicii*. The words are these: *Quorum nihil pernicii causa divino consilio, sed vi ipsa et magnitudine rerum factum putamus*.

We must presume, therefore, that Quadrigarius wrote either *facies* in the genitive case, or *facii*; but I certainly cannot find *facie* in any ancient book. But in the dative case, they who spoke with greatest purity did not say *faciei*, which is now in use, but *facie*. Lucilius in his Satires says:

Primum *facie* quod honestatis accedit.

The same Lucilius in his seventh book:

Qui te diligat ætatis *facieque* tuæ se
Fautorem ostendat, fore amicum polliceatur.

But there are neverthelefs many who, in both cafes, ufe *facii*. But C. Cæfar, in his fecond book on Analogy, thought it fhould be written *hujus die* and *hujus fpecie*. I myfelf alfo, in the Jugurtha of Salluft, a book of great credit and refpectable antiquity, find *die* in the genitive cafe. The words are thefe: *Vix decima parte die reliqua*. I cannot allow that the quibble is to be admitted, of underftanding *die* as if it were *ex die* *.

* *Ex die*.]—That is, fuppofing it to be an ablative cafe, governed by a prepofition underftood, rather than a particular mode of writing the genitive cafe.

C H A P.

CHAP. XV.

Of the species of controversy which the Greeks call ἄπορος.

DURING the summer holidays [1], being desirous to retire from the heat of the city, I accompanied Antonius Julianus the rhetorician, to Naples. There happened to be a young man of fortune, studying and exercising himself with his preceptors, in order to plead causes at Rome, and accomplish himself in Latin eloquence: this person entreated Julianus to hear him declaim. Julianus accordingly went to hear him, and I attended him. The young man appeared; and,

---

[1] *Summer holidays.*]—Rome, and what is usually termed the Campagna of Rome, has always been deemed unhealthy in the hotter months of summer. For which reason the wealthier of the old Romans always at this season retired to their country villas. For this purpose Naples was esteemed the most agreeable retirement, though many Romans had country seats in Sicily.

The time of recess from business in Rome, and particularly the business of the courts, was July and August. The same custom of leaving Rome for Naples in summer, still prevails; and is observed by all who travel from motives either of health or curiosity. The salubrity of the air of Naples has been a theme of admiration and praise among poets and descriptive writers, from the time of Augustus to the present period.

beginning

beginning an exordium with rather more arrogance and prefumption than became his years, he demanded the fubject of controverfy[z] to be propofed. There was with us a follower of Julianus, an ingenious and accomplifhed young man, who took offence that he fhould dare, in the prefence of Julianus, to rifque his reputation by the extreme peril of inconfiderate fpeaking. By way of trial, therefore, he propofed a controverfy not

[z] *Controverfy.*]—Thefe declamatory exercifes, the great and only excellence of which confifts in quirks and quibbles, incompatible with the dignity of genuine eloquence, fill a whole volume of the works of Seneca. The fpecimeh given in this chapter may perhaps be fufficient to fatisfy the reader; and it feems obvious enough, that the difcuffion of fuch queftions has an unavoidable tendency to pervert the public tafte, by fubftituting levity and impertinence in the place of real wit. Cicero and Quintilian have both of them reprobated, with becoming feverity, fuch idle and ufelefs difputations; and the introduction to Petronius Arbiter, at the fame time that it explains to how great a degree thefe vain declaimers abounded, fatisfactorily proves that there were not wanting thofe of more refined tafte, who defpifed and avoided them.

It appears, as well from this chapter as from various paffages in the ancient writers, that the young nobility of Rome had preceptors to inftruct them in declaiming on thefe controverfial queftions. Of thofe who attended the inftructions of fuch mafters, Petronius fays, acutely enough, " Qui inter hæc nutricentur non magis fapere poffunt quam bene olere qui in culina habitant. Pace veftra liceat dixiffe primi omnium eloquentiam perdidiftis. Levibus enim atque inanibus fonis ludibria quædam excitando effeciftis, ut corpus orationis enervaretur et caderet."

very

very confiftent, which the Greeks call ἄπορος; but which in Latin may not very improperly be termed *inexplicabile*. The controverfy was this: " Suppofe feven judges try a prifoner—that judgment is to prevail which the greater number fhall determine—the feven judges prefided—two of them thought the prifoner fhould be banifhed; two of them that he fhould be fined; the remaining three, that he fhould be put to death. Punifhment is demanded according to the decifion of the three, from which the prifoner appeals."

The young man, as foon as he heard this, without at all confidering the matter, or waiting to know what elfe was to be propofed, began with wonderful rapidity to affert I know not what principles upon this queftion, and to pour out expreffions, diftorted from their meaning, and a noify torrent of high-founding words. All his companions, who were accuftomed to hear him, applauded him with noify clamour. Julianus all this while was in the greateft perplexity, blufhing with confufion. After he had gabbled out many thoufands of fentences, we took our leave. His friends and acquaintance following Julianus, defired to know his opinion. " Do not," he replied, " enquire my opinion; *without controverfy*, this young man is eloquent."

---

³ *Without controverfy.*]—It is not poffible to tranffufe into our language the entire fpirit of this pun. The young man had no opponent, but the nature of the controverfy required an opponent. The friends of the young man defired to ex-

tort fome favourable expreffion from Julianus, whofe ambiguous anfwer implied, both that the declaimer had faid little
to the purpofe, and with nobody to make him any reply.

> No praife attends the warrior who returns
> To claim the palm of unconteſted fields.

CHAP. XVI.[1]

*That Pliny the Elder, a man by no means unlearned,
was not aware of that fallacy of argument, called
by the Greeks* αντιςτρεφον.

PLINY the Elder was thought the moſt
learned man of his time. He left fome
books, which he termed *Studiofi*, and which indeed are by no means to be defpifed. In thefe
books he has introduced many things gratifying
to the taftes of learned men. He relates a number of fentiments, which, in declamatory controverfies, he thinks urged with wit and fubtlety.

[1] This is in fa&ct the fame fubje&ct continued. A fimilar
controverfy is agitated in a preceding chapter; where a pupil refufes to pay his maſter for inſtructing him. Thefe controverfies were alfo called vindiciæ, from *vindico*, to claim.
See Feſtus de verborum fignificatione, at the word Vindiciæ.
Vindiciæ appellantur res eæ de quibus controverfia eſt.

The loſt book, called Studiofi, is mentioned with refpe&ct by
the Younger Pliny.

As

As this, for example, which he quotes from one of thefe controverfies. " A brave man is to have the reward which he folicits. One of this defcription demands the wife of another perfon, and receives her. He alfo whofe wife this had been, being entitled to the fame claim as the former, demands his wife again; which is refufed;"

The anfwer of this latter perfon demanding his wife to be given him again, is in his opinion very elegant and plaufible: " If the law is valid, reftore her; if it is not valid, reftore her." But Pliny did not know that this fentiment, which to him appeared very acute, was liable to the defect which the Greeks term ἀντιστρέφον. It is a fallacy concealed under the falfe appearance of an argument. Nothing can be more eafily applied to contradict itfelf; and it may be thus replied by the former perfon, " If the law is valid, I will not reftore her; and if it be not valid, I will not reftore her."

BOOK X.

CHAP. I.

Whether we ought to say tertium, *or* tertio consul? *and how Cnæus Pompey, when he was about to enroll his honours in the theatre which he consecrated, avoided, by the advice of Cicero, the doubtful usage of that word.*

WHEN I was at Athens I sent letters to an intimate friend at Rome, in which I reminded him that I had now written to him (*tertium*) a third time. He, in his answer, requested that I would explain to him the reason why I wrote *tertium* and not *tertio*. He added a request in the same letter, that I would give him my opinion, whether we ought to say, " Such an one was made consul *tertium et quartum, or tertio et quarto*." For he had heard a learned man at Rome use the latter term, and not the former [1].

Moreover,

---

[1] *The former.*] Mr. Boswell, in his Life of Dr. Johnson, informs us, that his learned friend never used the phrases

' the

Moreover, that Cælius[1] in the beginning of his book, and Quintus Claudius, in his eleventh chapter, had written, that Caius Marius was created conful *(feptimò)* a feventh time." To this I replied only in the words of Marcus Varro (a man of more learning, in my opinion, than Cælius and Claudius united) by which words each fubject he wrote to me upon, was determined. For Varro has clearly enough fhewn what ought to be ufed; nor did I choofe to be engaged at a diftance in a difpute with a perfon who had the reputation of being learned.

The words of Marcus Varro, in his fifth book of Rudiments, are thefe: " It is one thing to become prætor *quartò,* and another *quartùm. Quartò* marks the fituation, *quartùm* the time. Ennius has therefore, with propriety, written,

" Quintus pater, *quartùm* fit conful."

And Pompey, becaufe in the theatre he would not ufe either the term *tertiùm* or *tertiò,* has cau-

---

' the former,' and ' the latter,' from an idea that they frequently occafioned obfcurity. They neverthelefs are ufed by our beft original writers; and perhaps in a tranflation it would not only be difficult, but fometimes impoffible, to avoid them.

[1] *Cælius.*] Cælius Antipater, the hiftorian; he wrote an account of the Punic war, and is mentioned by Cicero with refpect; not, as Gronovius informs us, in the tract de Oratore, but in the 26th chapter of the Brutus, or de Claris Oratoribus. In this place Cicero commends his perfpicuity, calls him a good lawyer, and informs us that he inftructed L. Craffus.

tioufly omitted the concluding letters. What
Varro has briefly and obfcurely hinted at concerning Pompey, Tiro Tullius, the freedman of
Cicero, in one of his letters, has more fully mentioned in this manner : " When Pompey," fays
he, " was about to confecrate the temple of Victory, the entrance to which was to ferve as a
theatre ³, and to enroll in it, as in the theatre, his
name and titles, it was a fubject of debate, whether it fhould be written conful *tertiò* or *tertiùm*.
Which Pompey, with anxious enquiry, referred
to the moft eminently learned men of the ftate :

³ *Serve as a theatre.*] This is at firft fight a perplexing
paffage; and it feems almoft impoffible to reconcile with the
correct tafte and real magnificence of the Romans in the
time of Pompey, the confounding a theatre and a temple in
one edifice. The fact, however, undoubtedly was fo; and
Pompey, whatever were his motives, erected a temple, the
afcent to which formed the feats of a theatre, the area of
which was probably fo circumftanced and enclofed, as to
form one confiftent whole. The writers who mention this
building, feem at variance one with another, fome affert-
ing that it was dedicated to the goddefs Victory, others
faying it was dedicated to Venus. The truth is, as may be
eafily collected from comparing what is faid by Dion with
what Plutarch relates in his Life of Pompey, that it was dedicated to Venus Victrix. See Donatus de Urbe Roma, l. 3.
p. 196. ·

This unufual epithet of Victrix applied to Venus, is thus
explained by Varro. Venus is fo called, fays he, non quod
vincere velit, not from her wifh to conquer, fed quod vin-
cire et vinciri ipfa velit, but becaufe fhe wifhes to bind
others and be bound herfelf. See alfo Larcher fur Venus,
p. 91.

2

when

when they were of different opinions, and some proposed *tertium*, others *tertiò*, Pompey requested of Cicero to give orders that it should be written according to his opinion. But Cicero, fearing to sit in judgment on men of approved learning, left, by censuring their opinions, he might be thought to censure the men themselves, advised Pompey to use neither *tertium* nor *tertiò*, but to write it *tert.* concluding at the second *t*; so that, though the word was incomplete, the fact was told, and the ambiguous usage of a word avoided. But it is not now written in the same theatre, as Varro and Tiro have described; for some years after, when a part of it which had fallen down was repaired, the number of the third consulate was not distinguished as formerly by the first letters *t, e, r, t*; but by three small lines ||||" In the 4th Origin of Marcus Cato, we are told, " The Carthaginians broke their treaty (*sextùm*) a sixth time; which word implies, that they had acted treacherously five times before, and now did so a sixth time. The Greeks also, in distinguishing numbers of this sort, say, τριτον και τεταρτον; which answers to the Latin *tertium* and *quartùm*.

CHAP. II.

*What Ariftotle has recorded of the number of chil-
dren produced at one birth*[1].

THE philofopher Ariftotle has recorded,
that a woman in Egypt produced at one
birth five children; the utmoft limit, as he faid,
of

For the following note I am indebted to a medical friend,
of particular eminence and fkill in his profeffion.

There feems no reafon, from the ftructure of the human
uterus, to limit the number of fœtufes with which a woman
may become pregnant. But we know from experience, that
it is not very common to have more than one at a birth.
Dr. Garthfhore, by comparing a number of regifters, found
the proportion of twins to be as one to eighty of fingle children. When twins are produced, they are generally weakly,
and reared with difficulty. Triplets are of much lefs frequent occurrence, not oftener perhaps than once in twenty
thoufand births, and one or two of them commonly either born
dead, or much more diminutive and weak than the third.
Four children at a birth is fo very rare, that there is no cal-
culating the proportion, probably it does not happen oftener
than once in four or five hundred thoufand births; a greater
number is ftill lefs frequent, and the chance of their being
at the full time, or of their being all born alive, proportion-
ably lefs; the uterus feeming fcarce capable of fuch a degree of diftention as to permit more than two or three children to attain to maturity; whence it ufually happens, that
one or two of the moft vigorous and thriving children, by

preffing

of human parturition: nor was it ever known that more than that number were born together; and this number, says he, is very unusual. But in the reign of Augustus, the historians of those times relate, that a female servant of Cæsar Au-

pressing upon the others, destroys them while very young and feeble. The instances therefore mentioned in this chapter are rare and uncommon. But we have some similar examples in this country. In the Gentleman's Magazine for November 1736, there is an account of a woman in a milk-cellar in the Strand, who was delivered of three boys and one girl, but it is not said whether they were living or dead. In the same repository, there is an account of a woman in Somersetshire, who was delivered, in March 1739, of four sons and one daughter, who were all christened, and seemed healthy children. Among the writers of medical observa-tions, instances of much more numerous births are frequent; but there is generally so much fable mixed with their accounts, that little credit can be given them. Ambrose Parr, after quoting several stories of women who had been delivered of five, seven, twelve, and one of fifteen fœtuses, says, " Lady Maldemeure, in the parish of Sceaux near Chamberry, was delivered of six children at one birth, one of which succeeds to the title of Maldemeure, and is still living." As this account was published in the country where the family re-sided, and in the life-time of the young lord, it may, I should suppose, be depended upon as a fact. Dr. Garthshore re-ceived an account from Mr. Hull, surgeon at Blackbourne in Lancashire, of a woman who miscarried of five children, in April 1786, in the fifth month of her pregnancy; two of them only were born alive. They were sent to the Royal Society; and are preserved in the museum of the late Mr. John Hunter. The account, with some ingenious observa-tions on the subject of numerous births, is published in the Transactions of the Society for that year.

O 3

gustus,

guſtus, in the province of Laurentum, brought forth five children; that they lived a few days, and that the mother died not long after ſhe had been delivered; that a monument of the fact was erected by the command of Auguſtus in the Via *
Laurentina; and that the number of children ſhe produced (which we have mentioned) was inſcribed upon it.

* The road leading to Laurentum.

CHAP. III.

An examination of certain celebrated passages, and a comparison made between the orations of C. Gracchus, M. Cicero, and M. Cato.

CAIUS GRACCHUS is held to have been a powerful and strenuous orator. No one disputes it. But how is it to be borne, that in the eyes of some he appears more dignified, more spirited, more copious than Marcus Tullius [1]? Now I was reading lately a speech of Gracchus upon the promulgation of laws, in which, with all the indignation he is master of, he complains that Marcus Marius, and other persons of distinction from the municipal towns of Italy, were injuriously whipped with rods [2] by the magistrates of

the

[1] *Than Marcus Tullius.*]—It is certain that Hortensius was a very powerful rival to Cicero, and divided with him the palm of eloquence. This perhaps is the only passage in any ancient writer which even supposes him to have had any other competitor. The parallel betwixt Demosthenes and Cicero, as drawn by Plutarch, is known to every one.

[2] *With rods.*]—The person of a Roman citizen was in a manner sacred; of which we have a remarkable example in the history of St. Paul. See Acts, chap. xxii. ver. 25.

" And as they bound him with thongs, Paul said unto the centurion that stood by, Is it lawful for you to scourge a man that is a Roman, and uncondemned?

" When

the Roman people. His words upon this subject are thefe: "The conful lately came to Theanum[1] Sidicinum; he faid his wife wifhed to bathe
in the men's bath. Marcus Marius confided it
to the care of the quæftor of Sidicinum, that
they who were bathing fhould be fent away.
The wife tells her hufband that the baths were
not given up to her foon enough, nor were they
fufficiently clean. Immediately a poft was fixed
down in the market-place, and Marcus Marius,
the moft illuftrious man of his city, was led to it;
his garments were ftripped off, and he was beaten
with rods. When the inhabitants of Cales heard
this, they paffed a decree, that no one fhould
prefume to bathe when the Roman magiftrates
were there. At Ferentum alfo, our prætor, for a
reafon of the fame fort, ordered the quæftors to
be feized. One threw himfelf from the wall, the
other was taken and fcourged."—In a matter fo
atrocious, in fo lamentable and diftreffing a proof
of public injuftice, what has he faid, either full or

" When the centurion heard that, he went and told the
chief captain, faying, Take heed what thou doeft, for this
man is a Roman."

A particular law, called the Lex Porcia, ordained that no
one fhould fcourge a Roman citizen. See Livy, l. x. c. 9.
" Porcia tamen lex fola pro tergo civium lata videtur: quod
gravi pœna fi quis verberaffet necaffetve civem Romanum
fanxit."

1. *Theanum.*]—This place is now called Tiano, and is in
the vicinity of Naples: its adjunct, Sidicinum, now, according to D'Anville, Sezza, was from the ancient inhabitants named Sedecini.

fplendid,

splendid, or so as to excite tears or commiseration? What has he spoken expressive of exuberant indignation, or in a spirit of solemn and striking remonstrance? There is indeed a brevity, and terseness, and ornament in his speech, such as we usually find in the elegant wit of the stage. In another place, likewise, Gracchus speaks thus: "One example I will shew you of the licentiousness· and intemperance of our young men. Within these few years a young man was sent from Asia as an ambassador, who had not yet been in any magisterial office. He was carried upon a litter, when a herdsman from the peasantry of Venusium met him, and, not knowing what they were carrying, asked in joke whether they were bearing a dead body[4]? Having heard this, he ordered the litter to be set down, and the man to be beaten with the ropes[5] by which the

---

[4] *Bearing a dead body.*]—The original says, Is in lectica ferebatur. It was the office of the slaves, who were denominated Servi Lecticarii, to carry out the dead at funerals.

[5] *With ropes.*]—Struppis. This was an arbitrary and tyrannical abuse; but the ancient Romans certainly treated their own proper slaves with a cruelty which nothing could possibly excuse or justify. Their power over them extended even to life and death; it was not till the time of Constantine that this barbarous privilege was taken from masters. See Gibbon, vol. i. p. 65. "The progress of manners was accelerated by the virtue or policy of the emperors, and by the edicts of Hadrian and the Antonines, the protection of the laws was extended to the most abject part of mankind. The jurisdiction

the litter was faftened, till he died."—Now this fpeech of his, upon fo violent and cruel an outrage, differs nothing at all from the ftyle of common converfation. But when, in a fimilar caufe, in which Marcus Tullius was engaged, fome innocent Roman citizens are fcourged with rods, contrary to law, or put to death, what then is his mode of exciting pity? what is his fympathy? what is his ftrong reprefentation of the fact before our eyes? how does the current of his indignation and bitternefs rage and fwell? Truly when I read thefe things in Cicero, a certain image of him, the very found of his words, his invocations, his lamentations, take poffeffion of my foul—as, for inftance, where he fays of Verres, what (all I recollect at prefent) I have put down as my memory fupplied: " He himfelf, raging with vice and fury, came into the forum; his eyes glared, and cruelty might be traced in every feature of his countenance. All looked with expectation, to fee what act of villainy he would perpetrate; when on a fudden he orders a man to be brought out, to be ftripped naked, in the middle of the forum, to be tied up, and the rods to be prepared." By Hercules, thefe words alone—" to be brought out, to be ftripped, and

diction of life and death over the flaves, a power long exercifed, and often abufed, was taken out of private hands, and referved to the magiftrates alone."

The original is *ftruppis*, but it ought to be *ftuppis*, from the Greek στυππιον, which fignifies hemp.

tied

tied up," are of such terror-striking and horrible import, that you seem not merely to hear what was done, related, but absolutely to see it perpetrated. But our Gracchus, not in the spirit of one lamenting and complaining, but like a common retailer of a story, is content with saying, " A post was fixed [6] down in the market-place, his cloaths were stripped off, he was beaten with rods." But how gloriously does Marcus Cicero speak, when in the full representation of a fact, he says, not " a Roman citizen was scourged," but " a Roman citizen was in the act of being scourged with rods in the middle of the forum at Messana [7], when, amidst the anguish of his mind, and the repetition of the blows, not a groan escaped him, nor was a word observed to proceed from the wretched man, but these, ' I am a citizen of Rome.' By thus calling to mind his country, he trusted he might defy all their

[6] *Was fixed.*]—Palus destitutus, placed down. See also Tibullus, L. 1. E. 1. 11.

Nam veneror seu stipes habet *desertus* in agris.

Where *desertus* means planted down.
The form of the sentence, when any one was to be scourged, was this:

I lictor colliga manus deliga ad palum.

[7] *Messana.*]—Messina, formerly called Zancle. It is too well known to be here described; but the reader will find a most agreeable account of its modern condition in Brydone's tour through Sicily and Malta.

stripes,

stripes, and protect his body from torture." Violently too, and with energy and ardour, does he excite compassion in the Roman citizens, and detestation against Verres, when he says, " Oh the beloved name of liberty! Oh that right of our city, so peculiarly excellent! Oh the Portian and Sempronian laws! Oh the tribunary authority, grievously wanted, and once allowed to the Roman people! Have they all then at length fallen to this, that in a Roman province, in a town of our allies, in the public forum, a Roman citizen should be tied up, and scourged with rods, by him who, from the kindness of the Roman people, derived the ensigns of his authority? What! when flames, when hot irons, and other instruments of torture, were applied, though the bitter lamentations of the man, though his piteous tone of voice did not soften thee, wert thou unmoved also by the tears, by the repeated groans, of the Roman citizens who stood round?" Vehemently indeed, with solemnity, with copiousness, and propriety, did Marcus Tullius compassionate these events. But if there be any one of so unpolished, so barbarous an ear, that this splendour, this sweetness of speech, this harmonious position of words, gives him but little pleasure; or if he prefers the former because, being short, without cultivation, and without labour, they possess a certain native grace, and because there appears in them a

certain

certain shade and colour of dark [8] antiquity; let him examine, if he has any judgment, a speech of Marcus Cato in a similar cause, a man of remoter antiquity, to whose force and copiousness Gracchus never aspired. He will find, I think, that Cato was not content with the eloquence of his own time, but that he attempted to effect that which Cicero afterwards accomplished. For in that book which is entitled, " De Falsis Pugnis," he thus complained of Quintus Thermus,—he said " that his provisions had been ill taken care of by the decemviri; he ordered their garments to be stripped off, and themselves to be beaten with rods. The Brutiani scourged the Decemviri, and the eyes of many men beheld the fact. Who can support this insult, this act of tyranny, this slavery? No king had dared to do this; and do you, who are men of honour, allow these things to be done towards honourable men, who are sprung from honourable parents? Where are the bonds of society? where the faith of our ancestors? that you have dared to perpetrate these pointed injuries, tortures, blows, stripes, and pains, and butcheries, upon those whom, to our disgrace and insult, your own countrymen beheld, with many others? But how great grief, how many groans, how many tears, how much

---

[8] *Dark antiquity.*]—For *opacæ vetustatis* some would here read *opicæ vetustatis.* See Miscel. Observ. in Auctores Veteres et Recentes, Vol. IV. p. 437. That is rude or rustic antiquity, but the alteration seems of no material importance.

lamentation,

lamentation, have I heard ! Slaves do not eafily brook injuries ; but what fpirit do you think they poffefs, and ever while they live will poffefs, who are of illuftrious defcent, and diftinguifhed virtue ?" When Cato faid the " Brutiani fcourged them," left any one fhould enquire concerning the Brutiani, this is the meaning of the paffage : When Hannibal the Carthaginian was with his army in Italy, and had fought fome battle againft the Romans, the Brutii [9] were the firft inhabitants of Italy who revolted to Hannibal. The Romans, offended at this, after Hannibal left Italy, and the Carthaginians were overthrown, called this people by the ignominious diftinction of the Brutii, neither employing them as foldiers, nor confidering them as allies, but they commanded them to obey and wait upon the magiftrates who went into the provinces, and to ferve them as flaves. They accordingly went about

[9] *Brutii.*]—When Hannibal invaded Italy, many of the Italian ftates revolted from the Romans, and united themfelves with the Carthaginians. When Carthage was finally fubdued, many of thefe ftates returned to their allegiance to Rome, and many were fubdued by arms. Thefe latter were treated with great feverity, and reduced almoft to a ftate of fervitude, fome of them, like the Gibeonites of old, being little better than hewers of wood and drawers of water. The Bruttii, for example, were treated like their flaves, attendant upon ftage performances, and called Lorarii. Thefe feem to have been perfons whofe bufinefs it was to inflict punifhment upon their fellow flaves. The act of feverity here mentioned was impofed upon the Bruttii by Publius Sulpicius Galba, when dictator.

with

with the magiftrates, like thofe who in the play are called beadles, whofe office was (when order- ed) to bind people and fcourge them. They who came from Brutium were called Bruttiani.

CHAP. IV.

That Publius Nigidius, with great fophiftry, taught that words were not arbitrary but natural.[1]

PUBLIUS NIGIDIUS, in his Gram- matical Commentaries, fhews that names and words are fixed, not by accidental applica- tion, but by a certain power and order of nature; a fubject much celebrated in the differtations of philofophers, amongft whom it was a queftion, " Whether words are from nature or applica- tion?" Upon this matter he ufes many argu- ments, to prove that they appear rather natural

[1] Muretus, in his firft chapter, book xiii. of his Various Readings, laughs at Nigidius for thefe fanciful opinions. Nigidius, he fuppofes, borrowed them of Chryfippus; and he concludes his animadverfions in thefe words: " We could hardly believe that thefe chimerical things had been faid by fuch eminent men, did we not learn from Varro, that it is not poffible for a difordered perfon to dream any thing fo abfurd, which has not been ferioufly afferted by fome philofopher or other."

than

than arbitrary, amongſt which this ſeems ingenious and jocoſe : " When," ſays he, " we ſpeak
the word *vos* (you), we uſe a certain motion of
the mouth, agreeing with what the word itſelf
expreſſes ; we protrude by degrees the tips of
our lips, and thruſt forward our breath and mind
towards thoſe with whom we are engaged in converſation.   On the other hand, when we ſay *nos*
(we), we do not pronounce it with a broad and
expanded blaſt of the voice, nor with projecting
lips, but we reſtrain our breath and lips, as it were
within ourſelves.   This ſame rule takes place
likewiſe in the words *tu* and *ego*, *tibi* and *mihi*.
For as, when we conſent or diſagree, a certain
motion of the head or the eyes correſponds
with the nature of the thing expreſſed ; ſo in the
pronunciation of theſe words there is a certain
natural manner and ſpirit.   In Greek words too
the ſame rule is in force which we fancy prevails
in our own."

CHAP. V.

Whether avarus [1] *be a simple word, or, as it appears to P. Nigidius, a compound one.*

IN the twenty-ninth of his Commentaries Nigidius affirms, that the word *avarus* is not a simple but a compound word. That man (says he) is called *avarus* (covetous) who is *avidus æris* (fond of money); but in the union of the two words the letter *e* is worn away. So he says a man is called *locupletem* (rich) who holds *pleraque loca*, that is many possessions. What he says of *locuples* is more plausible, and stronger; but as to the word *avarus*, there is doubt. For why may it not seem to be derived from the single word *aveo* (to covet), and of the same formation as *amarus*, of which it can only be said that it is not a compound word?

---

[1] Vossius and others have supposed that *avarus* may be derived from *avidus auri*; and *locuples*, some are of opinion, is formed of *Joculi pleni*.

CHAP. VI.

A fine was impofed by the ædiles of the people [1] upon the daughter of Appius Cæcus, a woman of rank, for fpeaking impertinently.

SO inviolable did the dignity of the Roman difcipline deem it neceffary to preferve itfelf, that public punifhment was inflicted not on crimes only, but even on difrefpectful words; for the daughter of Appius Cæcus [2], going from the theatre, where fhe had been a fpectator of the games, was pufhed about by the multitude of people every where crowding in upon her. Endeavouring to extricate herfelf, fhe complained that fhe was ill : " And what," fays fhe, " muft now have become of me, how much more clofely fhould I

[1] *Ædiles of the people.*]—The ædiles of the people are to be diftinguifhed from the curule ædiles. The firft were elected from the Plebeians, as affiftants to the tribunes, and to determine leffer caufes; the latter were elected from the Patricians. The fame fact is related by Valerius Maximus, l. 8. De Judiciis Publicis, where other examples are enumerated of fevere punifhments inflicted capricioufly for trifling offences.

[2] *Appius Cæcus.*]—This was the Appius from whom the Appian Way took its name, and he is alfo celebrated for advifing the fenate, on the invafion of Italy by Pyrrhus, not to enter into any treaty of peace with the king till he fhould firft have evacuated the territories of the republic.

have

have been preffed upon, if my brother Claudius had not loft his fleet of fhips in the fea-fight, together with a vaft number of citizens? Surely I fhould then have been quite overwhelmed with the ftill greater influx of people. Oh that he were alive again! that he might conduct another fleet into Sicily, and carry that multitude to deftruction, which has now haraffed me almoft to death!" For thefe impudent and offenfive words, C. Fundanius, and Tib. Sempronius, ædiles of the people, impofed upon her a fine of twenty-five thoufand folid pounds of brafs [3]. Capito Atteius, in his Commentary upon Public Decifions, fays, this was done in the firft Punic war, in the confulate of Fabius Licinius and Titus Acilius Craffus.

---

[3] *Solid pounds of brafs.*]—*Æris gravis.* The moft learned commentators differ about the meaning of this expreffion. Servius explains it to be lumps of uncoined brafs. The ftandard varied at different times, according to the abundance or fcarcity of money; probably *æs grave* was ufed to mean the full ancient ftandard. The fine impofed on this occafion amounted to about twenty-five pounds of our money.

CHAP.

CHAP. VII.

Marcus Varro, as I remember, writes, that of those rivers which flow beyond the limits of the Roman empire, that of the first magnitude is the Nile, of the second the Danube, and next the Rhone.

OF all those rivers which flow within the confines of the Roman empire into the sea, called by the Greeks την εισω θαλασσαν, it is agreed that the greatest is the Nile[1]. Sallust has affirmed

[1] *The Nile.*]—Every thing which relates to the magnitude and excellence of this river I took pains to collect, in my notes to the second book of Herodotus, to which I beg leave to refer the reader. Ovid represents the Danube as equal to the Nile—

Innumerique alii quos inter maximus amnes,
Cedere Danubius se tibi Nile negat.

Ausonius calls the Danube second to the Nile—

————tibi Nile secundus
Danubius.

Arrian calls the Danube των ποταμων κατα την Ευρωπην μεγιστον. It is described at considerable length in the Melpomene of Herodotus. See my translation of that work, Vol. II. p. 225. Its ancient name was Danau; see Bryant. Milton thus speaks of the Rhine and the Danube—

A multitude

firmed that the Danube is the next in extent;
but Varro, when he defcanted upon that part of
the world which is called Europe, places the
Rhone amongſt the three firſt rivers in that quarter of the globe, by which he feems to confider
it as a rival of the Danube; for the Danube flows
likewife in Europe.

> A multitude like which the populous North
> Pour'd never from her frozen loins, to pafs
> Rhene or the Danaw.

Spenfer alfo calls it the Danaw.

CHAP. VIII.

That amongst the disgraceful punishments[1] by which soldiers were restrained, was the letting of blood; and what was the apparent reason of this.

IT was formerly a military sentence, to disgrace a soldier by ordering a vein to be opened, and blood to be taken from him. The reason of which is no where mentioned, that I can find, in the old records. But I suppose it was first practised towards soldiers, who were scarcely in their senses, and whose mind wandered from its usual habit, that it appears to have been not so much a punishment as a medical application. Afterwards, however, the same remedy perhaps was habitually applied, for many and various offences, as if all who committed crimes were seemingly unsound in mind.

[1] *Punishments.*]—The account which Gellius gives of the motive of this singular punishment, will hardly be deemed satisfactory. I find the following opinion concerning it in the Various Readings of Muretus, l. xiii. p. 199—" Ego id factum puto, ut sanguinem quem cum gloria fundere pro patria noluerant, eum cum ignominia amitterent." I think it was done that they might lose that blood with ignominy, which they were unwilling to spill with glory for their country. An explanation which, to me, seems reasonable enough.

CHAP. IX.

*By what means and in what form the Roman army
is ufually drawn up; and what are the names
of their divifions.*

THERE are military terms [1] applied to an
army drawn up in a certain manner, as
the front, the referve, the wedge, the ring, the
fquadron, the fheers, the faw, the wings, the
towers; thefe and other terms you may find in
our writers upon military topics. But they are
taken from the things which are properly fo
called; and in the drawing up of an army the
forms of thofe things which each word expreffes,
are reprefented.

[1] *Military terms.*]—All thefe will be found, with their
feveral explanations, in Vegetius, Frontinus, Polybius, and
others, and particularly in Lipfius de Militia Romanâ.

CHAP.

Chap. X.

Why the ancient Greeks and the Romans wore a ring upon the laſt finger but one of the left hand.

WE have been told that the ancient Greeks had a ring upon the laſt finger but one of the left hand. They ſay too that the Romans uſually wore their's in the ſame manner. Appion, in his books upon Ægypt, ſays, the reaſon of it is this, " That by diſſecting and laying open human bodies, as the cuſtom was in Ægypt, which the Greeks call anatomy, it was diſcovered

---

' *Wore a ring.*]—Much might be written on the ſubject of rings as worn by the ancients, and by the Romans in particular. They had their ſummer and their winter rings, their rings of dreſs and undreſs; ſome they wore only at home, others only abroad. It was the diſtinction of the gentleman from the ſlave, who, when made free, had a ring given him. Before they were free, ſlaves wore rings of iron. Ignorant people yet imagine that the wedding-ring is worn on the fourth finger of the left hand for the reaſon aſſigned in this chapter, namely, that from this finger there is ſome delicate nerve communicating with the heart. But this idea is properly expoſed by Brown, in his Vulgar Errors. The chapter is too long to tranſcribe, but the whole is curious and entertaining, and well deſerves the reader's attention. The ancients carried their ſuperſtitious prejudices with reſpect to this finger to ſo great a degree, that they mixed up their medicines with it,

that

that from that finger only, of which we have fpoken, a very fine nerve proceeded, and paffed quite to the heart: wherefore it does not feem without reafon, that that finger fhould particularly be honoured with fuch an ornament, which feemed to be a continuation of, and as it were united with, the principle of the heart."

CHAP. XI.

The meaning and formation of the word maturè; *the common ufage of it improper.—Likewife that the word* præcox *makes, in the genitive cafe, not* præcoquis, *but* præcocis. [*]

ACCORDING to our prefent ufage of the word, *maturè* (maturely) fignifies *properè* and *citò* (quickly, with expedition), contrary to the true meaning of the word. For *maturè* means one thing, and *properè* another. Publius Nigidius, a man of diftinguifhed eminence in all fcientific purfuits, fays, that *maturè* means neither too foon nor too late, but has a certain middle fignification. Well and properly has Nigidius

[*] The fubject of this chapter is difcuffed alfo by Macrobius, who indeed was no more than the echo of Gellius. See Satur. l. 3.

said

said this; for in corn and in fruits thofe are faid to be mature, which are neither crude and unripe, nor mellow and falling, but grown and ripened in their full time; but becaufe that has been called maturely done, which has been done with attention, fo the meaning of the word has been carried much farther, and a thing is now faid to be done maturely, becaufe it is done quickly, not becaufe it is done without indolence. Whereas thofe things which are haftened beyond moderation, may be more truely called immature. But Nigidius's middle fignification of the word, Auguftus moft elegantly expreffed in two Greek words[2], which he was accuftomed to ufe in his converfation, and his letters, " Σπευδε βραδεως." By which he recommended, that to accomplifh any thing we fhould ufe the promptnefs of diligence, with the delay of carefulnefs.   From

[2] *Two Greek words.*]—The correfpondent phrafe in Latin is *feftina lente*; concerning which proverb confult Erafmus, who has difcuffed it at confiderable length, drawing a parallel betwixt the characters of Agamemnon, whofe diftinction was the *lente*, and that of Achilles, whofe characteriftic was *hafte*. We have many modern proverbs of fimilar import.

The French fay—" Qui trop fe hafte en cheminant, en beau chemin fe fourvoye fouvent."   " He that walks too haftily, often ftumbles in plain way."

The Italians fay—" Prefto et bene non fi conviene."   " Haftily and well do not come together."

Sir Amias Paulet ufed this expreffion—" Tarry a little, that we may make an end the fooner." '

which

which two oppofite qualifications fprings *maturity*. Virgil alfo has very wifely feparated (if one obferves) the words *properare* and *maturare*, as having oppofite meanings :—

Frigidus Agricolam fi quando continet imber,
Multa, forent quæ mox cœlo *properanda* fereno,
Maturare datur.

" Whenever the winter[3] rains confine the hufbandman at home, many things may be done at leifure which afterwards, when the weather is fair, would be done in a hurry."

Moft elegantly has he diftinguifhed between thefe two words; for in rural affairs, during rainy feafons, the labour may be done at leifure, which in fine weather muft be done in hafte. But when any thing is to be expreffed which is done in too hurrying and fpeedy a manner, then it may be more properly called *prematurely* than *maturely* done. As Afranius[4], in his play called the Noμos, fays,

Appetis dominatum demens *præmaturè* præcocem.

[3] *Whenever the winter.*]—I have ufed the interpretation of Martyn, Vol. II. p. 74.

[4] *Afranius.*]—The fragments of this comic poet are collected in the Corpus Poetarum of Mattaire. He lived about one hundred years before Chrift. He is mentioned by Quintilian, who cenfures him for obfcenity. Fragments of his works are alfo found in H. Stevens's collection.

The

The foolifh youth, with wifhes *premature*,
Wou'd rule, ere yet his right to rule is fure.

In which line it muft be obferved, he ufes *præcocem*, not *præcoquem*; for the nominative cafe is not *præcoquis* but *præcox*.

Chap. XII.

Of certain marvellous tales which Pliny[1] the Elder moft unjuftly afcribes to Democritus the philofopher; likewife of the flying model of a pigeon.

PLINY the Elder relates, in the twenty-eighth chapter of his Natural Hiftory, that there is a book of that moft excellent philofopher Democritus, upon the Power and Nature

[1] Some of the commentators remark, that Gellius never introduces the name of Pliny, but to cenfure him. In the prefent inftance he has certainly cenfured him unjuftly, for in his preface to the very book where the circumftances here mentioned are recorded, Pliny does not fcruple to call them mendacia Græcæ vanitatis. He adds alfo, that many accomplifhed men doubted whether this book, afcribed to Democritus, were really written by him.

of

of the Cameleon [+], which he had read; and he hands down to us many foolish and intolerable abfurdities, as if written by Democritus, of which unwillingly, for they diftrefs me, I remember thefe—That the hawk, which is the fwifteft of birds, if he happens to fly over the cameleon when lying upon the ground, is drawn down, and falls with a degree of force upon the earth, and becomes a fpontaneous prey, to be torn in pieces by the other birds. There is likewife another ftory paft human belief—That if the head and neck of the cameleon be fet on fire with the wood called oak, on a fudden rain and thunder is produced; and that the fame thing ufually happens, if the liver of that animal be burnt upon the top of a houfe. There is moreover another relation, but fo very prepofterous that I hefitated about retailing it; however, I have laid it down as a rule, that we ought to fpeak what we think, of that fallacious feduction, by which men of the greateft wifdom, and particularly thofe who are ambitious of inftruction, are betrayed into by the power of admiration, even to their ruin. But

[+] *Cameleon.*]—Many ridiculous ftories concerning this animal have obtained belief, even in modern times. A vulgar opinion yet prevails, that it fubfifts wholly by air. But this is proved to be falfe, by the concurring teftimonies of the moft accomplifhed naturalifts, and is indeed evident from the very ftructure of the animal. It has not only a tongue but teeth, both of which would be ufelefs if air conftituted its only nutriment: and the tongue is peculiarly conftructed for the purpofe of catching infects.

I return

I return to Pliny:—" The left foot," fays he, " of the cameleon is roafted before a hot iron and a fire, with an herb called by the fame name, cameleon: each is mixed up in an ointment, formed into a pafte, and thrown into a wooden veffel; and he who carries that veffel, though he be openly in the midft of people, can be feen by no one." Such are the wonderful and delufive tales written by Plinius Secundus. Nor can I think that worthy the name of Democritus, which the fame Pliny, in his tenth book, afferts that Democritus wrote, namely, that by pronouncing certain words, and fprinkling the blood of certain birds, a ferpent was produced, which whoever accomplifhed could interpret the language and converfation of birds. Many ftories of this fort appear to have been given in the name of Democritus by ignorant men, who fheltered themfelves under the rank and authority of Pliny.

But that which Archytas [3] the Pythagorean is related to have devifed and accomplifhed, is

not

[3] *Archytas.*]—Of the great fkill of the ancients in mechanics we have various and fufficient teftimonies; and the name of Archimedes alone, as it is obferved by Mr. Dutens, in his Enquiry into the Origin of the Difcoveries attributed to the Moderns, would afford fufficient matter for a volume.

Archytas lived at the fame time with Plato, and his wooden pigeon has been celebrated by various writers. His life is given by Diogenes Laertius, who tells us that he was the friend and correfpondent of Plato.

The following is extracted from Middleton's celebrated Letters from Rome, p. 210.

" In

not lefs marvellous, though it appears lefs abfurd; for many men of eminence among the Greeks, and Favorinus the philofopher, a moft vigilant fearcher into antiquity, have, in a moft pofitive manner, affured us, that the model of a pigeon formed in wood by Archytas, was fo contrived, as by a certain mechanical art and power to fly: fo nicely was it balanced by weights, and put in motion by hidden and enclofed air. In a matter fo very improbable we may be allowed to add the words of Favorinus himfelf: " Archytas of Tarentum, being both a philofopher and fkilled in mechanics, made a wooden pigeon, which had it ever fettled would not have rifen again till now."

" In the cathedral church of Ravenna I faw, in Mofaic work, the pictures of thofe archbifhops of the place who, as all their hiftorians affirm, were chofen for feveral ages fucceffively by the fpecial defignation of the Holy Ghoft, who, in a full affembly of the clergy and people, ufed to defcend vifibly on the perfon elect in the fhape of a dove. If the fact of fuch a defcent be true, it will eafily be accounted for by a paffage in Aulus Gellius (whence the hint was probably taken) who tells us of Archytas the philofopher and mathematician, that he formed a pigeon of wood fo artificially, as to make it fly by the power of mechanifm juft as he directed it. And we find from Strada, that many tricks of this kind were actually contrived for the diverfion of Charles the Fifth, in his monaftery, by one Turrianus, who made little birds fly out of the room and back again, by his great fkill in machinery."

C H A P.

CHAP. XIII.

The reason why the ancients said partim [1] *hominum.*

WE often use the phrase " partim hominum venerunt," which means part of the men came, that is, some men. For the word *partim* is here an adverb, nor is it declined by cases. Thus we may say, " cum partim hominum," that is, with some men, or with a certain portion of men. Marcus Cato has thus written, in his speech upon the Florian affair : " There, like a woman of the town, she stole from the entertainment to the couch, and with (*partim* illorum) different parties of them, acted in the same manner." Ignorant people, when they read " partim," supposed it declined like a noun, not spoken as an adverb. But Quintus Claudius, in the 21st of his Annals, has used this figure in rather a more singular manner : " Enim [2] cum *partim*

---

[1] *Partim* is in fact the accusative case of the old nominative *partis*, the meaning is, " according to the part;" which terpretation will be found sufficient wherever the word *partim* occurs. It is in fact a Græcism.

[2] *Enim.*]—This sentence is at any rate imperfect, and probably corrupt. As it could not possibly convey any idea to an English reader, I have merely inserted the words in the text.

copiis

copiis *hominum* adolefcentium placentem fibi."
He has likewife, in his 23d Annal, thefe words :
"-Sed id circo [3] me feciffe quod utrum negligen-
tia *partim* magiftratuum, an avaritia, an calami-
tate populi Romani eveniffe dicam, nefcio."

[3] *Sed id circo.*]—I was induced to act thus, being unable
to fay whether it happened from the negligence of part of
the magiftrates, or from avarice, or the calamity of the Roman people.

CHAP. XIV.

*By what arrangement of words Cato said " Injuria '
mihi factum itur."*

I HEAR the phrases " *illi injuriam factum iri,*"
and " *contumeliam dictum iri,*" spoken univer-
sally, and it is certain that this is a common mode
of speech, examples are therefore unnecessary.
But " *contumelia illi,*" or " *injuria factum itur,*" is
somewhat more remote. We will produce an
example : Marcus Cato, defending himself against
Caius Caffius, says—" And thus it came to pass, O
Romans, that in the infult which, by the infolence
of this man, is about to be caft upon me (quæ
mihi per hujufce petulantiam *factum itur*), I
have caufe alfo to compaffionate the commonwealth." But as " *contumeliam factum iri*" fignifies " to go to do an injury," that is, to endeavour that an injury be done, fo " *contumelia factum
iri,*" in the nominative cafe, means the fame
thing.

* *Injuria.*]—There is no great acutenefs of criticifm difplayed in this chapter. The fentence, as it now ftands, can
never be confidered as pure Latin. It is by no means improbable that originally it was written *injuriam,* which makes
the conftruction natural and eafy.

CHAP. XV.

On the ceremonies of the prieſt and prieſteſs of Jupiter, and ſome words cited from the prætor's ediⁱt, in which he declares he will not compel either the veſtal virgins or the prieſts of Jupiter to take an oath. [1]

NUMEROUS are the ceremonies impoſed upon the prieſt of Jupiter, and many are the circumſtances [2] concerning them, which are collected in the books upon the prieſthood, and which we read in the firſt book of Fabius Pictor [3]. Of which theſe are the principal articles we can bring to mind: Firſt, " The prieſt of Jupiter

[1] This chapter is in ſome places exceedingly perplexed, and doubtleſs corrupt. Many of the injunctions and prohibitions are, according to our conception, ſo contrary to all meaning and common ſenſe, that I found it altogether impoſſible to ſatisfy myſelf in my attempts to make them intelligible to the Engliſh reader. I have only to ſay that I have done my beſt.

[2] *Circumſtances.*]—What I have thus rendered appears, in various editions of Gellius, *caſtus, cautus,* and *caſus.*

[3] *Fabius Pictor.*]—This perſonage is celebrated by Livy as the moſt ancient of the Roman hiſtorians. He lived about 216 years before Chriſt, or 500 after the building of the city.

is

is forbidden to ride on horſeback [4]: he muſt not ſee the ſoldiers marſhalled without the city walls: ſeldom [5] therefore is the prieſt elected conſul, becauſe the conduct of the wars was uſually committed to the conſuls. It is never lawful for the prieſt to take an oath: he is not allowed to wear a ring unleſs it be hollow [6] and perforated: it is not lawful for a flame to be carried from the houſe of the prieſt, ûnleſs for the purpoſes of religion: if a perſon bound enters his houſe he muſt be unbound, the bonds muſt be taken through the gutter to the roof, and thence thrown into the road: he has no knot on his cap, or cincture, or in any part of his dreſs: if any one

[4] *On horſeback.*]—This is a prohibition not very eaſy to explain. It appears to have been thought neceſſary to pay the Flamen Dialis every mark of honour. To ride on horſeback was always deemed honourable; why then deny this character alone ſo great a convenience and comfort? The latent intention might be, to prevent his becoming too familiar by appearing frequently in public.

[5] *Seldom.*]—The Flamen Dialis had from his office a ſeat in the ſenate, a diſtinction which no other prieſt enjoyed. He might, therefore, if ſuch was his temper and propenſities, occaſionally interfere in political diſcuſſions; and by rendering himſelf an object of popular favour, might eventually be propoſed as a candidate, and elected to the firſt office in the ſtate.

[6] *Hollow.*]—As all rings are hollow, it is not eaſy to comprehend what is here intended. It may mean a ring without a gem or ſtone; or more probably a ring, the circle of which had holes ſtamped in it.

is going to be flogged, and falls suppliant [7] at his feet, he may not be punished on that day: no one but a free man may shave the Dialis: he may not touch or even name a she-goat [8], raw flesh, or ivy, or a bean: he may not cut the long shoots of a vine: the foot of the bed in which he sleeps must have a thin coat of clay: he must not sleep from this bed three nights together; nor might any one sleep in this bed, nor at the foot of it might there be a chest with any

[7] *Falls suppliant.*]—Dr. Russel, in his entertaining History of Aleppo, tells us, it is usual for the Syriac christians to fall prostrate before their bishop, an act of servile obsequiousness, without example in any other period of the church.   In the East, indeed, the most humble prostration is practised from the vulgar towards the great, and the contagion probably, from time and circumstance, has been allowed to pollute an institution whose character is modesty and simplicity, and which revolts at such acts of humiliation from one frail being to another.

[8] *A she-goat.*]—This abhorrence of a goat does not seem very complimentary to the priest's great patron, Jupiter. The god, it seems, was nursed by a goat, to whose horn, *cornu* Amaltheæ, he gave what has been celebrated by numberless poets of ancient and modern times.   The curious observer will find a remarkable resemblance in the peculiarities enjoined to the Flamen Dialis, and the observancies which the Levitical law required of the high priest of the Jews. The high priest might not touch a body: he might not go into the open air when the anointing oil was upon him.   See also the description of the high priest's holy garments.   There were many more peculiarities relating to the Flamen Dialis than are mentioned here.   See in particular Plutarch's Roman Questions.

                                    sacred

facred cakes: the cuttings of his nails and hair muft be buried under a tree of the aufpicious kind [9]: with him, every day is holy [10]: he muft not be in the air without his cap: it has not long been determined by the priefts that he fhould go without it in the houfe." Maffurius Sabinus writes, that many of thefe peculiarities and ceremonious obfervances were remitted: " He might not touch any fermented meal: he did not put off his inner garment unlefs under cover, that he might not be naked in the air, that is in the eye of Jupiter: no one might take place of the Dialis at an entertainment, unlefs he who prefided at the facrifice [11]: if he loft his wife, he loft his office: his marriage could not be diffolved but by death: he never enters a place of interment: he never

[9] *Aufpicious kind.*]—Many trees were deemed of the inaufpicious kind, fuch were trees that bore no fruit; others were thought unlucky which bore fruit of a black kind.

[10] *Is holy.*]—The readings here are fo various as to render the tranflation of the paffage extremely difficult. We find *fertatus, feftatus, feriatus,* &c. &c. I have adopted the laft. There were in every month *dies feriati,* but to the Flamen Dialis, as I have rendered the paffage, every day was *dies feriatus.*

[11] *Who prefided at the facrifice.*]—Rex facrificatus. In the time of the kings, it was deemed a good omen for the king to be prefent at the facrifices, and taking the aufpices. This therefore they thought neceffary to continue in form after they became a republic. He therefore who prefided at the facrifice, on whatever occafion it was offered, was termed Rex facrificatus or *facrorum.*

touches

touches a dead body, but might attend a funeral[12].
It is said that the priesteffes of Jupiter, on their
parts, obferved nearly the fame ceremonies. The
garment of the prieftefs was dyed: fhe had fome
twig of an aufpicious tree twifted round her hood[13]:
fhe might not go more than three fteps up a ladder, unlefs of thefe which are called κλιμακες[14]:
when fhe went to the Argei[15] fhe might neither

[12] *Might attend a funeral.*]—It feems a little remarkable
that he fhould be allowed to attend a funeral, when it is certain that there was always a kind of bellman or trumpeter,
who went before at funerals, that the Flamen Dialis might
keep out of the way. See Magius de Tintinnabulis.

" Erant et alii codonophori qui atrati funus præcedebant.
Funeri autem adhiberi confueviffe arbitror, tum ut ad fpec-
tandam funebrem pompam homines accerferentur, tum ut
Flaminem Dialem admonerent funeris, ne ille ex improvifo
funeri occurreret et funebribus tibiis auditis pollueretur."

[13] *Hood.*]—Rica. This word is of very unufual occurrence. I find it thus explained in Terentius Varro; " Sic
rica a ritu quod Romano ritu facrificium feminæ cum faciunt,
capita velant."

[14] Κλιμακις.]—This is an obfcure paffage, and to me at
leaft not perfectly intelligible. Κλιμαξ is a part of a wag-
gon, (fee Pollux in voce) and it is not improbable but it
might mean fome particular kind of ladder enclofed be-
hind. The reafon of this prohibition was, doubtlefs, to prevent any body feeing what they ought not. Falfter refers
to the following paffage in Exodus, ch. xx. ver. 26. Neither fhalt thou go up by fteps unto mine altar, that thy na-
kednefs be not difcovered thereon.

[15] *Argei.*]—There were places in Rome confecrated by
Numa, where facrifices were offered, called Argei. According to Varro, there were twenty-four of thefe.

comb her head nor dress her hair." I have subjoined the Prætor's standing edict, concerning
the Flamén Dialis and the priestess of Vesta : " I
will not compel the priestess of Vesta, or the
Flamen Dialis, in the whole of my jurisdiction,
to take an oath." These are the words of Varro,
in his second book of Divine Things, concerning
the Flamen Dialis : " He alone has a white cap,
either because he is the greatest in his profession,
or because a white victim [16] should be immolated
to Jupiter."

[16] *White victim.*]—In all magic rites, and in particular to
the infernal deities, black victims were sacrificed, but to the
celestial gods white victims were offered. It was necessary
also, at least on some occasions, that the altar should be white:

——————Hoste repulso
Candida Pistori ponitur ara Jovi.

OVID.

See the same author in another place,—

Alba Jovi grandior agna cadit.

We have also this expression in Virgil, Georg. ii. ver. 146.

Hinc albi Clitumne greges et maxima taurus
Victima.

CHAP.

Chap. XVI.

Certain historical errors which Julius Higinus points out in the sixth book of Virgil.

HIGINUS censures Virgil, and thinks he would have corrected a passage in his sixth book. Palinurus is in the shades below, requiring of Æneas that he would take care to find out his body, and give it burial. He speaks thus—

> Eripe[*] me his invicte malis: at tu mihi ter-
> ram
> Injice (namque potes) portusque require Ve-
> linos.

For how, says he, could Palinurus be acquainted with, or mention the port of Velia ? How could Æneas discover the place from that name; since the town of Velia, from which he has called the

[*] *Eripe.*]—Thus translated by Dryden—

> Redeem from this reproach my wand'ring ghost,
> Or with your navy seek the Veline coast,
> And in a peaceful grave my corpse compose.

I do not know whether the reader will be satisfied with the vindication of this passage which occurs in Turnebus; see his Adversar. 435. *Velinus,* says the critic, in this place means no more than *palustris,* it is the same therefore as if he had said *require portum palustrem.* Virgil is certainly guilty of an anachronism.

harbour

harbour there the Velian, was founded in the province of Lucania, and so named when Servius Tullius reigned at Rome, more than six hundred years after Æneas came into Italy? For, he adds, they who were driven from Phocis by Harpalus[2], an officer of king Cyrus, built, some of them, Velia, and some of them Massilia. · Most absurdly therefore does he require that Æneas should find out the harbour of Velia, when at that time such a name was no where known. Nor ought that similar mistake to appear which occurs in the first book—

Italiam[3] fato profugus Lavinaque venit Littora.

A like mistake occurs in the sixth book,

Chalcidicaque levis tandem superastitit arce.

Although to the poet himself it may sometimes be allowed to relate by anticipation, in his own person, facts which he might know took place

---

[2] *Harpalus.*]—Ammianus Marcellinus, and Solinus, call this man Harpalus, but Herodotus, Pausanias, and the older writers, write his name Harpagus. See an account of his exploits in Herodotus, Vol. I. p. 115, &c. in my translation.

[3] *Italiam, &c.*]—This kind of anticipation is very frequent, and surely very allowable in poetry. A sublime use of it is made by Milton, when Adam hears from the angel an account of his posterity. All that Virgil remarks about Carthage is liable to the same objection, but no commentator that I know of has reprehended him for this.

afterwards. As Virgil knew of the city Lavinium, and the colony of Chalcis. But how could Palinurus know circumſtances that happened ſix hundred years after his time, unleſs one can imagine, that in the ſhades he had the power of divination, as indeed the ſouls of the deceaſed have? But if you underſtand it thus, though it is not thus expreſſed, yet how could Æneas, who had not the power of divining, find out the Veline port; the name of which, as we ſaid before, did not any where exiſt. He cenſures likewiſe another paſſage in the ſame book, and thinks Virgil would have corrected it, had not death prevented him: For, ſays he, when he had named Theſeus amongſt thoſe who had viſited the ſhades below and returned—

Quid Theſea [*]? magnum
Quid memorem Alciden? et mî genus ab Jove
ſummo.

Afterwards,

---

[*] *Theſeus.*]—For Theſeus in this place ſome authors would read Tereus. The reader will not here forget, that preciſely as Virgil, in this book, conducts Æneas to the ſhades below, Ulyſſes, in the Odyſſey, is ſent there by Homer. Mention is made by Pauſanias of the deſcent of Theſeus to the regions below by Heſiod; but this work is not come down to us. The popular ſtory of Theſeus is too well known to have a place here.

Jortin ſpeaks thus of this paſſage, in his ſixth Diſſertation :—

Sedet æternumque ſedebit.

This

Afterwards, however, he adds,

> Sedet, æternumque fedebit,
> Infelix Thefeus.

But how could it happen that he fhould for ever remain in the fhades, whom before he mentions with thofe who had gone down thither and re-turned again, particularly when the ftory of The-feus fays, that Hercules tore him from the rock, and dragged him into light? He fays too this Virgil falls into a miftake in thefe verfes:

> Eruet ille Argos, Agamemnoniafque Myce-
> nas,
> Ipfumque Æaciden genus armipotentis A-
> chilli,
> Ultus avos Trojæ, templa et temperata Mi-
> nervæ.

> He Argos fhall o'erturn, Mycene's walls,
> And of Achilles' race Æacides,
> Troy's fall avenging, and Minerva's fhrines.

He has confounded, fays he, different perfons and times, for the battle with the Achæans and Pyr-

This alone will not perhaps fully prove the eternity of pu-nifhments; for both the word *æternus* itfelf is fometimes of a lax fignification, as every learned man knows, and *fedet æter-numque fedebit* may mean, ' there he fits, and there he will fit always,' namely as long as he remains in Tartarus. If this interpretation be admitted, the objection in this chapter falls to the ground.

rhus

rhus neither happened at the fame time, nor between the fame perfons. For Pyrrhus, whom he calls the defcendant of Æacus, paffing over from Epirus into Italy, engaged with the Romans when Marcus Curius was their leader. But the Argive, that is, the Achæan war, was carried on many years after by Lucius Mummius, imperator. The middle verfe therefore, fays he, may be omitted, which very unfeafonably treats of Pyrrhus; and which Virgil, without a doubt, intended to have left out.

CHAP.

C H A P. XVII. [1]

For what reason, and in what manner, the philosopher Democritus deprived himself of his eye-sight; and the pure and elegant verses of Laberius upon that subject.

IT is told, in the records of Grecian history, that the philosopher Democritus, a man to be reverenced beyond all others, and of high authority, spontaneously deprived himself of sight, because he thought his contemplations and the exercises of his mind would be more exact in examining the laws of nature, if he should free them

from

[1] The circumstance related in this chapter, most incredible in itself, is positively denied by Plutarch, and doubted by Cicero. Neither is it mentioned by Laertius or Hesychius, but allusions to it are to be found in a multitude of writers. It is generally asserted and believed, that the privation of any one sense will necessarily make the others more acute and perfect. The beautiful apostrophe of Milton will here occur to most of my readers,—

> Wisdom, at one entrance quite shut out,
> So much the rather, thou celestial light,
> Shine inward, and the mind thro' all her powers
> Irradiate; there plant eyes, all mist from thence
> Purge and disperse, that I may see and tell
> Of things invisible to mortal sight.

What

from the allurements of fight, and the burthen of
his eyes. The poet Laberius, in a play called the
Rector, has defcribed in fome elegant and finifh=
ed verfes, this fact, and the manner in which, by
an ingenious contrivance, he became blind. But
he has feigned another inftance of voluntary
blindnefs, and has applied it not without elegance
to his own purpofe. The character which fpeaks
them in Laberius is that of a rich and covetous
man, lamenting the exceffive extravagance and
diffipation of his fon. The verfes are thefe :

> Democritus, Abdera's far-fam'd fon,
> Plac'd a bright mirror 'gainft the ftar of day,
> That his fair fight might perifh by the blaze;
> And thus his eyes, extinguifh'd by the fun,
> Might ne'er the wicked profperous behold;
> So do I wifh the fplendour of my gold,
> My life's remoter limit to obfcure,
> Rather than fee my prodigal poffefs it.

What is here told of Democritus, and his voluntary blind=
nefs, bears fome refemblance to the idea of Gray, in the fol=
lowing bold and animated defcription,—

> Nor fecond he who rode fublime
> Upon the feraph wings of extacy,
> The fecrets of th' abyfs to fpy.
> He pafs'd the flaming bounds of fpace and time,
> The living throne, the fapphire blaze,
> Where angels tremble while they gaze.
> He faw—but blafted with excefs of light,
> Clos'd his eyes in endlefs night.

CHAP.

C H A P. XVIII.

Story of Artemisia[1], and of the games instituted by her in memory of Mausolus, wherein celebrated writers contended.

ARTEMISIA is related to have loved her husband Mausolus beyond all the stories of amorous affection, nay beyond the limits of human

[1] This story of Artemisia is sufficiently familiar, and is to be found in a variety of places. The monument itself is described particularly by Pliny, Book xxxvi. chap. 5. See also the tract of Philo Byzantius, published at Rome by Leo Allatius, where every particular of this Mausolus is collected. Consult also Bayle, article Artemisia. The lines of Propertius on the vanity of the proudest monuments of art, are elegant and apposite—

> Nam neque pyramidum sumptus ad sidera ducti,
>   Nec Jovis Elei cœlum imitatà domus,
> Nec mausolei dives fortuna sepulchri
>   Mortis ab extrema conditione vacant.

Nor can I forbear to add the following from Beattie's Minstrel :—

> Let vanity adorn the marble tomb
> With trophies, rhymes, and scutcheons of renown,
> In the deep dungeon of some Gothic dome,
> Where night and desolation ever frown,
> Mine be the breezy hill that skirts the down,
> Where a green grassy turf is all I crave,

man attachment. Maufolus, according to Cicero, was king of Caria, or, as fome Greek hiftorians relate, he was the governor of a Grecian province, whom the Greeks call a fatrap. When this Maufolus died, and was entombed with a magnificent funeral, amidft the tears and lamentations of his wife, Artemifia, inflamed with grief and regret for the lofs of her hufband, had his bones and afhes mixed with fpices, and beaten to powder, fhe then infufed them into water, and drank them off; and is faid to have exhibited many other proofs of her violent love. She erected likewife, at a vaft expence of labour, for the fake of preferving the memory of her hufband, that very celebrated monument, which has been thought worthy to be admitted among the feven wonders of the world. When Artemifia confecrated this monument to the manes of her hufband, fhe inftituted likewife a literary conteft in his honour, and appointed pecuniary rewards, and moft munificent prefents of other things. To the celebration of thefe praifes, men are faid to have come, of illuftrious talents, and diftinguifhed oratory, Theo-

> With here and there a violet beftrown,
>   Faft by a brook, or fountain's murmuring wave,
> And many an evening fun fhine fweetly on my grave.

The appellation of Maufoleum has, as Bayle obferves, been given ever fince to all magnificent ftructures of this kind.

pompus [2], Theodectes [3] of Naucratis. There are also who have related, that Isocrates himself contended with them. But Theopompus was pronounced the victor in that contest. He was the pupil of Isocrates. The tragedy of Theodectes, which is entitled Mausolus, is now extant; in which, according to the examples cited by Higinus, Theodectes pleases more than in his prose works.

[2] *Theopompus.*]—He lived in the time of Alexander the Great, and was eminent as an historian. He is mentioned by many writers with respect.

[3] *Theodectes.*]—A difficulty here occurs of no great importance, but which has much perplexed and divided the commentators. The doubt is, whether a third eminent person is not to be added as a competitor at these games, and named Naucrites. The reader will adopt or reject my interpretation, as he thinks proper.

It may not be improper to add, as a conclusion to this chapter, that a story is told in Boccace, of a husband who obliged his wife to eat the heart of her gallant, whom he had put to death. The lady, when she was acquainted with what she had done, exclaimed, that it should not be said she ever took any food after so noble a repast; she then threw herself out of a high window, and was dashed to pieces. The husband relented, and buried the bodies of the lovers in the same grave.

CHAP. XIX.

That a crime is not done away or lessened by the defence which some offenders set up, namely a similarity of crimes in others; and a passage upon that subject from an oration of Demosthenes.[1]

THE philosopher Taurus reproved a certain young man with severe and vehement censure, because he had quitted his attendance upon

[1] Obvious as the folly must be of justifying our own indiscretions from the contagion and frequency of example, it is but too true, that the custom is, and perhaps always will be, prevalent in every age and country. The reproof, however of Taurus in this chapter may fairly be disputed as to its wisdom and its justice. The study of rhetoric and eloquence, as pursued in his time, appeared to have regard only to the external accomplishments and fleeting reputation of the individual. The study of philosophy, imperfect as it was, comprehended somewhat better, and by inculcating the necessity of at least some system of morals, necessarily had an influence on the good and happiness of society. Yet what Mr. Cowper observes on this subject, after all that can be favourably urged concerning it, is as just as it is forcible:

—Their answers vague
And all at random, fabulous and dark,
Left them as dark themselves. Their rules of life,
Defective and unsanction'd, prov'd too weak
To bind the roving appetite, and lead
Blind nature to a God not yet reveal'd.

the rhetoricians and the fchool of eloquence, for the ftudy of philofophy, which he faid was a tranfgreffion difingenuous and difgraceful. The young man did not attempt to deny the fact, but defended himfelf, by alledging that it was frequently done, and deprecated the bafenefs of the fault, by the citation of examples, and the excufe of cuftom. But Taurus, ftill more irritated by this kind of defence, " Foolifh and contemptible man!" fays he, " if the authority and laws of philofophy do not withdraw you from the effect of bad examples, yet does not that fentence of Demofthenes occur to you? which, as it is put together in a polifhed and elegant arrangement of words, might be more eafily impreffed upon your memory, as a fort of rhetorical tale : If I do not forget, what indeed I read in earlier youth — thefe are the words of Demofthenes, addreffed to one who (like yourfelf) endeavoured to blot out and excufe his own crime by the crimes of others. — Do not[2] fay that this is often done, but that it

ought

---

[2] *Do not, &c.*]—Thefe words occur at the beginning of the oration againft Androcion. This is one of the moft vigorous and animated of all the orations of Demofthenes, and this paffage in particular is highly extolled by Quintilian : " Optimum autem videtur enthymematis genus, cum propofito diffimili vel contrario ratio fubjungitur, quale eft Demofthenis, &c." That it may be more intelligible to the reader, he fhould be informed, that Androcion had, in the affembly of the people at Athens, propofed a decree, which was in oppofition to many eftablifhed cuftoms, and obnoxious to certain

tain

ought to be done; for if any thing be done contrary to the laws, and you follow the example, is it right that you fhould efcape the punifhment of the law? on the contrary, you ought to be more feverely punifhed; for, if any one of them had fuffered punifhment, you would not have propofed thefe things; fo if you are now punifhed, no one in future will propofe them." Thus did Taurus, by every mode of perfuafion and advice, incline his followers to the habits of good and virtuous morals.

tain exifting laws. But on being accufed, he alledged, in his vindication, that he had the fanction of example for what he had done.

Neither is it unworthy of remark, that Demofthenes made this, and the celebrated oration againft Timocrates, when he was no more than twenty-feven years old; and that Cicero made his oration in behalf of P. Quintius at twenty-fix, and that for Sex. Rofcius at twenty-feven,

CHAP. XX.

The meaning of the words rogatio, lex, plebiscitum, privilegium; *and wherein these words differ.* [1]

I HEAR enquiry made as to the meaning of the words *lex, plebiscitum, rogatio,* and *privilegium.* Atteius Capito, a man particularly skilled

in

---

[1] The terms *lex* and *plebiscitum*, which occur in this chapter, are so perspicuously explained by Bever, in his History of the Legal Polity of the Roman State, that I cannot fulfil my duty to the reader more effectually than by transcribing the passage.

When the Roman state increased in numbers and territory, fresh matters arose, which required new laws; all which are reducible to the following species:

" Such as were passed at the instance of a senatorial magistrate, by the whole of the aggregate body of the people, senators and Patricians, as well as Plebeians, in whom alone the majesty of the state resided—a law thus enacted was called " *Lex*" in its strict and proper sense.

" The second species of occasional written law was called " *plebiscitum,*" which was enacted by the Plebeian body alone, at the " *rogation*" of one of their own magistrates. The *Plebiscita* were originally made in the " *comitia tributa,*" at the instance of the tribunes, and were partial laws, binding the Plebeians only."

Thus far Bever. As to the term *privilegium*, it in a manner explains itself: *privilegia* are private laws. Anciently it was used in a bad sense, for a private law passed to punish

an

in the knowledge of public and private rights,
has thus defined the word *lex:* " *Lex* (law)" fays
he, " is the general decree of the people, or the
commons, upon a queftion propofed by the ma-
giftrate." If this definition be juft, neither the
iffue of the debate upon the command given to
Cnæus Pompey, upon the return of Marcus Cicero, the murder of Clodius, nor any decrees of
the like nature, can be called laws; for they are
not general decrees, formed on account of the
citizens as a body, but applied to particular individuals; wherefore they ought rather to be called
privileges. For the ancients called thofe *priva*
which we call *fingula*; which word Lucilius[a] has
ufed in his firft book of Satires,—

Abdomina Thynni
Advenientibus *priva* dabo cephaleaque a carne.

But Capito, in the fame definition, feparates *(ple-
bem)* the commonalty, from the people *(a populo)*;
for in the term *people*, every part of the city, and
all its ranks, are included. But that is called
plebs (the commons), in which the Patrician citizens are not included. The *plebifcitum*, therefore,
is, according to Capito, that law, which the commonalty, not the people, admits. But the head,

an individual, without the form of trial. Afterwards *privilegia* were underftood to be decrees of the emperors to punifh
or reward particular individuals, but they were not to be
confidered as precedents.

[a] *Lucilius.*]—So alfo has Horace. *Privos mutantur in
annos.*

and origin, and as it were fountain, of the whole circumſtance and law, is in the *rogatio*, whether the appeal is to the people, or the commonalty, a law for individuals, or a law univerſally binding. For all the other words are underſtood and contained in the very fundamental principle and meaning of the *rogatio*. For unleſs an appeal be made to the people or the commons, no decree of the people or commons can be paſſed. But notwithſtanding this, in old records we find no great diſtinction made between theſe words; for they have given the term *leges* both to the *plebiſcita* and the *privilegia*, and have called them all by the perplexed and undiſtinguiſhing title of *rogationes*. Salluſt too, who is particularly obſervant of propriety in the uſe of words, has yielded to cuſtom, and called the *privilegium* which was paſſed upon the return of Cnæus Pompey, a law (*lex*). His words are in his ſecond hiſtory: " For Caius Herennius, tribune of the people, oppoſed the law which Sylla the conſul wiſhed to paſs for his return."

CHAP. XXI.

The reason why Marcus Cicero scrupulously avoided the use of the words noviſſimus *and* noviſſimè.

IT is clear that Marcus Cicero was unwilling to uſe many words which are now in frequent circulation, becauſe he did not approve of them; as for inſtance *noviſſimus* and *noviſſimè*. For while Marcus Cato, and Salluſt, and others of the ſame age, generally uſed the word, and many men of learning introduced it in their works, yet he ſeems to have abſtained from it, as if not properly a Latin word. Wherefore alſo L. Ælius Stilo [1], the moſt

[1] *L. Ælius Stilo.*]—The commentators are much at variance about this perſonage, ſome calling him Ælius Gallus, ſome reading Lilius Stilo, &c. There ſeems little reaſon to doubt but the perſon here meant is the Ælius Stilo mentioned ſo honourably by Cicero in his Brutus, where he is called *eruditiſſimus et Græcis literis et Latinis*; and it is avowed that Varro was moſt materially indebted to him.

With reſpect to the word *noviſſimus,* Gellius has in this chapter been guilty of an unaccountable miſtake, for Cicero has not only once but ſeveral times introduced the word *noviſſimus* in his works. See his oration for Roſcius: " Itaque per brevi tempore qui ne in *noviſſimis* quidem erat hiſtrionibus, ad primos pervenit comœdos."

See alſo in the tract De Oratore, " Nec in hác modo re quæ ad vulgi ſenſum ſpectent et ad aurium voluptatem quæ duo ſunt ad judicandum *noviſſima*."

The

moſt learned man of thoſe days, avoided the uſe of that word, as new and illegitimate. What M. Varro thought of the expreſſion is evident from his ſixth book upon the Latin tongue, addreſſed to Cicero; what was anciently *extremum* began to be commonly called *noviſſimum*. But as Ælius Gallus, ſo certain old men in my memory, avoided this as too new a word. With reſpect to its origin, as *vetuſtius* and *veterrimum* are derived from *vetus*, ſo *novius* and *noviſſimum* come from *novus*.

The expreſſion may alſo be found in Pliny, Tacitus, Seneca, Quintilian, and all the writers of beſt authority; but it is a little remarkable, that it does not appear in any index to Cicero which I have ſeen, not even in Erneſtus.

C H A P.

CHAP. XXII.

*A passage cited from the book of Plato called Gor-
gias, on the abuses of false philosophy; in which
he lashes rashly those philosophers who are ignorant of the benefits of true philosophy.* [1]

PLATO, a man most studious of truth, and
prompt to enforce it upon all occasions, has
spoken justly and openly (though from the mouth
of no very grave or decorous character) all those
censures which may deservedly be cast upon such
sluggish and idle people, as, sheltered under the
name of philosophy, devote themselves to unpro-
fitable ease, and follow useless studies and a
mean course of life. For although Callicles,
whom he makes his speaker, is ignorant of true
philosophy, and heaps dishonourable and degrad-
ing reproofs upon its professors, yet what he says
is to be received as a caution, that we may not
in our own persons deserve such reproofs, nor by

---

[1] I think, with H. Stevens, that the title of this chapter
involves no little perplexity. Where is the temerity of
pointing out to censure the impudent or idle pretenders to
philosophy? Or, as Stevens observes, " If it be an act of temerity, why is the passage here inserted with so many and
such high encomiums."

idle

idle and foolish inactivity disgrace the cultivation and pursuit of philosophy. I have written down Plato's own words in his Gorgias, as I did not attempt to translate them, because no Latinity, much less any that I could supply [2], can emulate their force:

" Philosophy, O Socrates, is indeed becoming, if a man in his youth pursues it with moderation; but if he wastes his time too long upon it, it is a corruptor of men; for if he be naturally good, and follows philosophy when past his youth, he is of course ignorant of those things in which every one should be versed who aims to be a good and accomplished character. Such are ignorant of political science, and of the language which is essential in society, both in public and private concerns; neither is he acquainted with the pleasures and desires incident to men; nor, to say the whole at once, with manners. When, therefore, they are involved in any public or private business, they appear ridiculous. Just, indeed, as men engaged in civil life, if they should

---

[2] *I could supply*]—Many will perhaps be of opinion that this excuse would have come with much more propriety from myself. For if Gellius, a scholar and critic from profession, despaired of doing justice to the Greek, with which he must have been, from study and long residence in the country, so familiarly acquainted, it argues no small presumption in me to undertake what he thus evaded. I have examined the original as carefully as I could, and done my part as well as I was able.

enter

enter into your schools and difputations."
What Euripides' fays is pertinent:—

" That in which he is inferior, he avoids and
diflikes; the oppofite to this he praifes, thinking
this a proof of his complacency." I think it beft
to excel in both. The purfuit of philofophy, as
an accomplifhment of youth, is becoming, nor is
fuch a ftudy by any means difhonourable for a
young man. But when an older perfon perfifts
in fuch a purfuit, it is indeed, Socrates, a ridiculous thing. I feel the fame towards them who
philofophize as towards them who trifle and play;
and when I fee a young man in whom it is yet
becoming, fo trifling and playing, I am pleafed;
it feems to me graceful and liberal, and fuitable
to youthful age. If I hear a youth fpeaking too
readily, it is difagreeable to me, and wounds my
ears, and it feems to me as more proper for a
flave. But if any one hears a man trifling, or
fees him playing, it feems ridiculous, unmanly,
and worthy of ftripes. Juft fo do I feel about
thofe who philofophize. When I fee philofophy
in a young man, I am pleafed, it feems proper,
and I think it the mark of ingenuoufnefs. He
who does not ftudy philofophy, cannot be inge-

* *Euripides.*]—Thefe lines are among the fragments of
the Antiope, and I have ufed the verfion of Mr. Wodhull.
Every thing relating to thefe fragments is fo amply difcuffed
by Valcnaer, in his Diatribe in Euripidis perditorum dra-
matum reliquias, that it would be impertinent in me to do
more than refer the reader to that learned and ingenious
differtation.

huous, nor will he ever do any amiable or generous action. But when I fee an older perfon fo employed, and not about to defift, fuch a man, O Socrates! feems to me worthy of ftripes: for as I now faid, it happens to fuch a one, though naturally good, that he becomes unmanly, avoiding the bufinefs of the city and forum, in which the poet fays men become moft eminent. If he hide himfelf during life, whifpering in a corner with three or four young men, he will never accomplifh any thing liberal, great, or becoming. But for you, O Socrates! I have friendfhip and refpect; I rifk therefore that to happen to me with refpect to you, which happened to Zetho with refpect to Amphion, in the lines from Euripides juft quoted; for I have been induced to fay to you precifely what he faid to his brother—that you neglect, Socrates, what moft deferves your care, and that you injure your excellent talents by attention to childifh things; nor can you introduce any thing pertinent in the public courts, nor do you felect what is meritorious and becoming, nor can you give judicious counfel to others. Be not, my dear Socrates, offended with me, I will addrefs you with all mildnefs; does it not feem to be difgraceful to you to be efteemed, as I efteem you and all others whom philofophy allures? Now if any one fhould feize you, or one like you, and throw you into prifon, faying you had committed a crime, although you really had not, you could not vindicate yourfelf, but

*

would

would hefitate, and be perplexed, not knowing
what to fay: and being brought to trial, having
a vile and profligate accufer, you would fuffer
even death, if he fhould fo think proper. And is
this wifdom, O Socrates! if any purfuit, occupying
a man naturally ingenuous, makes him worfe,
fo that he can neither help himfelf nor fave himfelf, nor any one elfe, from the greateft dangers,
but muft fuffer every extremity from his enemies ?
He muft live unhonoured by his citizens. Such
a man, I almoft blufh to ufe the expreffion, we
may with impunity fmite upon the cheek.
Therefore, my friend, be perfuaded, and leave
off thefe trifles. Purfue things more honourable,
and from which you may appear to be really
wife. Leave to others thefe empty things, or, as
you may perhaps call them, infanities, ‘ which
make your houfes empty.’ Imitate not them
who follow thefe puerilities, but thofe who really
know how to live, who have glory and other
good things.

Plato [*] has fpoken thefe fentiments from the
mouth of one, as I faid before, of no great eftimation,

---

[*] *Plato.*]—The following fragment of Epicrates, as
preferved in Athenæus, is a pertinent illuftration of this
paffage. I copy the tranflation from Mr. Cumberland's Obferver:

A.   I pray you, Sir,
What are your wife philofophers engag'd in,
Your Plato, Menedemus, and Speufippus?

What

mation, yet with the repute of common fenfe and common underftanding, and with an inclination to fpeak the plain truth. For he does not defcant upon that fpecies of philofophy, which is the teacher of all virtues; which ftands foremoft in the difcharge of all public and private duties; which, if not prevented, regulates with firmnefs, fortitude, and wifdom, the government of the ftate. But he fpeaks of that futile and childifh attention to trifles, which conduces nothing to the guidance and regulation of life; in which people of that defcription (whom the vulgar confider as philofophers, and whom he confidered as fuch who delivered thefe cenfures) grow old in idlenefs.

> What mighty myfteries have they in projection?
> What new difcoveries may the world expect
> From their profound refearches?
>
> B.   Sir, you fhall know—at our great feftival
> I was myfelf their hearer—I muft fpeak
> Of things perchance furpaffing your belief,
> For ten moft fage academicians fat
> In folemn confultation on a cabbage.
>
> A.   A cabbage! what did they difcover there?
>
> B.   Oh Sir, your cabbage has its fex and gender,
> Its provinces, prerogatives, and ranks,
> And, nicely handled, breeds as many queftions
> As it does maggots.

See alfo the Nubes of Ariftophanes.

CHAP. XXIII.

A paſſage from an oration of Marcus Cato, on the ancient mode of life, and manners of women. That the huſband had power to put his wife to death, if taken in adultery.

THE writers on the food and dreſs of the Romans, inform us, that the women of Rome and Latium lived abſtemiouſly; that is, they abſtained from wine [1], which in the old language was called *temetum*. It was appointed by law, that they ſhould kiſs their relations, that it might be diſcovered by their breath whether

---

[1] *From wine.*]—The Greeks, though they did not poſitively forbid their women the uſe of wine, puniſhed any exceſs of this kind with extreme ſeverity. The teſtimonies of the fact here mentioned occur perpetually in the old Roman writers. Their idea was, that the uſe of wine excited amorous propenſities. Pliny ſays, "Non licebat vinum fœminis Romanis bibere, invenimus inter exempla Egnatii Mezennii uxorem, quod vinum bibiſſet a dolio interfectam furte a marito, eumque cædis a Romulo abſolutum." Many ſimilar paſſages might be eaſily collected.

Plato, in his Republic, forbids young men to drink wine till they are eighteen years old: they were not to get drunk till they were forty; after that period, they were to do as they pleaſed.

they had been drinking. But they relate that the women were accuftomed to drink the fecond brewing, raifin wine [a], fweet myrrhine, and other palatable liquors of that fort. And thefe things are publifhed in the books I mentioned. But Marcus Cato fays, that women were not only cenfured, but fined, if they had been drinking wine, with as much feverity as if they had com-mitted adultery. I have put down the words

[a] *Raifin wine.*]—Paffus in the original. Columella has particularly defcribed the making of this in his 12th book, chap. 39.—See Virg. Georg. ii. 53.

Et paffo Pfythia utilior.

Arnobius, in his tract adverfus Gentes, reproaching the Ro-mans for changing their manner of life, fays,

" Matres familias veftræ in atriis operantur domorum in-duftriàs teftificantes fuas? potionibus abftinent vini ?"

Bayle, at the article Lycurgus, tells us, that though there was no law in France to prohibit women the ufe of wine, in earlier times they were feldom known to drink any thing but water. A phyfician of Paris, who publifhed a book in 1696, fays, " Who would have thought that women would have added tobacco and brandy to fo many other vices they have gloried in for above thirty years paft ? They carry, as yet, but runlets of brandy at their fide: who knows but in time they will carry barrels ?" Ovid recommends a chearful glafs to the ladies :

Aptius eft deceatque magis potare puellas
Cum Venefis puero non male Bacche facis.

It is certain however, that the Roman wives were not allow-ed to keep the key of the wine-cellar.—See Cafaubon ad Athenæum, 725.

I

from

from Marcus Cato's oration (de Dote) in which it is also said, that husbands had a right to kill their wives when taken in adultery[s]. " A husband (says he) when he puts away his wife, judges his own cause as a censor, and has, it seems, entire controul in the matter. If she has committed any perverse or disgraceful act, she is fined: if she has drank wine, or contaminated herself by intercourse with another man, she is condemned: but upon the right of putting her to death, it is thus expressed: If you shall have caught your wife in adultery, you may kill her without any legal process; but she (should you be guilty of the crime) must not presume to touch you with her finger; the law does not permit it."

[s] *In adultery.*]—The punishment of adultery has been different in various times and nations; but, as a people have become more luxurious and corrupt, this punishment has become progressively less severe, till it has not only passed without public censure, but appeared with unabashed effrontery in all ranks of society.

Bayle, on the authority of Socrates Scholastius, mentions a punishment of adultery, so extremely preposterous, as to be reconciled to no principle of decency or common sense.

CHAP.

C H A P. XXIV.

They who spoke with elegance, used the words, die pristini, die crastini, die quarti, die quinti, *not as they speak them now* [1].

*D*IE *quarto* and *die quinto* (on the fourth and fifth day) which the Greeks exprefs by εις τεταρτην η εις πεμπτην, are words now in ufe among the learned, and he who fpeaks otherwife, is defpifed as unpolifhed and illiterate. But in Tully's time, and before that period, they did not, I think, ufe that phrafe. They faid *die quintè*, and *die quintì*, ufing it as a copulative adverb, the fecond fyllable being made fhort. Auguftus, who was well verfed in Latin, and an imitator of his father's elegance in converfation, has in that manner frequently diftinguifhed

[1] The fubftance of this chapter is to be found in the Saturnalia of Macrobius, l. i. The ftyle of Auguftus is fpoken of by Suetonius in terms of great refpect.

" Genus eloquendi fecutus eft elegans et temperatum: vitatis fententiarum ineptiis, atque incorcinnitate et reconditorum verborum, ut ipfe loquebatur fantoribus. Præcipuamque curam duxit fenfum animi quam apertiffime exprimere." Gellius in another place praifes the pure and fimple ftyle of Auguftus; and fo alfo do Tacitus and Quintilian.

in

in his Epiftles, the days he meant to point out.
But it will be the means of fhewing the ufual
cuftom of the ancients, if we put down the
formal words of the prætor, in which, according to eftablifhed cuftom, he proclaims the celebration of the feftival called the Compitalia[z].
The words are thefe: " *Die noni* (nine days
hence) the Compitalia will be holden in the affembly of the Roman people : when they fhall
have been begun, law bufinefs ceafes."   Here
the prætor fays, *die noni*, not *die nono*; and not
only the prætor, but almoft all antiquity fpoke
in the fame manner.   For I remember in Pom-
ponianus, a verfe from the farce[a] which is called
Mævia.

> Dies hic fextus, cum nihil egi, die
> Quarte moriar fame.

[z] *Compitalia*.]—Thefe feftivals were celebrated on the
fecond of May, to the Lares, in the public ways, at which
time anciently boys were faid to have been facrificed.—See
a long account of this feftival in Macrobius, l. i. Sat. vi. 16.
    See alfo Ovid. Fafti. l. v.

> Servat uterque domum domino quoque fidus uterque
>   Compita grata deo, compita grata cani,
> Exagitant et Lar et turba Diania fures
>   Pervigilantque Lares, pervigilantque canes.

[a] *Farce*.]—Atellana. Atellanus or Attellanus, was an epithet applied to a kind of farce which had its origin at
Attellanæ, a place in Campania.—See Juvenal, Sat. vi. 71.

> Urbicus exodio rifum movet Attellanæ
> Geftibus Autonoes.

Six days without a jot of work I've paft,
Four more,—and hungry I muft breathe my
   laft.

That paffage in Cœlius likewife furnifhes an inftance of it; in the fecond book of his hiftory—
" If you chufe to give me the cavalry, and follow
me yourfelf with the army, I will take care that
fupper fhall be prepared for you *(die quinti)*
five days hence, in the capitol at Rome." But
the ftory itfelf, and the words of it, Cœlius has
taken from Marcus Cato, where it is thus related :
" Therefore the mafter of the horfe thus advifed
the dictator of the Carthaginians, Send the cavalry with me to Rome, and five days hence
your fupper fhall be dreffed in the capitol."
But the laft fyllable of that compound, I find,
terminated either by the letter *e* or *i*, which
cuftom of ufing them indifferently was frequent
among the ancients, as in the words *præfefcine*
and *præfefcini, proclivi* (downwards) and *proclivè*;
and many others of the fame nature, they ufed
with various terminations. *Die priftini* (the day
before) was alfo applied, which fignified *die
priftino*, or *die priore*, which we commonly exprefs by *pridie*, changing the order of the compound, and deriving it as it were from *priftino
die*. By a fimilar procefs, *die craftini* (to-mor-
row) was ufed from *die craftino*. So the priefts
of the Roman people, when they fay, *in diem
tertium* (for three days) exprefs themfelves by
                                             die

die perendini; but as many people say, *die priſtini*,
ſo Marcus Cato in his ſpeech againſt Furius, has
ſaid, *die proximi* (next day). And Cnæus Matius, a very learned man, in his Mimiambi, has
uſed *die quarto*, inſtead of what we call *nudius-
quartus* (four days ago) in the following lines.

Nuper *die quarto* ut recordor, et certè
Aquarium urceum unicum domi fregit.

Four days ago—I have it in my book,
The only pitcher in my houſe he broke.

There only will remain this diſtinction, that we
ſay *die quarto*, ſpeaking of time paſt; *die quarti*,
or *die quartè*, of the future.

CHAP. XXV.

*The names of certain weapons, darts, and swords;
and the different sorts of ships mentioned in the
old books [1].*

WHILE we are sitting at ease in the carriage, in order to prevent one's mind
from being possessed by other trifling matters,
we may as well make some enquiry into the
names of the weapons, darts, and swords, which
are mentioned in the ancient books; as also into
the different kinds and appellations of the ships.
Those which occur are as follows: the spear,
the javelin, pikes, half-pikes, iron-crows, Gallic
darts, the lance, spears, rumigestri, torches, barbed
javelins, staves, missile spears, slings, Thracian
swords, the engine for flinging darts, scibones,
broad - headed javelins, short - swords, rapiers,
daggers, hangers, spades, wedges, ponyards, small
ladders. Of the wedge (lingula) since the use
of it is not very common, it is necessary to

[1] A long dissertation, or indeed a book, might be written
on the subject of this chapter. It will be sufficient, perhaps,
to refer the reader at once to Vegetius, and the other old
military writers. The vessels mentioned at the conclusion
are all enumerated and explained in Potter's Grecian Antiquities.

observe,

pbferve, that the ancients fo called an oblong fmall fword, made in the form of a tongue, of which Nævius makes mention in his Tragedy of Hefion. Thefe are his words;

> "Sine mihi gerere morem videar, linguâ verum lingulâ."

And the long fword (rhomphæa)[2] is a fpecies of weapon belonging to the Thracian nation, and its name occurs in the twenty-fourth of the Annals of Ennius. All the names of fhips we could call to mind are thefe; the gallies, merchantmen, ftore-fhips, long-veffels, tranfports, long-prows, pinnaces, or as the Greeks call them, κελητες, barques, frigates, rowing-veffels, light barges, which the Greeks call ιστυοποι, or επακτριδες, ketches or fpy-boats, or fifhing fmacks, cattæ, fkiffs, ferry-boats, nuctuciæ, mediæ, yachts, galliots, long-galliots, fcullers, capulices, fair-weather fhips, the cidarum, lighters, cruizers.

[2] *Rhomphæa.*]—Many of thefe words are written differently in different editions of Gellius, as *rumpia* for rhumphæa, *fibones* for fcibones, &c.

Chap. XXVI.

Salluſt was unwiſely cenſured by Aſinius Pollio, for ſaying tranſgreſſum *for* tranfretationem, *&c.* [1]

SALLUST has unjuſtly incurred the cenſure of Aſinius Pollio, in one of his letters addreſſed to Plancus, and indeed of others, becauſe. in the firſt book of his hiſtory he has called the act of tranſporting, and carrying over the ſea, *tranſgreſſum*, and the perſons carried over, which in our uſual phraſe is *transfretaſſe*, he. has called *tranſgreſſos.* Theſe are Salluſt's words: " Sertorius having left a ſmall guard in Mauritania, and taking the advantage of a dark night, was compelled, with a proſperous wind and great ſpeed, to avoid an engagement, by carrying his troops over the ſea." He afterwards

[1] The beginning of this chapter is different in different editions. H. Stephens has taken ſome pains to prove that it ſhould be read thus :—" Aſinio Pollioni in quadam epiſtola quam ad Plancum ſcripſit, et quibuſdam aliis C. Salluſtius iniquis dignum nota viſum eſt quod, &c."

As to the matter of the chapter itſelf, the reader has probably by this time diſcovered, that however agreeable the work of Gellius may be as a book of miſcellaneous entertainment, he certainly was himſelf no very. acute critic. What he alledges here is reaſonable enough.

ſays,

says, " *Tranfgreffos* omnis recipit mons receptus a Lufitanis." This (fay they) is fpoken improperly, and with the authority of no good author. For *tranfgreffus* and *ingreffus* are derived from *tranfgrediendo*, and that from *pedum gradu* (the ftepping of the feet). Pollio therefore thought that *tranfgreffus* was ill applied to thofe who fly, or creep, or fail, and that it fuited only thofe who walk, and meafure the ground with their footfteps. Therefore they deny, that in any good author *tranfgreffum* can be found, applied to fhips, or ufed to fignify the tranfporting of troops. But I afk, why, as they properly fay *curfus*[2] (the courfe) of a fhip, they may not likewife fay *tranfgreffus*, more efpecially when the narrownefs of that arm of the fea which flows between Spain and Africa is defcribed by a word[3] moft elegantly expreffive, of paffing over as it were the fpace of a few fteps. But let thofe who want an authority for it, and affirm, that *ingredi* and *tranfgredi* are not applied to failing, tell wherein the word *ingredi* differs from *ambulare*, (to walk). But Marcus Cato, in his book upon

---

[2] *Curfus.*]—Both the Greek and Latin writers of the beft authority ufed *currus* for a fhip. See Catullus:

Volitantem per mare *currum.*

See alfo the expreffion in Virgil, of ædificant naves. In Englifh alfo, we ufe the feemingly inaccurate expreffion, " I am fhipwrecked in my fortune, for I am in misfortune."

[3] *Word.*]—Fretum, now called the Straights, or the Straights of Gibraltar.

Agriculture,

Agriculture, says, " That a farm is to be chosen in such a situation, as to have a large town near it, and the sea, or at least a river where ships *(ambulant)* walk." Moreover, Lucretius bears testimony, that words taken from their literal sense are sometimes ornaments of speech. For in his fourth book, he speaks of the voice *(gradientem)* travelling through the arteries and the jaws. Which is somewhat more strong than what Sallust says of ships. Lucretius's [4] verses are these :

> All sound is body, for with painful force
> It moves the sense, when with an eager course
> It scrapes the jaws, and makes the speaker
> hoarse.

Besides, Sallust in the same book not only calls those who went in ships *progressus*, but also sailing skiffs. His words, as applied to the skiffs, I have subjoined : " Some of them making but little way, from being overweighted and unequally loaded, while fear agitated the persons in them, were sunk."

---

[4] *Lucretius.*]—The reference in Gronovius is wrong. The passage is in book iv. l. 532. We have an expression in English of a similar kind—" The noise grates my ears."

CHAP.

Chap. XXVII.

Account of the Roman and Carthaginian people.—
They were rivals of nearly equal strength [1].

IT is recorded in books of antiquity, that the
ſtrength, the ſpirit, and the numbers of the
Romans and Carthaginians were equal. Nor
was this opinion without foundation. For with
other nations the ſubjeƈt of diſpute was a ſingle
ſtate; but, with the Carthaginians, it was for the
empire of the world. A proof of this is exhibited in the ſpeech of each people, when Quintus
Fabius, the Roman general, delivered a letter
to the Carthaginians, in which it was declared,
that the Roman people had ſent them a ſpear
and a herald's ſtaff—two tokens, the one of war,
the other of peace—that they might chooſe which-
ever they pleaſed, and underſtand that as particularly ſent them, which they might think proper to accept. The Carthaginians anſwered, that
they would chooſe neither; that they who brought

[1] This ſubjeƈt is familiar to every ſchool-boy, and requires no elaborate diſcuſſion. The anecdote told in this
chapter, is a memorable inſtance of national ſpirit, and is recorded by Livy, book xxviii. c. 8. and by Florus, book ii.
c. 6, 7.

them

them might leave which they pleafed; and they would confider what the Romans left, as chofen by themfelves. Marcus Varro, however, fays, not that a fpear itfelf, or the ftaff itfelf, were fent, but two dice [2], upon one of which was engraven a ftaff, on the other a fpear.

[2] *Dice.*]—The teffera was a fmall tablet of wood, and ufed among the Romans for various purpofes. It was the foldier's watch-fignal; there was alfo (which feems here to be what is underftood) the teffera of hofpitality: this was a tally cut in two, whereof each party kept one. See a curious tract de Tefferis Hofpitalitatis, by Thomafinus. In the Medea of Euripides, Jafon, when about to fend Medea away, tells her he will give her a fymbol or teffera of recommendation to his friends.

Ὡς ετοιμος αφθονω δωναι χερι
Ξενοις τε πεμπειν συμβολ' οι δρασωσι σ'ευ.

Mr. Wodhull has not fufficiently marked the force of this in his tranflation.

> For with a liberal hand am I inclin'd
> My bounties to confer, and hence difpatch
> Such tokens as to hofpitable kindnefs
> Will recommend you.

To which Medea anfwers:

Ουτ αν ξεινοισι τοισι σοιο χρησαιμεθ' αν.

I will not ufe thofe with whom you are connected by the ties of hofpitality: that is, literally, Jafon fays, I will give you tefferæ hofpitalitis to my friends: No, fays Medea, I will not take them, nor be indebted to your friends.

CHAP. XXVIII.

On the distinctions of age—childhood, youth, and old age—taken from Tubero's history.

TUBERO, in his first book of history, has written, that Servius Tullius, king of Rome, when he divided the people into five classes [1], in order to number the young men, called those who were under seventeen years of age boys; from their seventeenth year, when they were deemed proper for service, he enrolled them soldiers; till forty-six, young men [2]; and be-

[1] *Five classes.*]—On this subject, of the classes into which the Roman people were divided, see Gellius again, l. vii. 13. The Romans were sometimes said to be divided into six classes; but the sixth class was called capiti censi, that is, reckoned only by their numbers, and considered as having no property; so that the general estimation reckoned five classes only. See Arnobius, p. 91.

" Numquid enim quinque in classes habetis populum distributum, vestri olim ut habuere majores.

[2] *Young men.*]—The expression of juvenis or junior, among the Romans, was certainly indefinable, and meant no more than those who were able to undergo a certain degree of labour or fatigue. Thus in our own language, it is certain, that in its primitive meaning yeoman signified a young man; and we know in how lax a sense it is now understood.

yond

yond that time elders. I have noted this, that the diftinctions which our forefathers obferved, might be known, between childhood, youth, and old age, according to the eftimate of that fagacious king, Servius Tullius.

CHAP. XXIX.

That the particle atque *is not only conjunctive, but has likewife a diverfity of fignifications.*

THE particle *atque* is called by the grammarians a copulative conjunction; and often indeed it unites and connects words. But fometimes it has other powers, not fufficiently obferved, except by perfons engaged in the diligent and attentive examination of ancient learning. For it has the power of an adverb, when we fay, " I acted otherwife *(atque)* than you." If it be repeated, it ftrengthens and increafes the fignification; as we find in the Annals of Quintus Ennius, unlefs my memory fails in the citation of the verfe:

Atque atque accedit muros Romana juventus.

It was likewife ufed by the ancients for the word *deque,* which has an oppofite fignification, and
moreover,

moreover for *ſtatim*, another adverb. As in theſe
verſes of Virgil, where that particle is thought
obſcure, and not properly introduced.

    ——Sic omnia fatis [a]
In pejus ruere ac retro ſublapſa referri
Non aliter quam qui adverſo vix flumine
    lembùm
Remigiis ſubigit, ſi brachia forte remiſit.
Atque illum in præceps prono rapit alveus
    amni.

[a] *Sic omnia fatis.*]—Theſe lines occur Georg. i. l. 199.
Thus tranſlated by Dryden:

    Thus all below, whether by nature's curſe
    Or fate's decree, degenerate ſtill to worſe;
    So the boat's brawny crew the current ſtem,
    And ſlow advancing ſtruggle with the ſtream;
    But if they ſlack their hands, or ceaſe to ſtrive,
    Then down the flood with headlong haſte they drive.

Dryden here has overlooked the force of *atque*, which
Martyn has not: he tranſlates the laſt line, " Immediately
the tide drives him headlong down the river."

    The expreſſion of " retro ſublapſa referri" is found alſo
in the ſecond Æneid.

    Ex illo fluere ac retro ſublapſa referri
    Spes Danaum.

BOOK XI.

Chap. I.

On the origin of the word Italy. *Of that fine which is called* ſuprema; *its meaning—the Aterian law —and in what terms the ſmalleſt fine uſed to be impoſed.*

TIMÆUS, in the Roman Hiſtory which he compoſed in Greek, and Varro in his Antiquities, agree in deriving Italy[1] from a Greek word, becauſe in the old Greek language oxen were called Ιταλοι, of which there were great numbers in Italy; and horned cattle in vaſt abundance were bred and paſtured in that country. Thence we may conjecture, that as Italy was ſo abundant in cattle[2], therefore the

fine

---

[1] *Italy.*]—It is certain that Heſychius has Ιταλος in the ſenſe of an ox; yet Heyne agrees rather with thoſe who derive the name of the country from Italus, one of its kings, according to Iſidorus. Bochart's derivation of it from a Phœnician word ſignifying pitch, has not obtained much currency, nor does it ſeem to deſerve it.

[2] *Abundant in cattle.*]—Armentoſiſſima. The indefatiga-

ble

fine was impofed which is called *fuprema*, of producing on particular days' two fheep and thirty oxen; which was levied in that proportion from the plentiful breed of oxen, and the fcarcity of fheep. But when that fort of fine which confifted of fheep and oxen was impofed by the magiftrates, fome of fmall and fome of greater values were produced, which made the payment of the penalty unequal. Wherefore, by the Aterian law, the value of the fheep was fixed at ten pieces of brafs, that of the oxen at an hundred: but the fmalleft fine impofed, is that of one fheep; the greateft, that of which we have fpoken. Beyond which, it was not lawful to fix any fine to be paid for one offence; and therefore it is called *(fuprema)* the laft, that is, the chief and greateft. When therefore this laft fine is now impofed, according to the manner of our anceftors, by the Roman magiftrates, it is ufually obferved, that the word *oves*, fheep, is

ble Barthius fpeaks highly of the advantage of making a gloffary of words ufed by each particular writer of any diftinction. He himfelf, with refpect to Gellius, has completed a gloffary of peculiar words beginning with *a*: Armentofiffima is among thefe; and the reader will find them all in his Adverfaria, p. 397.

• ⁹ *Particular days.*]—In fingulos: it is fometimes read 'in fingulos dies,' but I am inclined to think both readings wrong, and wifh to adopt what is propofed by Hotomannus, in his ufeful tract de Re Nummaria. He thinks it fhould be read 'in res fingulas,' which was a legal term for each offence.

T 2

ufed

ufed in the mafculine gender. So Marcus Varro has mentioned the legal terms by which the fmalleft fine was impofed. " Since, though called upon by Marcus Terentius, he has neither anfwered, nor excufed himfelf, I fentence him to pay a fine of one fheep." Unlefs this form was obferved, the fine was not deemed legal. This word *multa*, Marcus Varro, in his 19th book of Antiquities, fays is not a Latin but a Sabine word; and that in his memory, it was in ufe in the language of the Samnites, who came from the Sabines [*], But the upftart tribe of grammarians have affirmed, that this word, like many others, is fpoken (κατ' αντιφρασιν) by oppofi-tion.

But as our manner of fpeaking, and that which many of the ancients made ufe of, is *multam dixit*, and *multa dicta eft*, I have thought it not amifs to take notice that Marcus Cato has fpoken otherwife; for in his fourth book de Originibus, are thefe words: " Our general, if any one engages in battle, out of his rank, (*ei multam facit*) impofes a fine upon him. But he may appear, for the fake of elegance, to have avoided the word (*dicit*) fince the fine was levied ·in the

---

* *From the Sabines.*]—See Strabo, book v. " The Sabines are\the moft ancient nation, and from thefe the Samnites derive their origin. The Samnites were by the Greeks called Ζαυνιται." See Euftathius ad Dionyfium, and Pliny.

camp and the army, not proclaimed *(diceretur)* in the affembly, nor prefence of the people.

Chap. II.

That the word elegance, *among the ancients, was not applied to thofe diftinguifhed by their underftanding, but to thofe who were attentive to drefs and luxury, and was confidered as difgraceful.*

A MAN formerly was not called elegant, as a term of commendation; but till the time of Marcus Cato, that word was a reproach, and not a compliment. This we may obferve in other writers, as well as in that book of Cato, which is entitled, " Carmen de Moribus," wherein are thefe words: " They thought avarice included all vices; but the expenfive man, and who ever was thought ambitious, *elegant,* vicious, or foolifh, he was commended." From which it is plain, a man was not called by the ancients *elegant,* with reference to his genius[1],

but

---

[1] *To his genius.*]—We find that the term *elegans verborum* was applied by way of diftinction to Salluft, whilft Terence was called *compofitum atque elegans.* With us it is ufed invariably in a good fenfe; but it does not feem to have been a favourite expreffion with our older writers: I

do

but from a too frivolous attention to drefs and outward appearance. Afterwards, it ceafed to be a term of cenfure; but he was not thought worthy of commendation, whofe elegance was not very moderate. So Marcus Tullius pays a compliment to Lucius Craffus and Quintus Scævola, not for their elegance only, but their œconomy mixed with it. " Craffus (fays he) was the moft œconomical of *elegant* men, and Scævola the moft *elegant* of the œconomical." And in the fame book of Cato, we find it here and there mentioned. " It was cuftomary (fays he) to be dreffed handfomely in public, and plainly at home. They purchafed horfes at a dearer rate than cooks. Poetry was in no efteem [*]; and if any one addicted himfelf to the ftudy

do not remember to have met with it in Shakfpeare, and I know but of one place where it occurs in Milton. Milton ufes it in its claffical fenfe of correctnefs—

> Eve, now I fee thou art exact of tafte,
> And elegant.

[*] *In no efteem.*]—The fate of poets feems to have been much the fame in all ages—their productions honoured, and themfelves neglected. The maxim of Charles the IXth feems to have prevailed in every age: " Equi et poetæ alendi non faginandi." Though Otway, Chatterton, and fome others, would have been glad if even this cold comfort had been granted them. It is certain, that in the time of the republic, poets were held in no eftimation at Rome; they wandered from houfe to houfe, finging the praifes of thofe who would give them a dinner. When

Fulvius

study of it, or frequented entertainments, he was called a glutton." And in the same book, is that celebrated sentence of truth, " Human life is much like iron—if you use it, it is worn away, if you use it not, rust consumes it. So we see men worn away by exercising themselves, while sluggishness and torpor, without exercise, is yet more detrimental."

Fulvius went on some expedition as consul into Ætolia, he was abused for his effeminacy, in taking Ennius the poet in his suite. Plato, a very wise man, has in some part of his works, this remark: No one in his senses will knock at the door of the Muses.

CHAP. III.

Various usages of the particle pro, *with examples.*[x]

WHEN I find leisure from law causes, and business, and for the sake of exer-cife I walk or ride, I am accustomed to turn over in my mind matters trifling and of small consequence, and which appear despicable to the unlearned, which however are necessary to the clear understanding of antiquity, and particularly to the knowledge of the Latin language. As it happened lately in the retirement of Præneste, walking by myself in the evening, I considered of the various usages in the Latin language of certain particles, as for instance in the preposition *pro.* For at one time I observed they say, " that the priests have passed a decree *(pro collegio)* according to the power of their order;" at an-other, " a witness was brought in *(pro testimonio)* to give evidence." Marcus Cato one while writes, as in the fourth book of his Origins, that

[x] I believe it will be enough, if at this chapter I translate the remark of Quintus ·Carolus :—" As for this chapter, reader, go to the dictionary-makers, who have curiously in-vestigated the signification of this particle, and no one can be ignorant of the elements.

the

the battle was engaged in and fought *(pro castris)* before the camp: and in his fifth, that all the cities and islands were considered *(pro Illyrio)* as belonging to Illyricum. Sometimes they say *(pro æde Castoris)* for the temple of Castor: sometimes *(pro rostris)* before the rostra, before the tribune's chair, before the assembly, and sometimes that the tribune of the people interceded *(pro potestate)* by virtue of his authority. Now I thought that whoever imagined these words to be altogether like each other, or of equal efficacy, or yet differing from each other in every particular, falls into an error. For I was of opinion, that the variety of their signification was to be traced from the same origin and fountain, though not to the same end; which he will easily understand, who will consider the matter attentively, and use himself to consult our old books, and records of any celebrity.

C H A P. IV.

In what manner Ennius imitated Euripides.

THERE are some verses in the Hecuba of Euripides, charming in their language, and remarkable for their conciseness. Hecuba is speaking to Ulysses:

Τοδ᾽ αξιωμα καν κακως λεγητο σου [1]
Πεισει λογος γαρ εκ Τ᾽ αδοξκντων ιων
Καν των δοκκντων αυτος κ τάυτον σθενει

These lines Quintus Ennius, in his translation of that tragedy, has very well imitated in an equal number of verses.

> Hæc tu, & si perversè doces, facilè Achivos
>   flexeris,
> Nam cum opulente [2] loquuntur pariter, atque
>   ignobiles,
> Eadem dicta eademque oratio æqua, non
>   æquè valet.

Ennius,

[1] These lines are thus translated by Wodhull:
> Although you weakly argue, with your rank
> Convince them; for the self-same speech, when utter'd
> By th' ignoble, and men well esteemed,
> Comes not with equal force.

For πιισιι in the second verse, many would read ιικα; the difference is not great.

[2] *Opulente.*]—Alciatus thinks that Ennius wrote *opinati,*
which

Ennius, as I said before, has well tranflated the paffage, though the word *ignobiles* but ill anfwers to αυτι αδοξϗντων, and *opulenti* to αυτι δοκϗντων. For neither are all who are ignoble difefteemed, nor are all who are rich efteemed.

which the verfe requires as well as the fenfe; in which cafe the cenfure of Gellius falls to the ground, for *opinati* means men in honour and eftimation, and correfponds exactly with δοκϗντων. Gellius himfelf has the expreffion of *opera-tiffimi auctores*, for authors of great eftimation.

CHAP. V.

Certain things lightly touched upon concerning the Pyrrhonian philofophers, and the Academics; with the difference between them.

THOSE whom we call Pyrrhonian[1] philofophers, by a Greek furname are termed Sceptics, which fignifies as it were enquirers, doubters;

[1] *Pyrrhonian.*]—Pyrrho, the founder of this fect, if that can properly be called a fect which rejected all principles, was born at Elea, of obfcure parents, and was bred originally to the profeffion of a painter, but forfook that art for philofophy. This he ftudied firft under Dryfo, fon of Stilpo, then under Anaxarchus, with whom he went to India, in

the

doubters; for they determine nothing, they fix nothing, but are always examining and considering the nature of that on which they might determine. And indeed they seem to themselves not to see or to hear any thing clearly, but to undergo a certain affection like seeing and hearing: and upon those very things which produce these affections, they are always deliberating and contemplating what sort of things they are. And the confidence and veracity of all things is, they say, such an incomprehensible mixture of truth and falsehood, that every man who is not precipitate and rash in his judgment, should use the words which they report from Pyrrho, the founder of their sect. " Has not

the army of Alexander. The scepticism of Pyrrho naturally enough arose from the atomic philosophy of Democritus, which he studied under Anaxarchus, and from the fallacies of logic, which he exercised under Dryso. The accounts of his exposing his life to danger continually, by walking straight forward in spite of all obstacles, as not believing that any thing he saw before him was real, are probably fictitious. When we observe the subtlety of Gellius's distinction between this sect and that of the Academics, we cannot wonder that they have been often confounded. It was to very different philosophers than those of Pyrrho's maze or Epicurus's stye that Milton applies these charming lines:

> How charming is divine philosophy!
> Not harsh and crabbed, as dull fools suppose,
> But musical as is Apollo's lute,
> And a perpetual feast of nectar'd sweets,
> Where no crude surfeit reigns.

the

the matter rather this meaning, or that meaning, or neither?" For they deny that proofs of any thing, or its real properties, can be known and perceived; and they endeavour to inculcate and prove this by many arguments. Upon which subject Favorinus has compofed, with much fubtlety and logic, ten books, which he entitles, " Pyrrhonian Modes." For it is an old queftion, which has often been difcuffed by the Greek writers, in what things, and to what degree the Pyrrhonians differed from the Academics. For both were called Sceptics, enquirers, hefitaters, who affirm nothing, and think nothing can be comprehended. But they call all objeés (φαν-τασιας) appearances, not as the nature of the objeéts is, but as the affeétion of the mind or body is in them, upon whom thofe objeéts ftrike. Therefore all thofe things which aét upon the fenfes of men, they call " των προς τι," things which have a reference to fomething elfe; which phrafe means, that it has nothing confifting in itfelf, no inherent and natural power. But that all things have a reference to fomething, and appear to be fuch as their image reprefents them; and as they are formed by our fenfes which they touch upon, and not by that nature whence they themfelves proceed. But the Pyr-rhonians and Academics think alike upon thefe fubjeéts; yet they are thought to differ upon certain others, and particularly, becaufe the Aca-demics as it were underftand that nothing can

ever

ever be underſtood, and as it were determine
that nothing can ever be determined; while the
Pyrrhonians affirm, that this by no means ſeems
true, becauſe nothing ſeems true.

CHAP. VI.

The Roman women did not ſwear by Hercules, nor
the men by Caſtor.

IN ancient writings, neither do the Roman
women ſwear by Hercules, nor the men by
Caſtor.   Why the former did not ſwear by Hercules [1] is plain, for they abſtained from ſacrificing

to

---

[1] *By Hercules.*]—See Propertius, iv. El. 10.

> Maxima quæ gregibus devota eſt ara repertis,
>   Ara per has inquit maxima facta manus;
> Hæc nullis unquam pateat veneranda puellis,
>   Herculis eximii ne ſit inulta ſitis.

The Romans obſerved many peculiarities with reſpect to
the worſhip of Hercules.   When they ſacrificed to Hercules,
they introduced the name of no other god, nor ſuffered
any dog to come within the incloſure.   The reaſon of this,
according to Plutarch, was, firſt, that he was but a half-god;
and next, that he hated a dog, on account of the trouble he
had with Cerberus.—From the ſame authority, we learn

that

to him; but why the men did not call upon Caftor in their oath, is not fo eafily explained. It is no where to be found amongft good authors, that a woman fays *("Mehercule")* by Hercules, or that a man fays *("Mecaftor")* by Caftor. But *("Ædepol")* which is fwearing by Pollux, is common to man and woman. But Marcus Varro affirmed, that more anciently the men fwore neither by Caftor nor Pollux, but that this oath was ufed only by women, and was taken from the initiation to the Eleufinian myfteries. By degrees, however, through inattention to an-

that there were two altars to Hercules, a greater and a lefs; and that the women were not allowed to tafte of what was offered on the greater.

The children of the Romans were forbidden to fwear by Hercules in the houfe, but they might go out of doors and do fo. Plutarch fays, in his Roman Queftions, that hiftory relates of Hercules, that he never fwore but one oath in his life. With refpect to what Gellius fays of Mecaftor, there are exceptions to this rule, in the laft act of the Afinaria of Plautus, where Antemena fays, " Hoc Ecaftor eft, quod ille it ad cænam cotidie."

Ecaftor and Mecaftor are perfectly equivalent, and were ufed indifferently. According to Voffius, whofe opinion feems the beft on this fubject; both *e* and *me* are jurative particles, adopted from the Greek *m* and *μα*, the *s* being dropped from the former. Thus we have, in the Phormio of Terence, act. ii. fc. 2. *Ecere*, according to the old gloffary, for *by Ceres. Ejuno* and *Equirine* are alfo found for *by Juno* and *by Quirinus; e de Pol*, is per deum Pollucem; *me dius Fidius*, per Jovis filium. There is alfo *Mehercule*, for *by Hercules.* They who derive *Ædepol* from per ædem Pollucis, of courfe write it with an *æ* in the firft fyllable.

tiquity,

tiquity, the men began to fay *("Ædepol")* and it became a cuftomary phrafe: but *Mecaftor*, fpoken by a man, is to be found in no old writing.

Chap. VII.

Old and obfolete words not to be ufed.

TO ufe words which are become fomewhat obfolete and worn out, feems equally a fault with ufing unaccuftomed terms of harfh and vulgar novelty: But it is, I think, more difagreeable and more offenfive, to ufe new, unknown, and unheard-of words, than thofe which are low and mean. By new, I mean thofe which are unufual, or laid afide, though in date they may be ancient. But this is frequently the fault of late inftruction, which the Greeks call οψιμα-θία [1]. What you have never learned, you will be

a long

---

[1] Οψιμαθία.]—Our author has very happily hit off the moft prevalent caufe of this affectation of obfolete words, which he characterifes under the title of οψιμαθία, or late-acquired learning. Theophraftus has a chapter on the fubject of οψιμαθια; but in his acceptation of the term, it means a late paffion for learning, and particularly a defire to learn fuch things as are fit only for an earlier age.

Galen, .

a long time learning; and when at laft you be-
gin to know it, you make it appear of vaft
moment, wherefoever and whenfoever you fpeak
of it. As it happened lately at Rome, when
I was prefent, an old man, in repute as a pleader,
but who had become learned in an irregular and
fudden manner, was fpeaking before the prætor,
and intended to tell him that a certain poor man
lived in a miferable manner, eat bread made of bran,
and drank vapid and filthy wine. " This Roman
knight (fays he) eats chaff *(apludam)*, and drinks
vinegar *(floces)*." All who were prefent looked one
at another, at firft with a difturbed and inquiring
countenance, anxious to know the meaning of
each word; afterwards, as if he had fpoken
fomething in the Tufcan or Gallic language, they
joined in a loud laugh. Now, this man had
read, that the ancient farmers called the bran
(apludam) which he met with in that play of

Galen, in his book de Agnitione Pulfuum, fpeaks of the
kind of opfimathy mentioned by Gellius, defcribing men
who introduce into medical differtations fuch matters as
they ought to have learned at fchool, with other liberal
knowledge. " According," fays he, " to the cuftom of
men who acquire knowledge late, and are unable to keep
it to themfelves, though quite foreign to the art they treat
of."

Cicero, jefting on himfelf as having late in life become
a follower of Epicurus, and requiring therefore to be well
fed, fays, " Οψιμαθεις autem homines fcis quam infolentes
fint."—You know how impertinent they are who pick up
their knowledge late in life. *Ep. ad Div.* ix. 20.

Plautus (if it be his) called the Aſtraba[z]. He had likewiſe read that floces (*vinegar*) in the old language, ſignified the dregs of wine, like the lees of oil. This he had picked up from Cæcilius in his " Merchants," and had preſerved the two words as ornaments of ſpeech. Another taſtelefs fellow[3] of this ſtamp, when his adverſary required that the cauſe ſhould be put off, " I intreat you (ſays he) prætor, aſſiſt me, ſuccour me, how long does this *bovinator*, ſhuffler, intend to delay me?" and then three or four times, with a loud voice, he bawled out the word *bovinator*. A whiſpering took place among ſome who were preſent, wondering at this monſter of a word. When he, exulting, as in triumph, cries, " Have you not read Lucilius, who calls a ſhuffling double-dealer, *bovinator?*" The verſe is in his ninth book.

[4] This ſhifting ſhuffler, with abuſive tongue.

[z] *Aſtraba.*]—Αϛραβη is Greek for Clitella; this comedy is therefore conſidered as the ſame with that callĕd in Latin Clitellaria, or the Packſaddle. Perhaps Aſtraba was the name of one of the Dramatis Perſonæ. Nonius Marcellus ſpeaks doubtfully as to the point, whether this comedy is to be attributed to Plautus or not. Feſtus cites the word *apluda* from Nævius————Per hercle *apluda* eſt hodie quam tu nequior.

[3] *Taſteleſs fellow.*]—In the original ' aperocalus.' In Greek απειροκαλια was nearly equivalent to οψιμαθια in its uſage. It deſcribed that want of proper conduĉt which Gellius attributes to late inſtruĉtion.

[4] Hic ſtrigoſus, *bovinatorque* ore improbus duro.

CHAP.

CHAP. VIII.

What Marcus Cato thought and said of Albinus, who though a Roman, composed a history of his own country in Greek, at the same time apologizing for his ignorance.

MARCUS CATO is said to have censured Aulus Albinus • with great justice, and elegance. Albinus, who was consul with Lucius Lucullus, wrote a Roman history in Greek. In the beginning of his history he has expressed this sentiment, " That no one can blame him, if he shall have written any thing in those books incorrectly, or without elegance ; for, (says he) I am a Roman, born in Latium, and

---

• *Albinus.*]—This Albinus is mentioned with respect by Cicero in his Brutus, where he is called literatus atque disertus. A jest also of his against Carneades is related in the Lucullus, c. 45. Macrobius also relates the same incident as from Cornelius Nepos; but the life of Cato by this writer is obviously imperfect.

This kind of apology, introduced by Albinus, is very common, and may be found in many, and those the best writers, ancient and modern. See the beginning of Apuleius—Macrobius, i. 1. See also the Apophthegms of Plutarch.

ʻ The same anecdote is related also by Plato, in his History of Cato Minor.

ʻ U 2

the

the Greek tongue is quite foreign to me." Therefore he fought indulgence and favour towards his errors. When Marcus Cato read this, " Surely (fays he) Aulus, thou art a trifler, fince thou would'ft rather apologize for a fault, than avoid it. It is ufual to afk pardon, either when we have erred through ignorance, or done wrong from compulfion. But I defire to know, who compelled thee to do that for which you afk pardon, before you commit the fault?" This is in Cornelius Nepos's book upon Illuftrious Men.

C H A P. IX.

Story of the ambaffadors of Miletus, and Demof-thenes the orator, taken from Critolaus.

CRITOLAUS[1] relates, that ambaffadors came from Miletus to Athens upon public bufinefs, perhaps to requeft affiftance. They engaged what lawyers they thought proper, to fpeak for them, who, as they were inftructed, addreffed the people in behalf of the Milefians. Demof-

---

[1] *Critolaus.*]—The age of this hiftorian is uncertain; he is mentioned once or twice by Plutarch. See Voffius de Hift. Græc. l. iii.

thenes

thenes replied with feverity to the demands of the
Milefians, and contended that they were unworthy of affiftance, nor was it the intereft of
the ftate to grant it. The matter was deferred
to the following day. The ambaffadors in the
mean time came to Demofthenes, and with great
earneftnefs intreated that he would not oppofe
them. He afked for money, and they gave him
what he demanded. On the day following,
when the bufinefs was again debated, Demofthenes came into public with his neck and jaws
wrapped up in woollen, complaining that he had
a quincy, and could not fpeak againft the Milefians. On this one of the people called out, that
Demofthenes was troubled with the filver-
quincy[2]. Demofthenes (fays Critolaus) did not
afterwards

[2] -*Silver-quincy.*]—Argyranche. If the reader does not
think me tedious, I fhall not lament taking a little trouble
to refcue a man of fuch eminence as Demofthenes from an
imputation which probably had no foundation.

The fame reproach againft Demofthenes is related by
Plutarch, in his life of that orator, but with circumftances
perfectly different. His narrative is this, " It was not
long after this, when Harpalus quitted the fervice of Alexander, and fled out of Afia to Athens, he was confcious to
himfelf of many lewd practices occafioned by his luxury,
and feared the king, who was now grown terrible even to
his beft friends; yet this man had no fooner addreffed himfelf to the people, and delivered up his goods, his fhips, and
himfelf to their difpofal, but the other orators of the town
had their eyes quickly fixed on his money, and came in to
his affiftance, perfuading the Athenians to receive and pro-

tect

afterwards conceal the matter, but confidered it as a matter of triumph. For, having afked Ariftodemus the player, how much he received

for

tect their fuppliant. But Demofthenes at firft gave advice to chafe him out of the country, and to · beware left they involved their city in a war, upon fo unneceffary and unjuft an occafion. Yet fome few days after, as they were taking an account of the treafure, Harpalus, perceiving how much he was pleafed with the king's cup, and how curioufly he furveyed the fculpture and fafhion of it, he defired him to poife it in his hand, and confider the weight of the gold. Demofthenes being amazed to feel how heavy it was, afked him what price it would come for ? " To you, fir," faid Harpalus, " it fhall come with twenty talents;" and prefently after, when night drew on, he fent him the cup with fo many talents. This Harpalus, it feems, was a perfon of good fkill to difcern a man's covetoufnefs, by the air in his countenance, and from the pleafant caft of his eyes to difcern his nature.. For in fhort, Demofthenes could not refift the temptation, but receiving the prefent like a garrifon into his houfe, he was overcome, and wholly furrendered himfelf up to the intereft of Harpalus. The next day he came into the affembly, with his neck fwathed about with wool and rollers, and when they called on him to rife and fpeak, he made figns as if he had loft his voice. But the wits, turning the matter to ridicule, faid, that certainly the orator had not been feized that night with a fimple but a filver fquincy."

I have ufed the tranflation of Dryden, which is however in many places very inaccurate, and affords a ftrong proof of the carelefs and imperfect manner in which that job was performed. The pun upon αξι in particular is totally loft. Demofthenes afked ποσον αγιι, how much does

it

for acting, he answered, a talent. I (says Demosthenes) have had more for holding my tongue.

it weigh or bring? Harpalus answered, αξιι σοι εικοσι ταλαντα, it shall bring to you twenty talents.

In refutation of the above, I must now beg leave to insert the following translation from the second book of Paufanias, which carries with it every internal mark of authenticity and truth. " Demosthenes, in his old age, was compelled not only to go into exile, but to kill himself. Many things have been related of him by others, and asserted by himself, importing that of the riches which Harpalus brought out of Asia, Demosthenes received nothing. What was afterwards said, I shall here relate. Harpalus, flying from Athens, went with some ships to Crete, where, after a short time, he was murdered by some of his domestics. Some say he was by some artifice put to death by Paufanias, a man of Macedon. Philoxenes the Macedonian seized his treasurer when flying to Rhodes; and the same person had also required of the Athenians to deliver up Harpalus to him. When in possession of this man's person, he made rigorous enquiry concerning all who had received money of Harpalus; whom when he knew he sent letters to Athens. In these, he not only mentioned by name those who had taken any bribes, but the particular sum which each individual had received: but he made no mention of Demosthenes, although the orator was very obnoxious to Alexander, and although Philoxenes himself personally hated him.—Honours are paid to Demosthenes, both in other parts of Greece, and particularly by the inhabitants of Calaurea."

Erasmus, who hunted for proverbs wherever he could find them, has the phrase of Argentanginam pati, which he explains and exemplifies from the above story of Demosthenes, as given by Plutarch.

U 4

CHAP.

CHAP. X.

Caius Gracchus fixes the above story upon Demades and not Demosthenes. C. Gracchus's words quoted.

THE story which in the foregoing chapter we said was told by Critolaus of Demosthenes, Caius Gracchus, in his speech against the Aufeian law, has related of Demades [1], in these words:

[1] *Demades.*]—The story which is in this chapter related of Demades, is much more likely to be true of him than of Demosthenes. Demades was as remarkable for his avarice and extortion, as for his want of integrity. Plutarch relates, in the life of Phocion, that Antipater used to say, he had two friends at Athens, Phocion and Demades, on one of whom he could never prevail to accept any thing, to the other he could never give enough. Phocion gloried in his poverty, which he preserved to the hour of his death, though so often in command for Athens, and in friendship with many sovereigns; but Demades was proud of his wealth, even though dishonestly obtained. There was a law at Athens, that for every foreign dancer on the stage, the Choragus should pay a thousand drachmas. Demades exhibited a hundred foreign dancers on the stage, and at the same time paid down the fine of a thousand drachmas for each. When he celebrated the nuptials of his son Demeas, he said, ' When I married your mother, my next door neighbour

words : " For you, O Romans ! if you would be wife and virtuous, will find, if you enquire, that no one of us comes forward into public without being paid for it ; that all who addrefs you, have fome requeft to make ; nor does any one come before you for any other purpofe, than that he may carry fomething away. I myfelf, who am now fpeaking to recommend to you an increafe of your taxes, that you may be able to anfwer your own exigencies, and thofe of the ftate, do not deliver my fentiments without reward. What I feek of you is not money, but honour, and your good opinion. The orators who diffuade you from accepting this law, do not want your honours, but the money of Nicomedes. And they who perfuade you to accept it, they too do not look for your good opinion, but for the friend-fhip and the purfe of Mithridates ; whilft they who fit upon the fame feat, and are filent, they

bour hardly perceived the celebration of our nuptials, but the expences of your marriage are paid by kings and potentates.' He propofed at Athens, that Alexander fhould be the thirteenth of the great gods. He was fined for his impiety ; but he told the Athenians to take care, that in their fcrupulous anxiety about the heavens, they did not lofe the earth. In his account of this anecdote, at the article Olympias, Bayle with great acutenefs detects Erafmus of a material error, in not properly underftanding the words of Demades.

The Athenians afterwards deified Alexander, decreeing him the honours of Bacchus. ' Pray,' faid Diogenes, ' deify me too, and make me Serapis.'

are your bittereft enemies, for they receive a bribe from all parties, and are faithful to none. While you confider fuch people as not engaged in thefe matters, you compliment them with your efteem: but the ambaffadors' of princes, when they fuppofe orators hold their peace in compliment to them, are very lavifh in their gifts. As in Greece, when a tragedian boafted that he had received a whole talent for one night's acting, Demades, the moft eloquent man in the ftate, is reported to have anfwered, ' You feem to think it wonderful, that you have gained a talent by fpeaking. Now, I received ten talents from the king for being filent.' So too do thefe receive the greateft price for holding their peace."

CHAP.

Chap. XI.

The words of Publius Nigidius, in which he says there is a difference between lying and telling a lye. [1]

THESE are the words of Publius Nigidius, a man of great eminence in polite literature, and for whom Marcus Cicero had the highest respect, on account of his genius and accomplishments. " There is a difference between telling a lye, and lying. He who lies is not deceived himself, but attempts to deceive another: he who tells a lye, is himself deceived."

[1] These distinctions of Nigidius are little better than quibbles: *mentiri* and *mendacium dicere* do not necessarily differ in Latin, more than *to lye,* and *to tell a lye* in English; but it is evident, that a man may possibly tell or repeat a lye, either knowing it to be such, or not knowing it. In the former case, if he endeavours to make it pass for truth, he himself lyes; in the latter, he is only deceived. Polybius puts the thing much more plainly and sensibly. He says, " There are two ways of speaking falsely, either through ignorance, or by choice; the former is pardonable, the latter not." Apuleius, in his vindication of himself against the charge of magic, makes the same distinction betwixt the words *mentiri* and *falli* as Nigidius does betwixt *mentiri* and *mendacium dicere.*

He

He adds likewife, " He who lyes, deceives, as far as he is himfelf concerned ; but he who tells a lye, does not deceive as far as he is concerned." He moreover fays, " It behoves a good man to take care not to lye, and a wife one not to tell a lye." The former falls upon the man himfelf, the other does not. Diftinctly, in truth, and neatly, has Nigidius feparated his examinations of this fubject, in fuch a manner as to make them appear two different things.

CHAP. XII.

Chryfippus the philofopher fays, that every word is ambiguous and doubtful. Diodorus thinks, on the other hand, that no word is fo.

CHRYSIPPUS[1] affirms, that every word is by nature ambiguous, becaufe two or more interpretations may be given of it. But Diodorus,

---

[1] *Chryfippus.*]—Chryfippus, according to Diogenes Laertius, wrote two books upon ambiguous expreffions, and addreffed them to Apollas or Apellas. Quintilian alludes to the fame affertion of this philofopher, where he fays, ' There are fo many fpecies of amphibology, or dubious expreffion,

Diodorus, furnamed Cronus, fays, that no word is ambiguous, nor does any one fpeak a word or receive it in two fenfes; nor ought it to feem as if fpoken in any other fenfe than that which the fpeaker intends to give it. For (fays he) when I fpeak a word in one fenfe, and you receive it in another, it muft be rather fpoken obfcurely than

preffion, that, according to fome philofophers, there is no word that has not more than one meaning."

The diftinction of Diodorus Cronus, in oppofition to this, feems to contain only a refinement of no great ufe or importance. This Diodorus is alfo frequently quoted by Sextus Empiricus, but there feems to be a doubt whether the name of Cronus properly belongs to Diodorus. See Meibomius ad Diog. Laert. vol. ii. p. 126.

The name of Cronus occurs in an epigram of Callimachus, where he is called a wife man. Ο Κρονος εστι σοφος. A fingular anecdote is told of him by Diogenes Laertius, that being at the court of Ptolemy, and unable to anfwer fome ænigmatical queftion from Stilpo, he died of grief. An epitaph, or rather epigram, exifts, which I hope to be excufed for inferting.

Κρονε Διοδωρε τις σε δαιμονων κακη
   Αθυμια ξυνειρυσιν,
Ιν' αυτος αυτον εμβαλης εις ταρταρον
   Στιλπωνος ου λυσας επη
Αινιγματωδη; τοι γαρ ευρεθης Κρονος
   Εξωθεν τε ρω καππατι.

Literally thus :—" Cronus Diodorus, what deity could fo deprive you of your fenfes, as to induce you to put an end to your life, becaufe you could not folve the riddles of Stilpo? you will therefore appear to be really Κρονος, taking away the κ and the ρ."—— Anglicè, *an afs*, ονος being Greek for an afs.

ambiguoufly.

ambiguously. The nature of an ambiguous word should be, that he who speaks should seem to say two or more things; but no man says two or more things, that means to say but one.

CHAP. XIII.

What Titus Castricius thought of the words and the sentiments of Caius Gracchus, not allowing any dignity to what he said.

A SPEECH of Caius Gracchus, against Publius Popilius, was read before Titus Castricius, a teacher of rhetoric, and a man of strong and solid judgment. In the beginning of that speech, the words were arranged with more studied attention, and more harmony, than is usual in the orators of antiquity. The words I speak of are these: " The things which for years you have been anxiously* aiming at, and wishing for, if you

now

---

* *Anxiously.*]—We cannot easily find a more judicious criticism than this of Castricius. The words *cupidè* and *temere*, in the former part of the sentence, absolutely destroy its effect, and reduce it almost to nonsense. Whereas, without them, it is strong and well-constructed.

H. Stephens is of the same opinion, and thinks that the

words

now rashly throw aside, it cannot fail but you must either be said to have desired without judgment, or to have rejected without consideration."

The rhythm and sound of this flowing sentence particularly pleased us, and so much the more, as we perceived, even in those days, such sort of composition was studied by Caius Gracchus, a man of eminence and gravity. But when these words were often read over to us, who called for a repetition of them, we were advised by Castricius to consider wherein consisted the force of the sentence, and what we gained [2] by it, and not to allow our ears to be so gratified by the flowing measures of an elegant sentence, as to overpower our judgment. When by this admonition he had made us more attentive, " Examine," says, he, " what after all, these words avail; and let any of you say, whether there be any weight or elegance in this sentence: ' The things which for years you have been anxiously

words *cupide* and *temere* are either misplaced, or that there is some corruption in the passage.

There is certainly a kind of tautology in the sentence, not unlike the one adduced by Quintus Carolus, from Plautus, to exemplify the passage.

Cui homini dii sunt propitii, ei non esse iratus pute. The gods cannot be displeased and angry with those to whom they are propitious.

[2] *What we gained.*]—*Emolumenti* in the original.—H. Stephens proposes to read *momenti*. Some editions read *monumentum.* See H. Stephens, 161.

aiming

aiming at and wishing for, if you now rashly throw aside, it cannot fail but you must either be said to have desired without judgment, or to have rejected without consideration.' For who is not aware that it is usual *(ut quod cupidè appetieris cupidè appetisse)* to desire earnestly that which you earnestly desire, and to throw aside with rashness, that which you rashly throw aside? But, according to my opinion, the sentence was thus written: ' What you have sought and wished for these many years, if you now reject, you cannot but be said either to have sought too anxiously, or to have rejected too rashly.' If it were so spoken, the sentence would surely be more weighty and more solid, and would satisfy the expectation of the hearer. But at present, the words *anxiously* and *rashly,* upon which the whole weight of the sentence hangs, are not only placed in the end of the sentence, but appear before they are wanted in the beginning; and that which ought to arise from the subject, is spoken before the subject calls for it. For he who says, ' If you do this, you will be said to have done it with too much anxiety,' speaks what is completed with some regard to sense; but he who says, ' If you do this anxiously, you will be said to have done it anxiously,' says no more than, if you do it anxiously, you do it anxiously. I have warned you (says he) of these matters, not that I might cast a censure upon Caius Gracchus (for the gods have blessed me with a

better

better difpofition; and indeed, if any error could
be pointed out in a man of fuch powerful eloquence, the authority of his name, and the antiquity of his writing, has now done it away); but I
cautioned you to be on your guard, left the
modulated rhythm of any flowing fentence fhould
too eafily miflead you; and that you might firft
balance the weight of the fentiments with that of
the words; and if any fentence was fpoken
weighty, complete and entire, then, if you thought
proper, you fhould applaud it, in all its parts, with
the loudeft praife: but, if a meaning, cold,
trifling, and futile, be conveyed in words accurately and harmoniously arranged, you would
fuppofe it to be, as if men remarkable for their
deformity fhould come forward as players, to delight you with their buffoonery,"

CHAP. XIV.

The wise and elegant answer of King Romulus, upon the use of wine.

LUCIUS PISO FRUGI[1] has expressed himself with the greatest simplicity and sweetness, as to the sentiments and the words, in his first book of Annals, when speaking of Romulus's mode of life. His words are these: " They relate of Romulus, that being invited to supper, he drank but little wine ; because, on the day following, he was to be engaged in business. They say to him, Romulus, if all men were like you, wine would be cheaper. Rather, replied he, it would be dear, if every man were to do as I have done, drink as much as he chose."

[1] *L. Piso Frugi.*]—See book vi. chap. 9.

This author is mentioned by Cicero in his Brutus, but not in terms of very high respect.

Romulus, in abstaining from wine on account of business, seems to have been of the same opinion as Leotychidas, king of Sparta, who being asked why the Spartans drank so little wine, replied, " Because we mean to consult on our own affairs ourselves, and not to have others consider them for us."

CHAP. XV.

Upon the words ludibundus, errabundus, *and the lengthening of words of that sort.—Laberius used* amorabunda *in the same manner.—Sisenna, by a word of this kind, formed a new figure.*[1]

LABERIUS, in his Lacus Avernus, using a word in a new sense, has called a woman in love, *amorabundam.* That word Cæsellius Vindex,

---

[1] Scaliger derives the termination *undus* from *unda*, and says that it implies the notion of magnitude, because the sea was always considered by the ancients as illustrative of greatness. He proceeds thus—

" Eorum autem materia talis est, ut quædam B. habeant alia C. *Populabundus, iracundus, rubicundus, verecundus:* quorum origo a futuro verborum ducta, significationem expressit perpetuationis; ut *populabundus* non solum qui *populatur,* sed etiam *populabitur.* Pauca ut præsens respexere, ut *iracundus* ab eo quod est irasci, exempto sibilo, quasi qui semper irascatur, *rubicundus* qui semper rubricet."

De Causis Ling. Lat. B. xiv. c. 98.
Much more on the subject of these derivative adjectives may be found in the same place. *Populabundus* is explained in the manner of Scaurus:—"In rebus autem voluntate præditis indicant etiam ostentationem sive professionem, atque etiam ut ita dicam satagentiam, nam quem admodum differt verbale a participio, ita a verbali genus hoc nominum. *Pugnare* potest quis atque erit *pugnans, pugnator*

    longo

dex, in his Commentary upon Old Words, fays, is formed by the fame procefs as *ludibunda, ridibunda,* and *errabunda,* from *ludens, ridens,* and *errans.* But Terentius Scaurus, a very diftinguifhed grammarian in the time of Adrian, among other remarks of his upon the errors of Cæfellius, has affirmed, that in this word alfo he is miftaken, inafmuch as he has fuppofed *ludens* to mean the fame as *ludibunda, errans* as *errabunda, ridens* as *ridibunda.* Whereas *ludibunda* means one (quæ *ludentem* agit aut fimulat) who pretends to be fportive; fo of *ridibunda* and *errabunda.* But why Scaurus was induced to çenfure Cæfellius for this, in truth we have not difcovered. For there is no doubt but the words have the fame fenfe originally with thofe from which they fpring. But the meaning of *ludentem agere,* or *imitari,* we would rather feem not to underftand than accufe him of ignorance. But it would have been more becoming of Scaurus, cenfuring the commentaries of Cæfellius, to have remarked what the other has omitted, in what and how much *ludens* differs from *ludibundus, ridens* from *ridibundus, errans* from *errabundus,* and the like: whether they differ but little from their originals, and what particular force the

longe alio modo idem fignificat, addit enim habitum fciendi pugnas. Sic *populans* et *populator,* at *populabundus* hoc apponit infuper, ut palam præ fe ferat animum ac fpiritum *populatoris.*" He explains *vitabundus,* in Salluft, in the fame manner.

concluding

concluding fyllables of the words communicate. For this would have been a more pertinent enquiry in examining this figure, as in the words *vinolentus, lutulentus, turbulentus*; whether the addition be without any ufeful meaning, as in the Greek figure *paragoge*; or whether the concluding particles have any appropriate fignification. In noticing this criticifm of Scaurus, it occurred to me that Sifenna, in his fourth book, has ufed the fame figure: " Laying wafte (*populabundus*) the fields, he came to the town;" which means, when he actually laid wafte the fields, not as Scaurus fays of fimilar words, when he imitated one laying wafte. But on my enquiry about the reafon and origin of this kind of figure, as in *populabundus, errabundus, lætabundus,* and *ludibundus,* and many other fimilar words, our Apollinaris ingenioufly obferved, that the final and additional fyllables of fuch words marked the force of abundance and excefs. As *lætabundus* is faid of one exceffively joyful, *errabundus* of one who is very widely miftaken; and of the reft, where a fimilar figure is ufed, that this final addition marks the force of excefs and abundance [2].

---

[2] The reafon is affigned in the beginning of the preceding note.

CHAP.

CHAP. XVI.

The translation of certain Greek words into Latin is very difficult, as that which is called in Greek πολυπραγμοσυνη.

WE frequently obferve the names of things which cannot be expreffed in Latin as they are in Greek, by fingle words. Nor, if we ufed ever fo many terms, would they be fo clear and accurate, as the Greeks have before made them in one. Lately, when a book of Plutarch was produced to us, and we read the title of it, which was "περι πολυπραγμοσυνης," a certain perfon, who was unlearned and ignorant of Greek, inquiring the title and fubject of the book, we inftantly told him the name of the writer; but when we came to fpeak of the fubject of the book, we hefitated. Then indeed firft, (becaufe I did not

---

* This has been interpreted, by the tranflator of this part of Plutarch's Morals, an over-bufy inquifitivenefs into things impertinent; in other words, an impertinent curiofity: A perfon of this character was called in Latin ardelio. See Martial, lib. ii. ep. 7. and lib. iv. ep. 79.—

Vis dicare quid fis—magnus es ardelio.

Whoever has engaged in the bufinefs of tranflation from ancient authors, and from the Greek in particular, has frequently been impelled by neceffity to fubfcribe to the truth of what this chapter afferts.

think

think it a sufficiently apt interpretation to say that the book was written *de negotiositate*) I began to examine by myself the expression, as they say, word by word. But there was nothing which I remembered to have read, or that I was able to invent, which did not seem rough, absurd, and harsh; had I formed *multitudo* and *negotium* into one word, as we say *multijuga*, *multicoloria*, and *multiformia*. But it would found no less uncouth than if you were to translate in one word πολυφιλιαν, or πολυτροπιαν, or πολυμορφιαν. Wherefore, having remained silent for a short time in thought, I at length replied, that I did not think it could be expressed in one word, and therefore I had prepared to express the meaning of that Greek term by a compound phrase; " The engaging in many concerns, and undertaking to execute them all, is called in Greek, (said I) πολυπραγμοσυνη," concerning which, as the title tells, the book is written." Then, says this illiterate man, misled by my unfinished and incorrect terms; " So πολυπραγμοσυνη is a virtue; and this Plutarch, whoever he is, advises us, no doubt, to engage in business, and to take upon us as many concerns as possible; and properly enough he has written down in the title page the name of the virtue of which, as you say, he is about to speak in his book." " By no means," I replied, " for that is not considered as a virtue which is treated of in the book with a Greek name; nor does Plutarch do that which you suspect, or I

suppose

fuppofe I expreffed. For in this very book he diffuades us as much as poffible from the various, indecifive, and unneceffary thought and purfuit of too many concerns. But I conclude that your error is to be imputed," faid I, " to my imperfect expreffion, who was unable, without the greateft obfcurity, to fpeak that in many words which by the Greeks is faid in one, with the greateft neatnefs and perfpicuity."

C H A P. XVII.

The meaning of the phrafe " flumina retanda," found in the old prætorian edicts.

AS I was fitting by chance in the library of the temple of Trajan [1], and looking for fomething elfe, the Edicts of the Ancient Prætors fell into my hands, and I thought proper to read and look them over. In one of the oldeft edicts I found written, " If any one of thofe who have agreed with the public to fcour the rivers, fhall be brought before me on an information, that he has not done that which, by the condition

---

[1] *Trajan.*]—This was generally called the Ulpian Library. On the fubject of the Roman public libraries, I have before fpoken, in my notes to the fixth book, as well as in my obfervations on Herodotus.

of

of his agreement, he was bound to have done." Then we enquired the meaning of the word *retanda*. A friend who was sitting with me said, that he had read, in the seventh book of Gavius, on the Origin of Words, that those trees were called *retæ* which hung over the banks of rivers, or were found in their beds; and that they were so called *(a retibus)* from nets, because they impeded the progress of ships passing over them, and as it were netted or entangled them. Therefore he thought agreement was made to net, that is to cleanse, the rivers, that no delay or danger might happen to the vessels coming among the boughs of the trees.

C HAP.

CHAP. XVIII.

*The punishment which Draco the Athenian, in his
  Laws, inflicted upon thieves.—Those of Solon afterwards; those likewise of our Decemviri, who
  wrote the Twelve Tables, in which it appeared
  that among the Ægyptians thefts were allowed;
  among the Lacedæmonians encouraged, and commended as an useful exercise.—The memorable
  saying of Marcus Cato upon the punishment of
  thefts.*

THE Athenian Draco was held in great es-
teem; and considered as a man of consum-
mate wisdom. He was skilled in laws, human
and divine. This Draco was the first who made
laws for the use of the Athenians. In these he
decreed, and determined, that a delinquent taken
in a theft of any kind should be punished with
death; to this he added other laws, much too
severe. His decrees, therefore, being too sanguinary [1], passed into disuse, not by any open act or
ordinance, but by the tacit and unwritten con-

---

[1] *Too sanguinary.*]—Plutarch, in his Life of Solon, informs us, that Demades the orator used to say that Draco wrote his laws not with ink but blood. Plutarch says
also, that it was said of Lycurgus that he dipped his pen in
death.

sent

fent of the Athenians. They afterwards ufed milder laws, as inftituted by Solon, who was one of the feven illuftrious wife men. He thought proper by his law to punifh thieves (not as Draco had done, with death) but by a fine of double the value of the thing ftolen. But our Decemvirs, who, after the expulfion of kings, compofed laws in Twelve Tables for the ufe of the Roman people, neither punifhed with the fame feverity every fpecies of theft, nor ufed a lenity which was too remifs; for they permitted a thief taken in the fact to be put to death, if he either committed the depredation in the night, or if, when taken, he defended himfelf with any weapon. But other thieves taken in the fact, if free, were fentenced to be fcourged, and bound to the fervice of the plundered perfon, provided they committed the fact by day-light, and made no defence with weapons; if flaves, taken in the fact, they were to be fcourged, and thrown from the rock; if boys under age, they were to be punifhed at the difcretion of the Prætor, and their difgrace to be thus removed; and thofe thefts which were detected with a girdle and a mafk [2] were

punifhed

---

* *Girdle and a mafk.*]—The Athenians, from whom this was borrowed, had a cuftom of fearching for ftolen goods with no cloaths, except a girdle round the waift, and a mafk on the face. See Ariftoph. Nub. ver. 458.

The reafon of the mafk is thus explained by Feftus, at the word *lanx.*

" Lance

punifhed as if openly perpetrated. But we now depart in our practice from the obfervance of the Decemviral law; for if any one is willing to try a caufe upon an open theft, the action is brought for four times the value. But that, fays Maffurius, is an open theft which is difcovered in the fact; and the act is complete when the thing is conveyed away, the robbery of which was attempted. For the receipt of ftolen goods the penalty is threefold. But he who is defirous to underftand the meaning of the terms *conceptum*[3] and *oblatum*, and many other things of the fame nature, handed down from the admirable cuftoms of our anceftors, ufeful and agreeable to be known, may find them in a book of Sabinus, entitled, " Of Thefts," in which is told a circumftance, not commonly imagined, that not only men and moveables which may be felonioufly carried off, but eftates and houfes, may be the fubjects of theft; and that a farmer was convicted of theft in having fold a farm which he rented, and driven its owner from his poffeffion. Sabi-

" Lance et licio dicebatur apud antiquos, quia qui furtum ibat quærere in domo aliena licio cinctus intrabat, lancemque ante oculos tenebat, propter matrum familiæ aut virginum præfentiam."

[3] *Conceptum.*]—When the goods fought after in the manner defcribed in the preceding note, it was called *furtum conceptum*. *Furtum oblatum* was the offering of ftolen goods for fale. This fubject will be found explained at fome length by Heineccius, p. 549. &c.

nus further adds, what is ftill more extraordinary, that a perfon was condemned as having ftolen a man, who, when a flave was paffing within fight of his mafter, by holding out his robe, as if in the act of dreffing himfelf, he prevented the mafter from difcovering his fervant's flight. Upon all other depredations, which are not called open ones, they impofed a fine of twice the value. I remember to have read, in the books of Arifton, a lawyer of no inconfiderable learning, that amongft the ancient Ægyptians (a race of men evidently ingenious in their inventions, and wife in the purfuit of natural philofophy), all thefts were allowed [4] by the law, and were unpunifhed. With refpect to the Lacedæmonians, a prudent and active people, (the evidence of which is nearer to us than what is told of the Ægyptians) many eminent writers upon their cuftoms and laws affirm, that theft was frequent, and allowed

[4] *Thefts were allowed.*]—See Diodorus Siculus, l. i. c. 80. The law of the Ægyptians concerning thieves is fingular enough, it orders thofe who choofe to follow this profeffion, to enroll their names with the regulator of thefts (προς τον αρχιφωρα) and immediately to carry what they purloin to him. In like manner they who have loft any thing, leave with this perfon the defcription of each particular, with the day and hour when they loft it. Thus every thing may eafily be difcovered, and a fort of tax is levied, every one being permitted to have his property again, on paying a fourth part of its value. For, fince theft cannot be entirely prevented, the legiflator has found a method that the whole of what is loft may be regained, at the expence of a part of it.

by

by law, and that they did this from their youth, not for the fake of bafe profit, or providing money for the purpofes of luxury, or amaffing wealth, but to exercife and difcipline them in the art of war; becaufe the dexterity and practice of thieving fharpened and ftrengthened the minds of young men, fitting them for the contrivances of ambufcade, the toils of watchfulnefs, and the quicknefs of furprize. But Marcus Cato, in his fpeech on the divifion of fpoil among the foldiers, complains of their unpunifhed peculation and licentioufnefs, in ftrong and elegant terms. As the paffage pleafed me very much, I have fubjoined it:—" Thofe," fays he, " who are guilty of private depredations, pafs their life in confinement and fetters, while public plunderers are clad in gold and purple." But the pure and accurate definition given by wife men of " a theft" muft not, I think, be paffed over; left he alone fhould be thought a thief, who privately fteals, and, in a fecret manner, conveys any thing away. The words are thofe of Sabinus, in his fecond book of Civil Law: " He is guilty of theft who lays his hands upon any thing belonging to another, when he ought to know that he touches it contrary to the will of its owner." Alfo in another chapter, " Who filently takes away another's property for the fake of gain, is guilty of theft, whether he knows or is ignorant of its owner." Thus Sabinus, in the book above cited, has written concerning " things handled, in order to be ftolen."

But

But we ought to remember, according to what I have before said, that a theft may exist without any thing being touched, the mind alone, and the intention, consenting to it. Wherefore Sabinus says, he doubts not but the master may be convicted of theft who orders his servant [5] to commit felony.

[5] *Orders his servant.*]—The maxim of " qui facit per alium facit per se," makes a complete condemnation of a master who commands a slave to do any unlawful act.

B O O K XII.

C H A P. I.[1]

*Differtation of the philofopher Favorinus, in which
he perfuaded a lady of rank to fuckle her child
herfelf, and not to employ nurfes.*

WORD was brought once to Favorinus the
philofopher, when I was with him, that
the wife of one of his difciples was brought
to-bed,

[1] This will doubtlefs be thought by every reader an
entertaining and interefting chapter; and after making
due allowance for the variations of language and of manners, the precepts which it contains and communicates may
properly enough be recommended to the females of our age
and country. It is, I fear, but too true that many mothers,
from principles of perfonal vanity, or an exceffive love of
diffipation and pleafure, forego the delightful fatisfaction of
nurfing their children at their own breafts, left the employment fhould injure their beauty, or interfere with occupa-
tions comparatively contemptible. On the other hand, the
poor infants, who are thus removed from the tendernefs to
which they have fo powerful a claim, frequently fall the victims, often of neglect, and fometimes of cruelty. This remark does not apply to the higher ranks of life alone,

for

to-bed, and a fon added to the family of his pupil. " Let us go," fays he, " to fee the woman, and congratulate the father." He was a fenator, and of a noble family. We, all who were prefent, followed him to the houfe, and entered with him. Then, at his firft entrance, embracing and congratulating the father, he fat down, and enquired whether the labour had been long and painful. When he was informed that the young woman, overcome with fatigue, was gone to fleep, he began to converfe more at large. " I have no doubt," fays he, " but fhe will fuckle her fon herfelf." But when the mother of the lady faid, that fhe muft fpare her daughter, and find nurfes * for the child, that to the pains

of

for it is obferved, that the number of infants of all conditions, who perifh from the prevailing cuftom of putting out children to nurfe, is almoft incredible. I am alfo given to underftand by thofe whofe judgments in matters of this kind are fuperior to my own, that the females who refufe to fuckle their children, from the idea that the employment will be injurious to their beauty, frequently deceive themfelves ; that from the circumftance of unnaturally repelling the milk, cancers, tumours, afthmas, and a long train of dangerous and dreadful maladies, frequently enfue.

* *Find nurfes.*]—It is certain, that both among the Greeks and Romans, the fuckling of children was a fervile office. Among the Romans, Greek women were preferred for this purpofe. See Tacitus in Dial. de Caufis Cor. Eloq.

" At nunc natus infans, delegatur Græcula; alieni ancillæ cui adjungitur unus aut alter ex omnibus fervis, plerumque viliffimus."

of child-birth might not be added the toilſome and difficult taſk of ſuckling the child; " I entreat you, madam," ſaid he, " allow her to be the ſole and entire mother of her own ſon. For how unnatural a thing is it, how imperfect and half-ſort of motherly office, to bring forth a child, and inſtantly to ſend him from her; to nouriſh in her womb, with her own blood, ſomething which ſhe has never ſeen, and not with her own milk to ſupport that offspring which ſhe now ſees endued with life and human faculties, and imploring the tender care of a mother. And do you ſuppoſe," he continued, " that nature has given boſoms to women only to heighten their beauty, and more for the ſake of ornament, than to nouriſh their children. For on this account (which be it far from you) many unnatural women endeavour to dry up and extinguiſh that ſacred fountain of the body, and nouriſhment of man, with great hazard turning and corrupting the channel of their milk, leſt it ſhould render the diſtinctions of their beauty leſs attractive. They do this with the ſame infenſibility as thoſe who endeavour by the uſe

As ſoon as an infant is born, he is given to the care of ſome Greek female, to whom is joined one or more of the very meaneſt of the ſlaves.

Somebody once reproached a free-born Athenian woman, that ſhe had taken a child to nurſe for hire; ſhe exculpated herſelf by ſaying, that it was in time of war, when the Athenians had loſt much of their property, and it was not an eaſy thing for citizens to ſupport their dignity. The anecdote is ſomewhere in Demoſthenes.

of quack medicines to deftroy their conceptions [3], left they fhould injure their perfons and their fhapes. Since the deftruction of a human being in its firft formation, while he is in the act of receiving animation, and yet under the hands of his artificer, nature, is deferving of public deteftation and abhorrence; how much more fo muft it be to deprive a child of its proper, its accuftomed and congenial nutriment, when now perfect and produced to the world. But it is of no confequence, it is faid, provided it be nourifhed and kept alive, by whofe milk it is. Why does not he who affirms this, if he be fo ignorant of the proceffes of nature, fuppofe likewife that it is of no confequence from what body or from what blood an human being is formed and put together ? Is not that blood, which is now in the breafts, and has become white by much fpirit and warmth, the fame as that which was in the womb ? But is not the wifdom of nature evident

[3] *Deftroy conceptions.*]—The cuftom of procuring abortion I underftand to be very prevalent in oriental countries, and wherever polygamy is allowed. When a favourite fultana proves with child, fhe incurs great rifk of being fupplanted in the affections of her mafter, and has therefore recourfe to the abominable means of counteracting nature. See in particular Ruffel's Hiftory of Aleppo.

A fentence which follows I have not tranflated : " Ne æquor illud ventris irrugetur." Ovid has an expreffion altogether fimilar,—

>Scilicet, ut careat rugarum crimine venter,
>Sternetur pugnæ triftis arena tuæ.

Y 2

alfo

alſo in this inſtance, that as ſoon as the blood, which is the artificer, has formed the human body within its penetralia, it riſes into the upper parts, and is ready to cheriſh the firſt particles of life and light, ſupplying known and familiar food to the new-born infants ? Wherefore it is not without reaſon believed, that as the power and quality of the ſeed avail to form likeneſſes of the body and mind, in the ſame degree alſo the nature and properties of the milk avail toward effecting the ſame purpoſe. Nor is this confined to the human race, but is obſerved alſo in beaſts. For if kids are brought up by the milk of ſheep, or lambs with that of goats, it is plain, by experience, that in the former is produced a harſher ſort of wool, in the latter a ſofter ſpecies of hair. So in trees, and in corn, their ſtrength and vigour is great in proportion to the quality of the moiſture and ſoil which nouriſh them, rather than of the ſeed which is put into the ground. Thus you often ſee a ſtrong and flouriſhing tree, when tranſplanted, die away, from the inferior quality of the ſoil. What, I would aſk, can be the reaſon then that you ſhould corrupt the dignity of a new-born human being, formed in body and mind from principles of diſtinguiſhed excellence, by the foreign and degenerate nouriſhment of another's milk ? particularly if ſhe whom you hire for the purpoſe of ſupplying the milk be a ſlave, or of a ſervile condition, or, as it often happens, of a foreign and barbarous nation, or if ſhe be

diſhoneſt,

difhoneft, or ugly, or unchafte, or drunken; for often, without hefitation, any one is hired who happens to have milk when wanted. And fhall we then fuffer this our infant to be polluted with pernicious contagion, and to inhale into its body and mind a fpirit drawn from a body and mind of the worft nature? This, no doubt, is the caufe of what we fo often wonder at, that the children of chafte women turn out neither in body or mind like their parents. Wifely and with fkill has our poet Virgil fpoken in imitation of thefe lines in Homer,—

> Sure Peleus [*] ne'er begat a fon like thee,
> Nor Thetis gave thee birth: the azure fea
> Produc'd thee, or the flinty rocks alone
> Were the fierce parents of fo fierce a fon.

He charges him not only upon the circumftance of his birth, but his fubfequent education, which he has called fierce and favage. Virgil, to the Homeric defcription, has added thefe words:

> And fierce Hyrcanian tygers gave thee fuck.

Undoubtedly, in forming the manners, the nature of the milk takes, in a great meafure, the difpofition of the perfon who fupplies it, and then

---

[*] *Sure Peleus.*]—Thefe are the words of Phœnix, reproaching Achilles for his ftern and implacable temper. Iliad xvi. v. 33.

The quotation from Virgil is in the fourth Æneid, v. 367. See the note of Taubmannus at this paffage, p. 589. and the parallel chapter of Macrobius, l. v. c. 11.

Y 3

forms

forms from the feed of the father, and the person and fpirit of the mother, its infant offspring. And befides all this, who can think it a matter to be treated with negligence and contempt, that while they defert their own offspring, driving it from themfelves, and committing it for nourifhment to the care of others, they cut off, or at leaft loofen and relax, that mental obligation, that tie of affection, by which nature binds parents to their children ? For when a child is removed from its mother, and given to a ftranger, the energy of maternal fondnefs by little and little is checked, and all the vehemence of impatient folicitude is put to filence. And it becomes much more eafy to forget a child which is put out to nurfe, than one of which death has deprived us. Moreover, the natural affection of a child, its fondnefs, its familiarity, is directed to that object [s] only from which it receives its nourifhment, and thence (as in infants expofed at their birth) the child has no knowledge of its mother, and no regret for the lofs of her. Having thus deftroyed the foundations of natural affection, however children thus brought up may feem to love their

---

[s] *Directed to that object.*]—The converfe of this may alfo be ufed as an argument, if any fuch were wanting, to induce mothers to undertake this important office. See Letters to Married Women.

" That the tafk itfelf is a pleafure, the fondnefs of nurfes towards children at tne breaft fully proves ; and that it is an indifpenfable duty, the feelings of human nature explain."

father

father or mother, that regard is in a great meafure not natural, but the refult of civil obligation and opinion." Thefe fentiments, which I heard Favorinus deliver in Greek, I have, as far as I could, related, for the fake of their common utility. But the elegancies, the copioufnefs, and the flow of his words, fcarcely any power of Roman eloquence could arrive at, leaft of all any which I poffefs.

CHAP.

Chap. II[*].

Annæus Seneca, in his judgment upon Ennius and Cicero, expressed himself in a trifling and futile manner.

SOME people consider Annæus Seneca as a writer of little value, whose works are not worth turning over, because his style is low and vulgar; his matter and his sentiments are expressed with a foolish and empty parade, or a trifling and affected pertness; while his learning is of the

[*] The censure which Gellius in this chapter passes upon Seneca, a man in most instances far superior to himself, will not easily be approved by men of learning. The works of Seneca undoubtedly contain much valuable and important matter. Quintilian has discussed the subject of his merit and talents at some length, and though in many respects he thinks him reprehensible, on the whole he allows him a degree of excellence, which the testimony and praise of succeeding ages has confirmed. His memory has also found an able and indefatigable vindicator in Lipsius. It is no little praise which Seneca deserves, when we consider, that in the most profligate and corrupt times of the Roman empire, and in the reign of a prince who considered every advocate of virtue as his own personal enemy, he dared to censure the vices, which debased his country, with equal dignity and justice. The story of Seneca's connection with Nero, and his fatal end, are subjects too notorious for discussion in this place.

common

common ftamp, neither borrowing from the
fources of antiquity, nor poffeffing any grace or
dignity of its own. Some, however, do not deny
him the praife of elegance in the choice of words,
and even allow that he is not deficient in the
knowledge of thofe fubjects of which he treats;
and that he has cenfured the vices of the
times with becoming gravity and folemnity. It
is not neceffary for me to pafs my opinion upon
every effort of his genius, or each of his writings, but we will examine the fentence he has
paffed upon M. Cicero, Q. Ennius, and P. Virgil. In the twenty-fecond book * of his Moral
Epiftles, addreffed to Lucilius, he fays, that
Quintus Ennius has written thefe foolifh verfes
concerning Cethegus, a man of antiquity:

—— dictus ollis popularibus olim,
Qui cum vivebant homines atque ævum agi-
　　tabant,
Flos delibatus populi et Suada medulla,

He then criticifes thefe lines thus: I wonder that
thofe illuftrious men, who were fo devoted to

* *Twenty-fecond book.*]—The works of Seneca are not now
divided into books; the part to which there is here an allufion is loft. The fragment of Ennius may be thus interpreted: " All his fellow citizens, who lived at that time,
agreed in calling him (Cethegus) the chofen flower of the
people, and the very marrow of eloquence." The expreffion
of Suada medulla occurs in Cicero. Suada was the goddefs
of eloquence, called by the Greeks Peitho.

Ennius,

Ennius, fhould have commended thefe ridiculous verfes, as the beft of that author's production. For Cicero quotes them as an example of good verfe. He then fays thus of Cicero: I no longer wonder that there are found thofe who will write fuch lines, fince there are not wanting thofe who commend them; unlefs perchance Cicero was pleading fome caufe, and wifhed to make them appear excellent. He then adds this very ftupid remark; even in the profe compofitions of Cicero there are paffages, from which you may difcover that he has read Ennius, not without fome profit. He alfo cites from Cicero, paffages which he blames, as being imitations of Ennius, as in his books de Republicâ, where he fays that Menelaus was endowed with a *fuavilo-quens jucunditas* [3]; and in another place, he obferves in fpeaking a *(breviloquentiam)* concife-

---

[3] *Jucunditas.*]—A fweet fpeaking pleafantnefs. Homer thus fpeaks of Menelaus:

When Atreus' fon harangued the lift'ning train,
Juft was his fenfe, and his expreffion plain;
His words fuccinct and full, without a fault;
He fpoke no more than juft the thing he ought.

It may not be impertinent to add what Cicero and Quintilian fay on this fubject.

Cicero.—Menelaum ipfum dulcem illum quidem tradit Homerus, fed pauca loquentem.

Quintilian.—Homerus brevem cum animi jucunditate et propriam, id enim eft non errare, verbis et carentem fupervacuis, eloquentiam Menelao dedit.

nefs.

nefs. Then this trifling man proceeds to apologize for the errors of Cicero, which, he fays, " was the fault, not of the author, but of the age. When it was thought worth while to read fuch verfes, it was neceffary to write fuch criticifms." He adds, that " Cicero inferted this, that he might efcape the cenfure of being too diffufe, and ftudious of terfenefs in his ftyle." In the fame book, he paffes this judgment upon Virgil. " 'Our poet Virgil too, from the fame reafon, has written fome harfh and irregular lines, of unufual length, that the popular tafte for Ennius might difcover fomething of antiquity in a modern poem." But I am weary of Seneca's remarks; yet I cannot omit thefe jokes of this foolifh, infipid, and ignorant man. " There are (fays he) fome fentiments in Ennius fo ftriking, that although written amongft the *(hircofos)* loweft vulgar, yet give delight amongft the *(unguentatos)* moft polifhed." And having cenfured the lines before quoted upon Cethegus, he fays, " the man who likes fuch verfes as thefe, may as well like the beds of Sotericus [4]."

Worthy, no doubt, muft Seneca appear of the perufal and attention of young men, who has

[4] *Sotericus.*]—This was probably fome rude artificer of fome celebrity in the lefs polifhed times of the republic In after times, the beds of the Romans were fumptuoufly decorated with gold and filver. The beds of Sotericus became a proverbial expreffion for any thing of mean and inelegant workmanfhip.

compared the dignity and beauty of ancient compofition to the beds of Sotericus, that is, as poffeffing no excellence, and as obfolete and contemptible. I fhall however, in this place record and relate a few things which this Seneca has written well. Such is that which he has faid of a mifer, one covetous, and as it were thirfting for money. "What does it fignify how much you have, there is ftill much more which you have not." This is very well indeed. But the tafte of young men is not fo much improved by good, as it is corrupted by bad writing. And fo much the more, if the bad far exceeds the good, and part of the former is not given merely as a comment upon fome fimple and unimportant matter, but is communicated as advice in fomething of a dubious nature.

CHAP. III.

Meaning and origin of the word Lictor; *different opinions of* Valgius Rufus, *and the freedman of* Tullius Cicero.

VALGIUS RUFUS, in his second book, intituled, " de Rebus per Epistolam quæsitis," says, the *lictor*[1] takes his name from *ligando*, because when the Roman magistrates ordered any one to be whipped with rods, his legs and hands were accustomed *(ligari)* to be bound by a beadle; and he whose office it was as beadle to bind the criminal, was called *Lictor.* He quotes likewise upon the subject the authority of Marcus Tullius, in his speech for Caius Rabirius. " *Lictor* (says he) bind his hands." Thus says Valgius, and I am indeed of his opinion. But Tiro Tullius, the freedman of Cicero, derives *lictor* from *(linum)* a rope, or *(licium)* a

---

[1] *Lictor.*]—Nonius Marcellus is of the same opinion.

 Lictoris proprietatem a ligando dictam putat vetustas,
 Ita enim antiquitus carnificis officium fungebatur. .

See also Festus:

 Lictores dicuntur quod fasces virgarum ligatos ferunt,
 Hi parentes magistratibus, delinquentibus plagas ingerunt.

thread,

thread. For (fays he) they who attended upon the magiftrates were girded with a twifted cord called a rope. Now, if any one thinks Tullius's opinion more probable, becaufe the firft fyllable in *lictor* as in *licium* is long, and in *ligo* fhort, that is of no confequence, for *lictor* comes from *ligando*, as *lector* from *legendo*, *victor* from *vincendo*, *tutor* from *tuendo*, *structor* from *ftruendo*, the vowels originally fhort being made long.

Chap. IV.

Lines from the feventh book of Ennius's Annals, in which the difpofition and conciliating conduct of an inferior toward a fuperior friend is defcribed and defined.

IN the feventh book of Ennius's Annals is de-fcribed with exactnefs and fkill, in the cha-racter of Geminus Servilius [1], a man of rank, the difpofition,

[1] *Geminus Servilius.*]—When Tullus Hoftilius, took and deftroyed Alba, he removed many of the more noble families to Rome, and placed them in the fenatorial order. Sufficient teftimony of this incident appears from Livy and Dionyfius Halicarnaffenfis. The Servilian family was among thefe, and always enjoyed the higheft reputation and dif-tinction.

difpofition, the complaifance, the modefty, the fidelity, the reftraint, and the propriety of fpeech; the knowledge of ancient and modern fcience; the ftrict obligation to preferve fecrecy, with the various remedies to diminifh the cares of life, by means of its relaxations and comforts, which ought to adorn him who profeffes himfelf the friend of one fuperior in rank to himfelf. Thofe verfes are, I think, no lefs worthy of frequent and attentive perufal, than the decrees of philofophers upon the duties of life. Befides, there is fuch a facred tafte of antiquity in his lines, fuch an unmixed fweetnefs, fo removed from all obfcurity, that in my opinion they are to be remembered and obferved as the ancient and confecrated laws of friendfhip. Wherefore I thought them worthy of being tranfcribed, if there be any one who has not feen them.

> Thus faying, on his faithful friend he called,
> A friend, with whom in free and open talk
> The table's focial joys he oft had fhar'd;
> With whom he many a lengthen'd day had
>   pafs'd,

tinction. The Servilius Geminus here mentioned was conful with Lucius Aurelius, and according to a paffage in the firft book of the Tufculan Queftions, chap. xxxvii. he fignalized himfelf at the battle of Cannæ.

The verfes quoted in this chapter are certainly corrupt. Turnebus has taken fome trouble to explain them, and has in part fucceeded. See his Adverfaria, p. 620.

On

On ſerious or on trifling ſchemes, in council
    deep;
On legal topics, ſenatorial power,
On high exploits, or gayer lighter themes,
Still ſpeaking each his thought, approv'd or
    not,
There lurk'd no baſe deſigns with miſchief
    fraught;
But virtue, learning, mildneſs, eloquence,
Contentment, knowledge, and a happy mind,
Still prompting wiſe advice, reſtraining ſtill
The flippancy of ſpeech, with antique lore
Well grac'd, nor leſs with modern wiſdom
    ſtor'd;
A mind alike prepared the knotty points
Of human laws, or laws divine, to ſolve,
The veil of cautious ſilence to employ,
Or grace with eloquence the cauſe of truth:
On him, amid the battle's fierceſt rage,
Servilius called, and thus his thoughts ex-
    preſs'd.

They ſay that Lucius Ælius Stilo was accuſtomed
to aſſert that Q. Ennius wrote theſe verſes on
himſelf, and that this was a repreſentation and
deſcription of his own manners and talents.

CHAP. V.

Discourse of the philosopher Taurus, upon the manner of supporting pain, according to the decrees of the Stoics. [a]

WHEN the philosopher went to Delphi to see the Pythian games, and to meet an assembly of almost all Greece, I was one of his attendants, and on the journey we came to Le-

---

[a] I have before had occasion to speak of the peculiarities of the Stoic discipline; the more curious reader may compare the contents of this chapter, with Cicero, l. iii. de Finibus, and l. ii. of Tusculan Questions. Zeno, to avoid the peculiarities of Epicurus as far as possible, who made happiness consist in an exemption from fatigue and pain, made his wise man free from all passions of every kind, and capable of happiness in the midst of the severest anguish. What opinion our Milton entertained of all these philosophers, and their different systems, may be collected from the following passage:

> Others apart sat on a hill retired,
> In thoughts more elevate, and reasoned high
> Of Providence, foreknowledge, will, and fate,
> Fix'd fate, free-will, foreknowledge absolute,
> And found no end, in wandering mazes lost.
> Of good and evil much they argued, then
> Of happiness, and final misery,
> Passion and apathy, and glory and shame,
> Vain wisdom all and false philosophy.

badia [1], an old town in Bœotia.   Word was here brought to Taurus, that a friend of his, a man of rank, and a philosopher of the stoic school, was oppreſſed with a grievous fit of ſickneſs; checking therefore the ſpeed of our journey, ·which otherwiſe required diſpatch, and leaving the carriage, he proceeded to viſit his friend, and I (as it was my cuſtom to go with him everywhere) followed.   When we came to the houſe in which the ſick man was, we perceived him lying under great pain and anguiſh, afflicted with a diſorder which the Greeks call colon [3]; and in a raging fever [4]; his groans, half-ſtifled, burſt from him, and the deep ſighs which eſcaped from his inmoſt breaſt [5], diſcovered no leſs the

* *Lebadia.*]—Here was anciently an oracle of Trophonius, which was delivered from ſome den or cavern.   Its modern appellation is Livadia.

[3] *Colon.*]—The colon, in anatomy, is one of the thick inteſtines, and it is from this part that the diſeaſe called the colic takes its name; and it was probably this which afflicted the poor philoſopher, who is here mentioned as ſtruggling betwixt his ſyſtem, and his feelings of pain.

[4] *Raging fever.*]—In Gronovius, febri rabida; but it may be reaſonably doubted, whether Gellius did not write febri rapida; which expreſſion occurs in book xviii. chap. 10. —accedente febri rapida.

[5] *Inmoſt breaſt.*]—Similar to this is the expreſſion of Virgil:

> Ingemuit, deditque has imo pectore voces.

Again,

> Suſpirans, imoque trahens a pectore vocem.

See alſo Apuleius, page 5. the edition of Pricæus.

> Imo de pectore cruciabilem ſuspiritum ducens.

pain

pain he fuffered, than his ftruggles to overcome it. When Taurus had fent for his phyficians, and converfed with them on the means of cure, and had alfo encouraged the patient to fupport his calamity, by mentioning the inftances of his fortitude to which he had been witnefs, we returned to our carriage and companions. " You have feen," fays Taurus, " no very pleafant fight indeed, yet one which is not without its ufe, a philofopher contending with pain. The power and nature of the diforder was what produced his anguifh and torture of limbs, while the faculty and powers of his mind, which was equally their property, fupported and reftrained within bounds, the violence of an agony almoft ungovernable. He allowed no loud groans, no complaints, no indecorous words to efcape him; and yet (as you faw) there were manifeft proofs of a conteft between mind and body for the poffeffion of the man." Then a young man, a difciple of Taurus, not ignorant of philofophy, remarked, that, if fuch is the bitternefs of pain, that it ftruggles againft the will and the judgment, and compels a man involuntarily to utter groans, and to confefs the evil of his violent diforder, why is pain among the Stoics called a thing indifferent, and not an evil? How does it happen that a Stoic can be moved, or that pain can move him; fince the Stoics affirm, that nothing can move them, and that a wife man is moved by nothing? To this Taurus replied, with a more cheerful countenance (for he feemed pleafed at being allured into the argument) " If our friend were in better health, he would defend the unavoidable complaints of this kind from calumny, and would, I dare fay, refolve your queftion; but you know I am no great friend to the Stoics, or rather to their doctrine; for it often appears contradictory to its own tenets and to ours, as is proved in my treatife on the fubject. But as my cuftom is with you, I will fpeak unlearnedly (as they call it) and at large, what, if any Stoic were prefent, I fhould think it neceffary to deliver in a more logical and ftudied manner. For you know, I fuppofe, that old and common proverb, " fpeak without ftudy[6], and you make the fubject clear." Then beginning upon the topic of pain, and the groans of the fick Stoic, he thus proceeded: " Nature (fays he) when fhe produced us, implanted in thofe firft principles with which we were born, a love and affection for ourfelves, to fuch a degree, that nothing is dearer or of greater concern to us than ourfelves. And this fhe confidered would be the fource of perpetual prefer-

---

Without ftudy.]—This proverbial expreffion is taken from Suidas, or rather perhaps from the frogs of Ariftophanes. The correfponding proverb in Latin is much neater, though with precifely the fame meaning, rudius ac planius.

The interpretation of Erafmus is far-fetched. It was cuftomary, he obferves, for the learned men of old to veil the myfteries of fcience in dark and ænigmatical expreffions. In the paffage of Ariftophanes referred to above, Bacchus reproaches Euripides with obfcurity.

§   vation

vation to the human race, that every one, as foon as born, fhould receive a knowledge of thofe things, which are called by the ancient philofophers, the principles of nature, fo that he might delight in the things which are agreeable to his bodily fyftem, and fhrink from thofe which are otherwife. Afterwards, in the growth of age, reafon fprings from her feeds, with deliberation, the knowledge of juftice, and one's real intereft, with a wifer and more balanced choice of advantages, while, above all the reft, the dignity of virtue and propriety is fo pre-eminent, that every outward object is defpifed which oppofes our poffeffing and preferving that quality. Nor is any thing efteemed a real good, but what is honourable, nor any thing evil, but what is bafe. As for all other things of an indifferent nature, which are neither honourable nor difgraceful, they are determined to be neither good nor evil. But things produced from, and bearing a relationfhip to other things, are diftinguifhed and divided by their own qualities, which the philofophers call[7] προηγυμενα and αποπροηγυμενα. Therefore, pleafure and pain, as far as each relates to the end of living well and happily, are efteemed in-

---

[7] *Philofophers call.*]—Primary and fecondary caufes. See Cicero, lib. iii. de Finibus. Laertius calls thefe principles προηγμενα and απροπονημενα, that is, proper objects of preference or rejection. See the fubjects of the turpe et honeftum, or vice and virtue, moft agreeably difcuffed in the feventy-fourth epiftle of Seneca.

Z 3

different,

different, and neither good nor evil. But since a man just born is endowed with these first sensations of pain and pleasure; before his knowledge and his reason have appeared, and since he is by his nature attached to pleasure, and averse to pain, as to an enemy, therefore reason, which is given him afterwards, can scarcely pluck from him, or check or extinguish those affections which are born with him, and have taken deep root: yet he contends with them for ever, restrains them when licentious, and compels them [3] to submission and obedience. Thence you behold a philosopher, relying on the efficacy of his system, enabled to struggle with the violence of a raging disorder; neither giving way to his complaint, nor expressing his pain, nor (as it frequently happens) groaning and lamenting, with exclamations upon his own misery; but only utter-

---

[3] *Compels them.*]—It was a very different and far superior philosophy which Akenside had in view, when he wrote the following animated lines:

> The immortal mind, superior to his fate,
> Amid the outrage of external things,
> Firm as the solid base of this great world,
> Rests on his own foundations.   Blow, ye winds;
> Ye waves, ye thunders, roll your tempest on;
> Shake, ye old pillars of the marble sky,
> Till all its orbs, and all its worlds of fire
> Be loosened from their seats, yet still serene
> The unconquer'd mind looks down upon the wreck,
> &c. &c.

ing fhort. breathings, and fuch deep fighs, as are
proofs not of his being overcome and worn out
with pain, but of his ftruggles to opprefs and
fubdue it. But I know not (fays he) whether
it may not be afked, as to his ftruggles and
groans, that if pain be not an evil, why is it neceffary to- engage in thofe ftruggles, or give
vent to thofe groans? For all things, though not
evil in themfelves,- are however not deftitute of.
inconvenience: but there are many things in:
themfelves great evils, and of private detriment,
which are neverthelefs not bafe; yet they are
oppofite and hoftile to the gentlenefs and lenity
of nature, by a certain myfterious but effential
confequence of its qualities. Thefe therefore a.
wife man can patiently endure, though he cannot
make them participate the fuperior qualities of
his nature. For what they call apathy is not
only in my opinion, but according to many of
the moft fagacious of that fect, as Panætius, a
grave and learned man, difapproved and rejected.

But why is a Stoic philofopher, who they
affirm can be compelled to nothing, obliged
againft his will to utter groans? Surely a wife
man cannot be overcome, while he has an opportunity of ufing his reafon. But when nature
compels, reafon, given by nature, is compelled
alfo. You may afk, if you pleafe, why a man
involuntarily winks his eyes, when another fuddenly raifes his· hand before his face? why,

when

when the sky is illuminated by a flash of light, a man involuntarily holds down his head ? why, amidst loud peals of thunder, does he feel terror ? why does he start, when any one sneezes ? why does he grow hot in the parching of the sun, or cold in severe frosts ? These things, and many others, are neither under the guidance of inclination, wisdom, nor reason, but are the decrees of nature and necessity. But that is not fortitude, which strives against nature, like a prodigy, and steps beyond the usual natural powers, either by an astonishing effort of the mind, or some act of fierceness, or some great and distressing exercise of the faculty in suffering pain; such as we have heard of in a certain gladiator of Cæsar's, who was accustomed to laugh when his wounds were probed. But that is true and genuine fortitude, which our ancestors called the power of distinguishing things supportable, from those which are insupportable; by which it appears, that some are intolerable things, from which men of fortitude may shrink, as neither to be engaged with nor supported." When Taurus had said thus much, and seemed about to say yet more, we arrived at our carriages, and pursued our journey.

C H A P.

Chap. VI.

What the Greeks call ænigma, *the ancient Latins call* scrupos.

THAT species of composition, which some of our ancient authors called *scrupos* [1], the Greeks call *ænigma*; such as that which we find in three verses of six Iambic feet, of very ancient date, and of great wit. The ænigma we leave unexplained, that we may excite the conjectures of readers, in attempting to discover it. The lines are these:

" Semel [2], minusne, an bis minus fit, non sat scio,
" An utrumque horum, ut quondam audivi dicier,
" Jovi ipsi regi noluit concedere !"

He

[1] *Scrupos.*]—This word is as frequently read scirpos, which means a rush without a knot—it is also read *sirpus*, which is synonymous with *scirpos*. *Scrupos* is the same with *scrupus*, and signifies a little stone.

[2] *Semel*, &c.]—Literally thus: I do not well know whether he is once *minus* or twice *minus*, or both these, as I have formerly heard it said, who would not give place to great Jove himself?

Both

He who is unwilling to puzzle himself about its meaning, will find what it is, by confulting the fecond book of Marcus Varro upon the Latin language, addreffed to Marcellus.

Both thefe means three times *minus*, that is, in Latin, *Terminus*, the god of boundaries or limits.

The circumftance of his not giving place to Jupiter, is thus introduced by Ovid, Fafti, l. ii.

> Quid nova cum fierent capitolia, nempe deorum
>   Cuncta Jovi ceffit turba, locumque dedit,
> 'Terminus, ut memorant veteres, inventus in æde
>   Reftitit et magno cum Jove templa tenet.

In honour of this Terminus there were annual feafts at Rome, called *Terminalia*; and the tradition of his not giving way to Jupiter, was underftood to imply the perpetuity of the Roman empire.

I remember to have feen fome old monkifh verfes, which had a fimiliar play upon the word *ter*:

> Domini Scropi hac in fofsâ
> Tandem requiefcunt offa
> En, en, en, &c.

Where en, en, en, mean *terrena*.

CHAP. VII.

Upon what occasion Cnæus Dolabella[1], the proconsul, referred the trial of a woman accused of having given poison, and confessing the fact, to the court of the Areopagites.

WHEN Cnæus Dolabella was proconsul in Asia, a woman of Smyrna was brought before him. This woman had destroyed, at the same time, her husband, and her son, by giving them poison; nor did she deny the fact. She alledged as the cause of her having done so, that the husband and son had by some artifice put to death another son of her's by a former husband, an excellent and blameless youth. Nor was the truth of this fact disputed. Dolabella referred the matter to his council. No one in so doubtful a point ventured to give his opinion, because the acknowledgment of the crime, by which her husband and son had been put to death, seemed to require punishment, yet it was justly perpe-

[1] *Cnæus Dolabella.*]—The same story is told not only in Valerius Maximus, whom indeed Gellius quotes, but in Ammianus Marcellinus, book xxv. chap. 2. The commentators differ about this Dolabella, for though Gellius calls him Cnæus, he is by Valerius Maximus named Publius. Bayle, at the article Dolabella, enters at some length into this question.

trated

trated upon very wicked men. Dolabella referred the matter to the Areopagites [*] at Athens, as judges of greater wifdom and experience. The Areopagites being made acquainted with the nature of the caufe, fummoned the woman and her accufer to appear at the period of an hundred years. By thefe means, neither was the act of adminiftering poifon pardoned, which would have been illegal, nor was the guilty woman condemned and punifhed, for a crime, which was deemed pardonable. This ftory is told in the eighth book of Valerius Maximus, on Memorable Sayings and Occurrences.

[*] *Areopagites.*]—It is unneceffary to detain the reader on this fubject of the Areopagites; but by way of reviving it in his recollection, I may be excufed adding, that this tribunal was inftituted by Cecrops; that it was confirmed in its jurifdiction by Solon; that its decifions were highly revered; and that after it loft its power, it retained its reputation.

A cafe not very unlike the one introduced in this chapter, is mentioned fomewhere in Ariftotle. A woman had a faithlefs lover, and agreeably to the old fuperftitions concerning the power of magic and incantations, fhe adminiftered a potion to him, which fhe prefumed would reftore him to her affections: unluckily he died in the operation. She was brought before the Areopagites, who being convinced that her intention was certainly not to deftroy him, deferred paffing any judgment on her crime. The Abbé Barthelemy, in his Voyage du Jeune Anacharfis, has collected many interefting particulars concerning the court of Areopagus. The fubject alfo is acutely and agreeably handled by Meurfius.

C H A P.

Chap. VIII.[a]

Reconciliations between great men, worthy of record.

PUBLIUS AFRICANUS the Elder, and Tiberius Gracchus, the father of Tiberius and Caius Gracchus, men illustrious from
their

[a] The fact recorded in the commencement of this chapter is to be found at length in Livy, Plutarch, and Valerius Maximus. In Livy, Book xxxviii. c. 57.—in Plutarch, in the lives of the Gracchi—and in Valerius Maximus, book iv. c. 2. and 3.

The latter anecdote also is told by Valerius Maximus, Livy, and Cicero. See Valerius Maximus, book iv. c. 21. Livy, book xl. c. 45, 6. and in Cicero de Provinc. Consul. 9.—Many parallel anecdotes might easily be collected from modern history, and indeed it seems to be one of the characteristics of a great and noble mind, to make all private and personal considerations give way to the public good. Two examples of public reconciliation occur in Shakespeare, one of which excites abhorrence, the other a smile. The first is in Richard the Third, when king Edward obliges the queen's relations, and Hastings, Dorset, &c. to be publicly reconciled, concerning which the king says to the duke of Gloucester,—

> Brother, we have done deeds of charity,
> Made peace of enmity, fair love of hate,
> Between these swelling, wrong incensed peers.

The other is in Henry the Eighth, who is represented as compelling Gardiner, bishop of Winchester, and others of
his

their exploits, loaded with honours, and diſtin-guiſhed by the purity of their lives, frequently diſagreed upon public affairs, and from that or ſome other reaſon were not united in friendſhip. Their ſecret diſlike of each other had long pre-vailed, till on the uſual day the feaſt of Jupiter was held, upon which occaſion the ſenate ban-queted[z] in the capitol, and it happened that theſe two men were placed next each other at the ſame table. When, as if the immortal gods were arbiters in the quarrel, in the feaſt dedicat-ed to Jupiter, joining their hands, they became immediately allied by the ſtrongeſt friendſhip; nor was that all, for alliance by relationſhip ſoon took place. Publius Scipio having a daughter that was now marriageable, betrothed her upon that ſame occaſion to Tiberius Gracchus, whom he had choſen and approved at a time when the judgment is moſt ſevere, namely, when he was at enmity with him. Æmilius Lepidus alſo,

his privy council, to embrace Cranmer, Archbiſhop of Can-, terbury, whoſe ruin they had plotted—

    Make me no more ado, but all embrace him—
    Be friends—for ſhame, my lords.

There is ſomething extremely ludicrous in the repreſenta-tion of this ſcene on the ſtage.

[z] *The ſenate banqueted.*]—*The jus epulandi publice* was peculiar to the ſenate. This took place on ſolemn feſtivals, and the ceremony was called *epulum Jovis,* or *cæna Dialis.* The ſenators were dreſſed on the occaſion in their ſenatorial robes, and the feaſt was celebrated ſometime in the month of November.

and

and Fulvius Flaccus, two men of illuftrious birth, accumulated honours, and exalted ftations, were oppofed to each other, with bitter hatred, and long-indulged enmity. When the people made them cenfors at the fame time, on being nominated by the herald, in the Campus Martius, before the affembly was difperfed, each of them was united in attachment and embraces to the other. And from that day, during their cenforfhips, and afterwards, they lived in the ftricteft and moft friendly intimacy.

CHAP.

Chap. IX.

Some words are of double meaning, and even the
word honos *was so considered formerly.*

ONE may very often see and observe in old
writers, many words which have now only
one fixed meaning in our usage of them, yet formerly had a sense so indifferent and indeterminate,
that they might bear two significations contradictory to each other. Of which some are
well known; as " *tempestas* ', *valetudo, facinus,
aolus, gratia, industria.*" These words almost
every body knows bore a double signification,
and were spoken either in a good or bad sense.
You will find by many examples, that *periculum* ',
venenum, and *contagium,* were not used as they are

' *Tempestas,*]—means a good or bad season, *valetudo* good
or bad health, *facinus* a good or bad action, *dolus* an act of
wisdom or low cunning, *gratia* a good or bad turn, and *industria* with care or with a mischievous intention.

Muretus observes, at p. 83. of his Various Readings,
that as the Latins used *honos* in an ambiguous sense, so did
the Greeks use οννιδος and κλιος, and he quotes two passages
from Euripides in confirmation of his opinion. The expression of αισχρον κλιος occurs in the Helen.

' *Periculum,*]—is used both for hazard and experiment,
venenum is either poison or simple medicine, *contagium* is
either infection or a contact, *a contingendo.*

now,

now, only in a bad fenfe, and that the word *ho-*
nos alfo had a middle fignification, and was fo
ufed that *malus honos* was the fame as *injuria,*
though this very feldom occurred.   But Quintus
Metellus Numidicus, in a fpeech he delivered
upon his triumph, has ufed thefe words : " In
the fame degree as all of you, O Romans, are
of more confequence than myfelf alone, fo does
he heap greater injury and difgrace upon you,
than upon me; and as honeft men would rather receive than offer an infult, fo has he fhewn
worfe regard towards you than me.   He wifhes
me to bear, and you to offer, an injuftice.   Thus
with one party is left a fubject of complaint, with
the other difgrace."   This fentence, he has
fhewn a worfe regard towards you than me, is
expreffed by *pejorem honorem,* and is the fame as
what he before fays, he heaps a greater difgrace upon you, than upon me.   Befides this
ufage of the word, I thought proper to produce
the fentiment of Quintus Metellus, that we
might determine it to be a decree of Socrates,
which fays,

Καχιον ειναι το αδιχειν τ8 αδιχεισθαι.

It is worfe to be unjuft, than to fuffer injuftice [1].

[1] *Injuftice.*]—The fentiment here afcribed to Socrates is
taken from the Gorgias of Plato.

CHAP. X.

Meaning of the Latin word æditimus[1].

ÆDITIMUS is an old Latin word, formed like *finitimus* and *legitimus*. But inſtead of it the word *ædituus* is now uſed by many, from a new invented term, as if it were derived (a tuendis ædibus) from guarding the temples. This might be ſufficient to warn thoſe ignorant and furious diſputants, but that they are not to be reſtrained without authority. Marcus Varro, in his ſecond book addreſſed to Marcellus upon the Latin language, thinks we ought rather to uſe *æditimus* than *ædituus,* becauſe the latter is fabricated by late invention, the former pure from its ancient original. Lævius[2] alſo, I think, in his Proteſilaodamia, has uſed the word *clauſtritimus,* one who guards the gates, a word formed by the ſame proceſs as *æditimus,* one who guards the temples. In the moſt correct copies of Tully's ſpeech againſt Verres, I find it written " *æditimi cuſtodeſque maturè ſentiunt,*" while in

---

[1] *Æditimus.*]—Conſult Varro and P. Feſtus concerning this word; ſome explain it, and I think not impertinently *ædis intimus.*

[2] *Lævius.*]—Some editions read Lævius, ſome Nævius, and others Livius.

the common books it is written *æditui.* There
is a dramatic ftory of Pomponius's, called *Æditi-*
mus, in which this line appears,

> Qui poftquam tibi appareo atque *æditimos* [3]
> in templo tuo.

And Titus Lucretius [4], in his poem, inftead of
ædituos, calls the guards of the temple *ædituentes.*

[3] *Æditimos in templo tuo.*]—We have an expreffion in
our verfion of the Pfalms correfponding with this, and
which may be offered properly enough as a tranflation of it:
" I had rather be a door-keeper in the houfe of my God."

[4] *Lucretius.*]—See Book vi. ver. 1271.

> Onerataque paffim
> Cuncta cadaveribus cæleftum templa manebant;
> Hofpitibus loca quæ complerant *ædituentes.*

I do not think that Creech has given the full force of this
paffage: he renders it thus,—

> Death now had filled the temples of the gods;
> The priefts themfelves, not beafts, are the altar's load.

CHAP.

C H A P. XI.

They are miſtaken who commit ſins with the hope of remaining concealed, ſince there is no perpetual hiding-place for ſin.—The words of the philoſopher Peregrinus upon that ſubjeƈt, from a ſentiment of the poet Sophocles.

I SAW, when I was at Athens, a philoſopher named Peregrinus[1], and ſurnamed afterwards Proteus, a man of dignity and fortitude, who reſided in a little cottage without the city. As I uſed to go to him frequently, I heard from him many uſeful and excellent remarks, among which this is what I chiefly remember: He ſaid, " that a wiſe man would not be guilty of ſin, although gods and men were alike ignorant of it[2]."

For

[1] The life of this Peregrinus is given by Lucian, and indeed a more extraordinary charaƈter never appeared on the world's great theatre.   See what I have ſaid concerning him at chap. 3. book viii.

[2] *Ignorant of it.*—This accords with what is expreſſed in the lines—

> Oderunt peccare boni virtutis amore;
> Oderunt peccare mali formidine pœnæ.

It is ſurely a noble and charming ſentiment, though, as Gellius on a former occaſion has obſerved, it comes from an

unworthy

For he thought a wife man fhould avoid fin, not
from the fear of punifhment or difgrace, but
from his fenfe of duty, and love of virtue. But
of thofe who were not of fuch a difpofition, or fo
taught, that they could eafily reftrain themfelves
from fin, by their own power and will, he
thought they would be more readily induced to
fin, when they expected their guilt would be concealed, and that fuch concealment would produce
impunity. "But," fays he, " if men know that nothing can be long concealed, they will fin in a
more guarded and fecret manner. Wherefore,"

unworthy mouth. The idea of man being produced for the
purpofe of leading a life of wifdom and virtue, in noble dif-
dain of fenfual gratifications, is thus exquifitively reprefented by Akenfide,—

> Say, why was man fo eminently rais'd
> Amid the vaft creation; why ordain'd
> Thro' life and death to dart his piercing eye
> With thoughts beyond the limit of his frame,
> But that the omnipotent might fend him forth,
> In fight of mortal and immortal powers,
> As on a boundlefs theatre, to run
> The great career of juftice; to exalt
> His generous aim to all diviner deeds;
> To chafe each partial purpofe from his breaft;
> And thro' the mifts of paffion and of fenfe,
> And thro' the toffing tide of chance and pain,
> To hold his courfe unfaltring, while the voice
> Of truth and virtue, up the fteep afcent
> Of nature, calls him to his high reward,
> The applauding fmile of heaven.

A a 3

he

he added, " thofe lines of Sophocles, the wifeft of poets, were worthy to be remembered—

> Nor vainly think your fkill can ought conceal,
> Time, that knows all things, fhall all truths reveal."

Another of the old poets, whofe name I do not now recollect, has called Truth [3] the daughter of Time.

---

[3] *Truth, &c.*]—The Platonifts confidered truth as no lefs effential to the happinefs of man in a more elevated ftate of being, than virtue. Indeed it cannot be very eafy to confider them as detached from each other. The fame philofophers, in a very beautiful allegory, called Truth the body of the fupreme being, and Light his fhadow. There is a fine paper in the Rambler, defcribing the qualities and influence of Truth, Falfhood, and Fiction, where the moralift reprefents Truth to be the daughter of Jupiter and Wifdom.

CHAP. XII.

*The witty reply of Cicero, excusing himself from the
charge of a manifest falshood.* [1]

THIS too is one of the arts of rhetoric, that
upon an attack it enables a man, with wit,
to acknowledge the truth of an accusation in such
a manner as to escape, by some jocular reply, the
turpitude of that which cannot be denied, and to
make the deed appear worthy rather of laughter
than of serious censure. This, we are told, Cicero did, when, by an elegant and facetious turn,
he did away that which he could not deny. He
wanted to purchase a house upon the Palatine
Mount, but had not the money; he received
privately from Publius Sylla, who was then under
a public accusation [2], twenty thousand sesterces.
Before he made his purchase, this circumstance
became known to the public, and he was accused
of having received money, for the purpose of buy-
ing the house, from an accused man. Cicero, fur-

[1] Macrobius has given a collection of the jests of Cicero,
which it is my intention to insert in a future work.

[2] *Under accusation.*]—Sylla was accused by L. Torquatus
of being concerned in the Catilinarian conspiracy. The
oration which Cicero made in his defence yet remains.

A a 4

prized

prized by the sudden reproach, denied the receipt of it, and professed that he had no intention of making the purchase. " Therefore," says he, " let it be considered as a truth if I buy the house." Afterwards, however, when he *did* buy it, and this falshood was objected to him in the senate by his opponents, he laughed heartily, and in the midst of his doing so, " Why," says he, " you are destitute of common sense [3], if you do not know that it is the part of a cautious and prudent master of a family to deny his intention of making any purchase, that he may prevent competitors in the sale."

[3] *Common sense*.]—In Gronovius it is ακοινονοντοι, without common sense; but it is read in various editions ακοινωιντοι, which means *in communes*. See also H. Stephens at this passage—he would prefer αροικομητοι, that is, ignorant of things relating to domestic matters, or of œconomy, in its literal acceptation. This is plausible and ingenious,

Chap. XIII [1].

The meaning of the phrase " intra calendas," whether it signifies before the calends, or upon the calends, or both.—The meaning of the phrase " intra oceanum," and " intra montem Taurum," in the speech of Marcus Tullius, and the usage of " intra modum," in a certain epistle.

BEING appointed by the consuls a judge extraordinary [2] at Rome, when I was to give judgment within the calends, I enquired of Apollinaris

---

[1] This is a very intricate and perplexing chapter; and I do not know that in my progress through Gellius I have met with any thing less easy to render in intelligible English. After all that I have done, many of my readers would perhaps have commended me, if I had followed the example of the French translator, and omitted it altogether; but this would have been inconsistent with my plan and determination, to insert every thing contained in my original. To say that the calends in the Roman chronology were the first day of the month, and that they were reckoned backwards, so that, for example, the last day of May was the second of the calends of June, seems almost superfluous.

The matter which Gellius wished to have defined was, whether his duty allowed him to pass judgment on the day of the calends only, or whether he was allowed the latitude of doing so before the actual day of the calends.

[2] *Judge extraordinary.*]—The circumstance which Gellius here relates of himself is highly to his honour, as the Romans

linaris Sulpitius, a man of learning, whether in the phrafe *intra calendas* (within the calends), the calends themfelves were included? I ftated to him, that I was appointed judge, that the calends was the limit, and that I was to pafs judgment *intra eum diem.* " Why," fays he, " do you enquire this of me, rather than of thofe learned and ftudious men [3], whofe affiftance you ufually rely upon in matters of law." To this I replied, " If I wanted information upon any matter of right eftablifhed or received, contefted or ambiguous, new or ratified, I fhould know that I muft apply to thofe whom you mention. But when the meaning, application, and reafon of any Latin terms are to be examined, I fhould be foolifh [4] and blind indeed, if, having an opportunity

were remarkably tenacious of the character and talents of thofe whom they appointed to fituations fo delicate and arduous. They were obliged to be of a certain age, and they could not enjoy this fituation if they had been expelled the fenate. The oath taken by each judge was, that he would decide according to his confcience and the law. It fhould feem by this and other fimilar paffages, that in any extraordinary cafes affiftant judges were appointed.

[3] *Men.*]—The commentators are greatly at variance at this paffage, fome contending that it fhould be read *peritis ftudiofifque viris,* others that it muft be *peritis ftudiofifque juris.* Fortunately the nature of the Englifh idiom has enabled me to render it in a manner which gives the force of both expreffions.

[4] *Foolifh.*]—The original is a very unufual word, *fcævus,* for which fome would read *lævus,* as in Virgil, fi mens non

lævu

opportunity of confulting you, I fhould go to any other." " Hear then," fays he, " my opinion of the word, but fo that you may be impreffed, not from my obfervation on its nature and meaning, but from what you have known and remarked to be its common acceptation. For not only the true and proper fignifications of common words are changed by long ufage, but even the decrees of the laws themfelves become, by filent confent, obfolete." He then fpoke upon the fubject in my hearing, and that of many others, nearly in this manner, " When the day," fays he, " is fo fixed, that the judge gives fentence *(intra calendas)* within the calends, it occurs immediately to every one, that there is no doubt but, properly fpeaking, it fhould be *(ante calendas)* before the calends. It is only doubtful, whether the word calends, which you enquire about, be properly ufed. Now, without doubt, the word is fo conftituted, and has fuch a fignification, that when the phrafe *intra calendas* is ufed, it ought to be underftood only as meaning the calends, and including no other day. For thefe three words, *intra, citra,* and *ultra,* by which certain boundaries of places are fignified, by the ancients were contracted into fingle fyllables, as *in, cis, uls.* Since thefe

læva fuiffet. *Scævus* comes from the Greek word σκαιος, which, as Turnebus obferves, the Latins have borrowed, and made their own, interpofita digamma, by the interpofition of the digamma. See his Adverfaria, L. 50. p. 691.

particles

particles were expreſſed rather obſcurely, from the brevity and tenuity of their ſound, to each of them was added the ſame ſyllable, and that which was called *cis Tiberim* [s], and *uls Tiberim*, began to be called *citra Tiberim*, and *ultra Tiberim*, and that which before was called *in*, by the addition of the ſame ſyllable, became *intra*. For he who ſays *intra oppidum, intra cubiculum, intra ferias* (within the town, &c.), means no more than *in oppido, in cubiculo, in feriis*. *Intra calendas* (within the calends) therefore does not mean *before* the calends, but *upon* the calends, that is, on the very day upon which the calends fall. So according to the meaning of the word itſelf, he who was ordered to pronounce any thing *intra calendas*, unleſs he were to do it on the calends, would not perform what his duty required. If he pronounces before, he cannot be ſaid to do it *intra* but *citra*. But I know not from what cauſe it is that the common abſurd acceptation of the phraſe ſhould prevail by which *intra calendas* (within the calends) ſeems to ſignify, either within the calends, or before the calends, which is exactly the ſame. It is moreover doubted, whether it could be done *ante calendas*, whereas it ſhould neither be beyond nor within, but what is betwixt both, *intra*, that is, on the calends. But cuſtom has got the better, which, as it governs every

---

[s] *Cis Tiberim.*]—Thus alſo it was a common mode of expreſſion at Rome to ſay, *cis Alpes*, and *trans Alpes*, for this ſide the Alps, and beyond them.

thing,

thing, has a particular influence on words[6]."
When Apollinaris had thus learnedly and perspicuously handled the argument, I made this reply, " I had intended, before I applied to you,
diligently to enquire in what manner our anceftors applied the particle in queftion. I find that
Cicero, in his third oration[7] againft Verres,
wrote thus : ' There is no place *(intra oceanum)*
on this fide the ocean, nor indeed fo remote or
inacceffible, where, in thefe times, the injuftice and
licentioufnefs of our countrymen, has not reached.' He fays *intra oceanum*, contrary to your
mode of reafoning. He would not, I think, fay, *in*

[6] *Influence on words.*]—The following extraƈt from the preface of Mr. Nares to his Effay on Orthoepy feems pertinent
in this place.

"The arbitrary caprice of fafhion, and the fpirit of improvement mifdireƈted, are daily making changes in the ftruƈture
and found of language, which, though feparately inconfiderable, are, after fome time, important in the total amount:
and as the celeftial figns had nearly changed their places before the flow but conftant motion of the equinoxes was de-
teƈted, fo a language may have departed confiderably from
the fixed point of purity, and the harmony of its conftruƈtion
may be materially injured, before thofe minute changes,
which affeƈt only fingle words or fyllables, fhall have attraƈt-
ed the public obfervation."

[7] *Third oration.*]—It is in the 89th chapter or divifion.
The infertion of the paragraph preceding may make the
prefent quotation more perfpicuous.
" All our provinces mourn and complain, every free nation remonftrates againft us, every kingdom of the globe ex-
claims againft our avarice and injuftice. There is no place,
&c."

oceano.

oceano. He speaks of all the regions which the ocean surrounds, and which our countrymen were able to approach, which cannot be interpreted by *in oceano,* though it may by *citra oceanum.* For he cannot be supposed to speak of I know not what islands, which may be said to be *in* the waters of the ocean." Then Sulpicius Apollinaris smilingly replied, "You have objected from Cicero with sufficient acuteness; but Cicero has said *intra,* and not as you interpret, *citra oceanum.* For what can be denominated *citra oceanum* (on this side of the ocean), when the ocean circumscribes and surrounds all regions [8]? For that which is *citra* is *extra,* but how can *extra* be applied to that which is *intra?* But if the ocean were in one part of the earth alone, the land towards that part might be called *citra,* or *ante, oceanum.* But as the ocean surrounds the earth on every part, nothing is *citra,* on this side of it; for the earth in every limit being walled in by its waters, every thing included in its margin is within it. Thus the sun moves not *citra cælum* [9], but *in cæle,* and *intra*

---

[8] Perhaps better in English; " For that which is on this side a thing is without its limits, and how can that be without which is within ?"

[9] *Citra cælum.*]—That is, not on this side of the region of the sky, but in or within it. The expression is *vertitur,* which may be understood of the revolution of the sun round its axis, though it is not probable that Cicero understood enough of the motion of the heavenly bodies so to apply it. Indeed, the philosophy of his time acknowledged none but the system which made the earth the fixed centre, round which the other planets moved in certain orbits.

cælum,

cælum, not on this side of the sky but within it." Thus far Apollinaris seemed to reason with learning and acutenefs. But afterwards, in the letters of Tully to Servius Sulpicius, I found *intra* applied to *modum*, as they say *intra calendas*, who mean to say *citra calendas*. Thefe are the words of Cicero [10], which I have added: " But yet, as I avoided giving him offence, who perhaps would have thought that if I had been perpetually filent, I fhould feem to think that ours was not a republic, that I may fatisfy both his will and my own feelings, I fhall do this not only moderately, but *intra modum*." He had firft faid *modice*, which means with an equable and temperate fpirit, when, as if this expreffion difpleafed him, and as willing to correct it, he added, or even *intra modum*. By which he fignified, that he would do this lefs than he might have done even to have been thought moderate. That is, not all that moderation required, but a little on this fide of it, or as it were, *citra modum*. In the oration which he

[10] *Cicero.*]—The paffage occurs in the fourth book of Cicero's Familiar Letters, and in the fourth letter. The queftion was, whether, on fome occafion or other, the fenators fhould publicly thank Cæfar, which fome individuals at firft, and Cicero for a time, refufed to do. It feems from this quotation, and indeed from many places in the writers of that time, that it was cuftomary for the fenators to take opportunity of publicly thanking Cæfar for his moderation, clemency, magnanimity; this, however, fays Cicero, " I fhall do not only moderately, but even lefs than moderately, that is, very fparingly indeed."

3

made

made for P. Seftius ", he fays *intra montem Taurum*, that is, not on Mount Taurus, but as far as Mount Taurus, comprehending the mount itfelf alfo. Thefe are his words, from the oration juft quoted :

" Our anceftors obliged Antiochus the Great, whom in continued hoftilities they overcame both by fea and land, to confine his dominions *intra montem Taurum*. They took Afia from him, and affigned it to Attalus for his empire."

They ordered him to confine his dominions *intra montem Taurum*, which does not mean, as we fhould fay, *intra cubiculum*, unlefs the term *intra montem* could be underftood to apply to the countries which Mount Taurus by its pofition feparates. For as he who is *intra cubiculum* (in the chamber) is not in the walls of the chamber, but within the walls which inclofe the chamber, fo he who reigns within Mount Taurus reigns not only on Mount Taurus, but over thofe countries alfo of which Mount Taurus is the limit. According, therefore, to the analogy to be drawn from the words of Cicero, he who is directed to judge any thing *intra calendas*, may legally and properly do fo both before the calends, and on the calends ; nor is this by a certain privilege, as it were, of inveterate cuftom, but by the rule of right reafon, becaufe the

---

" *Seftius*,]—or Publius Sextius. The place here quoted is in the 27th divifion of the oration. *Intra montem Taurum* doubtlefs means the countries in the vicinity of Mount Taurus.

2

period

period of time which is included in the day of the calends may properly be termed *intra calendas* (within the calends).

CHAP. XIV.

Force and origin of the particle saltem [1].

WE were enquiring about the particle *saltem*, what was its original signification, and whence it was derived. It seems to have been

---

[1] *Saltem* is anciently written *saltim*; Heyne, however, who usually prefers the old method of writing Latin, has, in his edition of Virgil, used *saltem*. See Æneid iv. ver. 327.

> *Saltem* si qua mihi de te suscepta fuisset
> Ante fugam soboles.

See *saltem* used in a similar sense by Terence, Andria, act ii. scene 2. " *Saltem* accurato." So also Adelphi, act ii. scene 2. " *Saltem* quanti empta est, Syre." Donatus seems to incline to this abreviation of *saltem* from *salutem*, which he denominates το εσχατον, or the last thing, namely, life, which a captive entreats from his conqueror.

The curious reader may also see what Janus Gulielmius says on this subject, in his first book de Verisimilibus. This critic observes, that the best of the ancient writers used *saltim*, which he thinks may be derived from the supine *saltu*, as *raptim* from *raptu*, *sensim* from *sensu*, *cursim* from *cursu*, &c.

been firſt formed, not like ſome of thoſe expletives of ſpeech which are aſſumed without any definite meaning, or attention to regularity. There was one preſent who ſaid he had read in the Grammatical Commentaries of Publius Nigidius, that *ſaltem* was formed from the phraſe "*ſi aliter*," which phraſe was elliptical, *ſi aliter non poteſt* forming the perfect ſentence. But I never met with this in the Commentaries of Nigidius, a book which I think I have read with ſome attention. However, theſe words (*ſi aliter non poteſt*) do not ſeem to be far diſtant[2] from the meaning of the word concerning which we are enquiring; but to include ſo many words in ſo very few letters, ſeems too minute and ſubtle a contrivance. There was alſo another man, well verſed in books and learning, who ſaid, that *ſal-*

He obſerves, that Priſcian, enumerating the adverbs terminating in *em*, makes no mention of *ſaltem*. Priſcian ſubjoins this remark :

" In *im* et denominativa inveniuntur, et verbalia, et participialia; ut a parte partim, a viro viritim, a vice viciſſim, a ſtatu ſtatim, a raptu raptim, a ſaltu ſaltim et ſaltuatim."

[2] *Far diſtant.*]—*Aberrare.* A learned and ingenious critic, in the fourth volume of Miſcellaneous Obſervations on Authors Ancient and Modern, propoſes to read *abhorrere*, which reading, he obſerves, has the authority of ſome manuſcripts. Gellius often uſes *abhorret* in this ſenſe. See l. x. c. 4.

" Quorum verborum ſignificatio a ſententia Salluſtii non *abhorret*." See alſo l. xvii. c. 13. " Motus oculorum a natura rei quam ſignificat non *abhorret*."

tem feemed to him formed by the omiffion of the
letter *u* in the middle, and that *falutem* was formerly fpoken where we now fay *faltem.* " For," fays
he, " when we have been requefting many things
in vain, then we are accuftomed, as if making our
laft petition, which cannot be denied, to fay, this
(faltem) at leaft ought to be done, or to be granted ; as if at laft afking a favour which it is very
reafonable both to require and to grant."   But
this, although ingenious and pleafant enough,
feems too far-fetched ; I therefore thought it a
fubject worthy of further inveftigation.

<hr>

C H A P.   XV.

*That Sifenna, in his Hiftorical Records, has fre-
quently ufed fuch adverbs as* celatim, velitatim,
faltuatim.

HAVING often read Sifenna's hiftory, I
obferved in his compofition the frequent
occurrence of fuch adverbs as thefe, namely, *curfim*[1], *properatim, celatim, velitatim, faltuatim,* the

[1] *Curfim.*]—*Curfim* may be rendered in a curfory manner,
properatim in a hafty manner, *celatim* in a private manner,
velitatim in a fkirmifhing manner, *faltuatim* in a defultory
manner.

Quintus Carolus enumerates many other adverbs in *im,*
fuch as *examiffim, unciatim, alternatim,* &c.

two firſt of which, being more common, do not require to be illuſtrated by examples; the others are thus introduced in the ſixth book of his hiſtory: " He placed his men in ambuſcade, (quam maxime *cclatim* poterat) in as ſecret a manner as he could."   So in another place, " Having paſfed one ſummer in Aſia and Greece, in purſuit of literature, I wrote my hiſtory in a regular ſtyle, left by expreſſing myſelf in a ſkirmiſhing[z] or deſultory manner I ſhould burthen the minds of my readers."

[z] *Skirmiſhing.*]—Vellicatim et ſaltuatim.